BRITISH SUBMARINES AT WAR 1914-1918

BRITISH SUBMARINES AT WAR
1914-1918

EDWYN GRAY

Pen & Sword
MARITIME

First published in Great Britain in 1971 by Charles Scribner's Sons

Republished in 2001 and again in this format in 2016 by
PEN & SWORD MARITIME
An imprint of
Pen & Sword Books Ltd
47 Church Street, Barnsley
South Yorkshire
S70 2AS

ISBN 978 1 47385 345 4

Printed and bound in England
By CPI Group (UK) Ltd, Croydon, CR0 4YY

Pen & Sword Books Ltd incorporates the Imprints of Pen & Sword Aviation,
Pen & Sword Family History, Pen & Sword Maritime, Pen & Sword Military,
Pen & Sword Discovery, Pen & Sword Politics, Pen & Sword Atlas,
Pen & Sword Archaeology, Wharncliffe Local History, Leo Cooper,
Wharncliffe True Crime, Wharncliffe Transport, Pen & Sword Select,
Pen & Sword Military Classics, The Praetorian Press, Claymore Press,
Remember When, Seaforth Publishing and Frontline Publishing.

For a complete list of Pen & Sword titles please contact
PEN & SWORD BOOKS LIMITED
47 Church Street, Barnsley, South Yorkshire, S70 2AS, England
E-mail: enquiries@pen-and-sword.co.uk
Website: www.pen-and-sword.co.uk

CONTENTS

MAPS

Drawn by Boris Weltman

ILLUSTRATIONS

The author and publishers are grateful to the following for permission to reproduce the copyright illustrations: The Imperial War Museum, Nos. 1, 4, 5, 6, 7, 8, 9, 10, 11, 13, 14, and 18; Lord Keyes, No. 12; The Mansell Collection, No. 15.

Author's Note

WHEN, IN 1620, the Dutchman Cornelis Drebbel sailed up the Thames in the world's first submarine and 'calmly dived under the water while he kept the King and several thousand Londoners in the greatest suspense', no one in the watching crowd could have foreseen where his invention would lead.

Today, the nuclear-powered missile-submarine stands supreme as the world's most powerful warship. Able to circumnavigate the globe without surfacing, it can sail beneath the polar ice-caps, and travel 120,000 miles without refuelling. And, at the touch of a button, its megaton destructive power can obliterate half a continent.

Not surprisingly, many things have happened in the history of the submarine since that day, 350 years ago, when Drebbel first submerged his primitive boat in the Thames. This volume deals only with that part of the story between the years 1900 and 1918 and it recounts the dramatic history of the Royal Navy's early submarines and their pioneer crews during the First World War when the traditions and legends of the modern Submarine Service were created.

The story has been written mainly for the general reader who has neither the facilities nor time to ferret facts from the hundreds of naval histories in which they hide and, for this reason, footnotes and technical details have been omitted. I hope, however, that the serious student of naval affairs will discover many new facts and that he will gain a fresh insight into the scope and effect of British submarine operations in the First World War.

I would like to acknowledge my personal debt to the many

authors and historians who, since 1918, have unravelled the complex details of the submarine story for without their hard work and painstaking research this book could not have been written. I must also thank Associated Book Publishers (International) Ltd for allowing me to quote extensively from the naval memoirs of Sir Roger Keys, and to Cassell & Co, Hodder & Stoughton Ltd, HM Stationery Office, Doubleday & Co. Inc., The Hamlyn Publishing Group Ltd, George G. Harrap & Co Ltd, Hutchinson Publishing Group Ltd, Faber & Faber Ltd, and Rupert Hart-Davis, for permitting me to use their copyright material. I am grateful, too, to M. Brennan, Photographic Librarian of the Imperial War Museum, and his staff, for their willing assistance in tracing the photographs.

Like all writers I owe a great deal to those who helped me on the background work and research including my father, Dr A. E. Gray, who assisted with the maps and diagrams.

Finally may I express my admiration for the gallant crews of the British Submarine Service whose stirring deeds made this history possible. May this book stand as a humble tribute to those who never returned.

EDWYN GRAY
Attenborough,
Norfolk.
November, 2000

CHAPTER ONE

'A Damned
un-English Weapon...'

SO FAR AS the Royal Navy was concerned the war against
the Boers in 1900, was a mere side-show of no interest to anyone except, possibly, the soldiers concerned and the halfpenny
Press.

The enemy had no warships and their erstwhile allies,
despite the sabre-rattling threats of Kaiser Wilhelm II, had no
desire nor intention of disputing Britain's sea power. Only the
shuttle service of steamships carrying troops and supplies to
Cape Town and returning home with the sick and wounded,
served to remind the complacent admirals that England and
her Empire were fighting a bloody war.

Not that the sailors themselves failed to support their comrades in the field. HMS *Powerful*, diverted en route from China,
landed half a battalion of the Mauritius garrison at Durban,
and played a crucial role in the defence of the Cape Colony.
Her prompt action, however, was not taken on receipt of
orders from the Admiralty, but stemmed from the personal
initiative of her Commanding Officer, Captain Lambton. Not
content with acting as a mere troop ferry, Lambton sent a
contingent of the cruiser's own Bluejackets to help the
defenders of Ladysmith.

With similar enterprise Percy Scott, captain of the *Terrible*,
landed a number of 45 pdr naval guns, equipped with wheeled
carriages of his own invention, to add the Navy's fire-power
to the Army's pitifully inadequate artillery. He also devised
and manned an armoured train, but what their Lordships had
to say about a gold-braided Captain operating a railway is
unfortunately not known.

Officially the Royal Navy did nothing, except to criticize
the mistakes of the generals and bemoan the Army's system of
command. Admiral Fisher's comments in a letter two years
after the war typify the seaman's view: '... its almost incon-
ceivable blunders ... our "Army of Lions led by Asses" ... so
needlessly slaughtered.'

The Admiralty had its own problems. The Naval Estimates
had been presented and considerable pressure was being exerted
by the Press and public for the Navy to take an interest in the
new-fangled submarines which the French were developing.
At the turn of the century France, not Germany, was still
regarded as our main potential enemy and the Fashoda
Incident was still fresh in the minds of many.

During the Debate on the 1900 Naval Estimates, George
Goschen, the First Lord of the Admiralty told the House: 'The
submarine boat, even if practical difficulties attending its use
can be overcome, would seem ... to be eventually a weapon
for Maritime powers on the defensive.'

Nevertheless, when the First Lord received a note to say that
a certain Mr Rice of the American Electric Boat Company was
in Europe, he was more than anxious to see him, for he already
knew that the American company had taken over Mr Holland's
patents for a prototype submarine and could now produce a
workable model. He was also well aware that the United States
had adopted this form of underwater defence a few months
earlier. But he knew, as well, that the professional heads of the
Royal Navy would oppose any suggestion emanating from a
mere civilian on principle.

Anxious though he was to adopt this novel weapon,
Goschen had the shrewdness to realize that it was useless to
interfere at this stage. He passed the note, without comment,
to Rear-Admiral Wilson VC, Third Sea Lord and Controller
of the Navy. Such matters were *his* affair.

The 'salt-water' Admirals had always been strongly opposed
to this 'underhand' form of warfare, as Wilson described it.

Almost a hundred years earlier, Pitt had watched Robert Fulton's *Nautilus* nose her way under the waters of Walmer Roads before attacking and sinking the Danish brig *Dorothea*. To his untutored, civilian imagination this novel method of blowing holes in the bottoms of French warships brought a new dimension into the science of naval warfare. His enthusiasm was promptly suppressed by the First Lord of the Admiralty, the Earl of St Vincent, in no uncertain terms: 'Pitt was the greatest fool that ever existed to encourage a mode of warfare which those who commanded the sea did not want and which, if successful, would deprive them of it.'

Wilson shelved the matter in typical civil-service style. 'Any communication Mr Rice wishes to make in writing will receive consideration' he minuted the file. And *that*, he assumed, was *that*.

But Goschen, once he had the bit between his teeth, was not so easily circumvented. He was convinced that Britain could use the submarine to advantage and, acting in his capacity as political head of the Royal Navy, he wrote to Rice privately. The correspondence led to meetings and soon some hard figures emerged. The American company could deliver a Holland-type boat for £34,000 and they guaranteed to hold this price for a period of five years. Presented with this offer, and realizing that Goschen meant business, the admirals changed their tactics.

Wilson enlisted the aid of the Director of Naval Construction, Sir William White, who did some rapid calculations and declared the price too high—the French were building submarines for £25,000 apiece. He forgot to mention, however, that the French boats were decidedly inferior in every way to the Holland design. But he knew from long experience in the Civil Service that the Treasury would seize on this like a dog on a bone.

Fortunately for Wilson, the man most likely to support the submarine venture, Vice-Admiral Sir John (Jacky) Fisher, was safely on board his flagship HMS *Renown*, as Commander-in-Chief of the Mediterranean Fleet. Later, when he became First Sea Lord, Fisher gave submarine building almost as high priority as his beloved Dreadnoughts. But, for the time being at least, Jacky was conveniently out of the ring.

Despite determined opposition to the adoption of the submarine, the Admiralty yielded to Goschen and agreed, on 8 October, 1900, to order five Holland-type boats from the Electric Boat Company. A fighter to the last, even in a lost cause, Wilson announced his agreement because, as he put it, 'Our primary object is to test the value of the submarine boat as a weapon in the hands of our enemies', and he promptly dubbed it a 'damned un-English weapon'.

At this stage a General Election intervened and Goschen found himself replaced as First Lord by Lord Selborne, who was, significantly, a great friend of Sir John Fisher, as was also the new Parliamentary and Financial Secretary, H. O. Arnold-Foster.

So it fell to Lord Selborne, introducing the 1901 Naval Estimates in March, to make the first public acknowledgement that the Royal Navy had committed itself to the submarine.

A few days before the Estimates were introduced Wilson made one final effort to veto the new weapon, even though the submarines had already been ordered. Giving up the technical, financial, and historical arguments of the past few months, he turned to the ethical and tried to persuade the new First Lord to include a statement in his speech that 'HM Government considers it would be to the advantage of all Maritime nations of the world if the use of the submarine boat for attack could be prohibited.' Waxing in enthusiasm, Wilson, who had won his VC during a *land* battle in the Sudan, went on to suggest that we should 'treat all submarines as pirates in wartime and . . . *hang all the crews.*'

The first five boats to be commissioned were constructed

under licence by Vickers at Barrow-in-Furness and it was originally intended that these five boats should be allocated one each to Chatham, Portsmouth and Devonport, and to the two Torpedo Schools, with a view to exercising with destroyer flotillas. The influence of Wilson was clearly visible in this original appraisal. But the plan was soon scrapped.

Captain (later Admiral Sir) Reginald Bacon, the Navy's leading torpedo expert and later Fisher's biographer, was appointed Inspecting-Captain of Submarines and ensconced in a small room at the Controller's Department of the Admiralty. But his chief technical adviser, Sir William White, the Director of Naval Construction, was still strongly opposed to the submarine. He advised Bacon never to go below water in one —a remark which suggested that financial considerations were not the only ones in his mind when he originally allied himself with Wilson against Goschen in 1900. And Sir John Durston, Engineer-in-Chief and inventor of the water-tube boiler which Fisher introduced into the Navy against fierce opposition, refused to have anything to do with petrol engines working in a confined space.

Left on his own, Bacon was able to take complete control of the newly-formed Service and, aided by Vickers, began devising his own improvements to the Holland boats before they were even in service.

HM Submarine *No. 1* was launched on 2 November, 1902, and was followed shortly afterwards by her sister, *No. 2*. A design fault, said by some to have been deliberately interpolated into the plans by Holland's Fenian Society associates, resulted in *No. 1* capsizing when she was launched, but Captain Reginald Bacon quickly pin-pointed and corrected the trouble and the little submarine soon showed great promise. After fitting-out, the two boats, under the direction of Captain Cable, USN, underwent their diving trials and were put through rigorous tests before they were considered ready to be handed over to the Navy.

Finally the great day arrived and the torpedo-gunboat *Hazard*, commissioned as depot-ship to the newly-formed Submarine Branch, sailed for Barrow with Bacon on board to escort the first two boats down the West Coast via the Irish Sea and Land's End to Portsmouth.

Admiral of the Fleet the Earl of Cork and Orrery, then serving as a lieutenant on *Hazard* recalled the voyage as a series of mishaps with the primitive petrol engines breaking down every few miles. The little flotilla proceeded on the surface all the way and, on Admiralty instructions, took refuge in harbour every night. But Captain Bacon safely shepherded his flock into Portsmouth and the Navy was able to take its first close look at these underwater marvels.

By modern standards HM Submarine *No. 1* was a primitive and pitifully inadequate vessel. Displacing 104 tons on the surface and 122 tons submerged, she was 63′ 4″ long and had a maximum beam of 11′ 9″. Her four-cylinder petrol engine developed 160 h.p. giving a top surface speed of between eight and nine knots. For progress under the sea a sixty-cell battery fed the electric motor which, struggling to produce a puny 74 h.p., pushed the boat along at a maximum of five knots. The armament consisted of a solitary fourteen-inch torpedo tube set in the bows and her crew of seven had, as can be imagined, very little room in which to move, let alone live.

The interior stank of raw petrol-vapour, bilge-water, and dampness tinged with oil. When submerged, the unshielded electrical components emitted violent sparks which, in a confined atmosphere already saturated with petrol-vapour, added the danger of explosion to the other ever-present hazards of underwater running.

There was no gyro-compass. An ordinary standard compass was mounted on the *outside* of the hull, to keep it free from the magnetic influences inside the boat; the submarine commander could only view it through an unreliable optical tube fitted with a primitive mirror system, and there was no conning-tower.

When running submerged the single, fixed periscope could be neither raised nor lowered and, when coming in to make an attack the submarine had to be 'porpoised' so that the tip of the 'scope only broke the surface at intervals. To make matters worse, the uncorrected optical construction of the periscope gave the captain an upside-down view of the world above the waves—and this did not exactly assist accuracy when making a torpedo attack. But, despite the many defects, the submarine could move underwater and fire her deadly torpedo submerged.

Assembling at Portsmouth in 1903 the five Holland boats set out on a joint exercise which required them to sail around the Isle of Wight *on the surface*. Even this proved too much for the temperamental machinery. Three broke down before they had covered four miles, the fourth wallowed on a little further, and only one finally managed to reach Cowes under its own power. But Captain Bacon was undismayed.

Hard work and bitter experience gradually sorted out the faults in the engines and long technical discussions with the submarine commanders slowly ironed out the other defects. By 1904 the little flotilla was ready to show a disbelieving Navy their true potential.

Conceived for coastal work and too small for the open waters of the Channel, the five Hollands were assigned to the defence of Portsmouth during the Naval Manœuvres that followed in March. They were soon to make their mark; for they 'torpedoed' four battleships of the Channel Fleet, including the Fleet Flagship, to the undisguised fury of the same Admiral Wilson who had done so much to prevent the acceptance of the submarine by the Royal Navy.

The first of Bacon's improved Hollands, the *A.1*, took part in the exercises and proved that her larger size—at one hundred feet she was nearly forty feet longer than the original vessels—

DUW—B

and higher speed were a great advance. The class, as such, were not good sea-boats and had an unfortunate tendency to plunge through the waves when running in a heavy swell from either ahead or astern. But the newly-devised conning-tower helped to make things more comfortable for the captain when the submarine was cruising on the surface.

On the last day of the manœuvres, 18 March, 1904, the pioneer flotilla left harbour and sailed out into the Solent to set an ambush for the cruiser *Juno*—due to return to Portsmouth on completing her part in the exercises. *A.1*, prototype of the new class, took her place as one of the flotilla.

Juno was sighted coming down the Solent off the Nab Tower at noon and Submarine *No.2* edged into an attacking position, fired off an oblique shot and missed. Closing to within 400 yards, *No.3* loosed off her practice torpedo and, to the surprise of her young captain and the consternation of the cruiser's officers, scored a direct hit. Delighted with this proof of his flock's capabilities, Bacon signalled *A.1* to join in the attack. It was now Lt Mansergh's turn, but so intent was he on his quarry that he failed to notice the liner *Berwick Castle* bearing down upon him.

Spotting something lying half-submerged in the path of his ship the Master of the liner rapped out an order to the helms-man and then jerked the handle of the engine-room telegraph to full astern. The steamship, her helm jammed hard to starboard, responded slowly and a collision was inevitable. With a screech of ripping metal the submarine rolled over and plunged to the bottom of the Solent with all hands. Unaware of the tragedy, and signalling that she had apparently struck a practice-torpedo, the *Berwick Castle* resumed her voyage to Hamburg.

A few hours later Bacon realized that *A.1* was long overdue. When he was passed the liner's signal a sudden fear gripped his heart and he set out in *Hazard* to try and locate the missing submarine.

A large patch of white water created by the air-bubbles escaping from the shattered hull of the *A.1* was mute testimony to the tragedy which had taken place so close to home. There was no equipment on board for salvage and nothing could be done to rescue the trapped crew—if, indeed, any of them were still alive. Staring at the troubled waters, the crew of *Hazard* stood at the rails in silence as their ship reverently circled the grave of their comrades.

The new service had experienced its first disaster and one all the more horrifying for happening so close to the safety of Portsmouth Harbour. The big question was, what effect would the tragedy have on the morale of the other submarine crews?

Sir John Fisher, newly returned from the Mediterranean and serving as Commander-in-Chief, Portsmouth, hastily penned a private report on the accident to the Prince of Wales who had visited the unfortunate *A.1* only a few days earlier. Then, having completed the letter he composed a General Signal to his Command:

'Time has not permitted the Commander-in-Chief until now to express publicly his great personal sorrow for the grievous calamity that has befallen us. Practically our gallant comrades died in action. Their lives are not thrown away if we consider their splendid example of cheerful and enthusiastic performance of a duty involving all the risks of war.

The Commander-in-Chief cannot delay expressing his admiration of the manner in which the Officers and men of the Submarine Flotillas have carried out the recent manœuvres, as the risks have been those which usually are only incurred in war, and the pluck and endurance which have been shown leave nothing to be desired, but is only what the Admiral expected.'

It was a fitting epitaph not only to Lt Mansergh and his crew of brave pioneers who had gone to the bottom in *A.1*, but also to the hundreds of British submariners who were to subsequently perish.

Despite her tragic loss off the Nab Tower, *A.1*'s career was not over. A month after the accident she was salvaged, repaired, and refitted for service. And in the cramped confines of her primitive control-room the submarine's new captain, a dark-haired twenty-two-year-old lieutenant, Max Kennedy Horton, learned to master the arts of undersea warfare. And, as we shall see later, he learned his lessons well.

Later the same year the submarine *A.4* almost met with a similar fate. Commanded by Lt Martin Nasmith, another pioneer who was to win fame during the war, she was sent out into the Solent for an experiment into underwater-signalling.

A.4 had to lie submerged with the tip of a slim brass ventilating-tube poking out of the water while her commander listened as a torpedo-boat circled on the surface ringing a bell at intervals.

Unaware of the dangerous trials in progress, a passing steamer came too close, and her wash engulfed the open ventilator. Sea-water surged down the brass tube flooding the submarine's cramped interior and, before anything could be done, the bows tilted and *A.4* plunged to the bottom ninety feet below. As the horrified men on the torpedo-boat watched the air-bubbles streaming to the surface it seemed a repeat of the *A.1* disaster.

Inside *A.4* the rising sea-water soon reached the batteries and clouds of chlorine gas filled the hull making the crew cough and choke in the darkness. But there was no panic. While some of the men held back the water by wedging clothing into the base of the open tube Lt Herbert, the First Lieutenant, groped his way through the poisonous blackness, located the controls, and blew the tanks. After minutes which seemed an eternity the little submarine rose slowly to the surface and Nasmith, Herbert, and the rest of the crew staggered out of the hatchway into the fresh air.

The 'A' class suffered more than their fair share of disaster. Sir John Durston's fears proved to be well-founded when an explosion on *A.5* caused by an electrical spark igniting the ever-present petrol-vapour, killed six of the submarine's crew and injured another twelve.

And the inherent design-fault of the class, their tendency to plunge through a head sea instead of riding the waves, brought sudden tragedy to *A.7* a few years later. Cruising on the surface in a heavy swell she dived out of control, without warning, taking her entire crew to the bottom.

On Trafalgar Day, 1904, Sir John Fisher was appointed First Sea Lord. His support for the submarine was already well known and, a few months earlier, he had written: 'It is astounding to me, perfectly astounding, how the very best amongst us fail to realize the vast impending revolution in Naval warfare and Naval strategy that the submarine will accomplish.'

Once firmly placed in the seat of power, with characteristic energy he began a large building programme. 'More submarines at once,' he demanded. 'At least twenty-five in addition to those now building and ordered, and 100 more as soon as practical.'

The building slips at Vickers were now busier than ever and the Royal Dockyards, those bastions of conservatism, were dragged into the urgent production of 'Fisher's Toys'—as his hated rival Lord Charles Beresford once scornfully termed them. The 'B', 'C', and 'D' classes were designed, built, and commissioned between 1905 and 1910—each larger and more powerful than its predecessor.

Fisher's vision sent these new vessels far away from the sheltered coastal waters of Britain. Six 'B' class submarines were posted to Gibraltar and Malta and, in 1910, three of the larger 'C' class boats, escorted by the sloop *Rosario*, were towed to the Far East to join the China Squadron at Hong Kong; an epic voyage for submarines in those early pioneer days.

When, in the same year, Captain Roger Keyes took over command of the Submarine Flotillas the Navy boasted a total of twelve 'A's, eleven 'B's, thirty-seven 'C's, and the newly-commissioned Overseas Submarine 'D.1'. The original five Hollands were no longer considered operational but they remained in service for experimental and training purposes. Fisher's job of expansion had been well and truly accomplished.

Although at heart a destroyer man, Keyes took the new service in his stride and, within a year, had reorganized it on a war footing. One of his first achievements was the adoption of the retractable periscope. Realizing that the new boats were too large and unwieldy for 'porpoising' Keyes saw that some form of mechanically-powered 'scope was essential. Persuading a reluctant Financial Secretary to supply the money required, he purchased the best French and German models available, and then proceeded to pass them over to British manufacturers with orders to copy them. This foresight resulted in British submarines having very efficient periscopes when they sailed to war four years later. Less successful was the borrowing by Armstrongs of the French Laubeuf design and by Scotts of the Italian Laurenti type. Both classes proved decidedly disappointing in service and all had been sold to Italy by the end of 1916.

Anxious to obtain higher surface speeds, Keyes next turned his attention to the possibilities of steam-engines, 'a simple and well-tried means of propulsion' as he called it. Experienced submarine commanders were openly hostile to the idea of funnels and steam boilers for obvious reasons and Fisher's comment when he heard of the suggestion was bitterly scathing: 'Like damned fools . . . we are hankering after steam-engines in submarines.' The disastrous results of this experiment in steam-submarines will be seen later. Suffice it to say, at the moment, that the first attempt, the *Swordfish*, built by Scotts, was such a lamentable failure that it was finally converted into a surface patrol boat. There was a similar lack of success in another big submarine, the Vickers-built *Nautilus*, who ended her days ignominiously as a battery-charging vessel.

There is no doubt that Roger Keyes did a great deal for the British Submarine Service and at every opportunity he brought the submarine to the notice of the admirals and the Admiralty. He was an immensely popular man with his subordinates and did all he could to help his captains reach a peak of war efficiency. Nevertheless, his enthusiasm often over-rode his better judgement and some responsibility for the introduction of inadequate submarine designs must be laid at Keyes' door.

Submarine tactics were still in the strictly experimental stage but under Keyes' imaginative control a pattern gradually began to emerge. In the 1911 exercises the impossibility of maintaining a close blockade of the enemy coast was proved and, in 1912, Max Horton in *D.6*, and Lambton in *D.2*, both penetrated the Firth of Forth and 'sank' warships at anchor off Rosyth. But despite these demonstrations of the submarine's potential all was not well with the service.

Due to Keyes' policy of breaking the Vickers' monopoly and borrowing foreign designs no new submarines had been produced for two whole years. In October, 1914, the Navy had twelve *less* submarines than in January, 1910, and the constant search for better and faster submarines, though praiseworthy in attempt, hampered the production of proven lines. The proper role of the early submarines, with their mechanical unreliability and archaic communications was by no means clear. For it must be remembered that no senior serving officer in the Navy had any personal experience of submarine warfare or submarine handling.

Within the Submarine Service the submarine-commanders were all young men of junior rank. Despite the fact that they were the *only* men qualified to speak with authority on submarine matters their views were ignored by the senior officers. The stringent class system of the Victorian navy still permeated the command structure of the Royal Navy before 1914 and many of the failures in the coming war can be attributed to the resultant stifling of personal initiative. As Beatty himself commented after Jutland, 'there seems to be something wrong with our bloody ships—*and with the system.*'

But there was no lack of personal initiative, heroism and skill in the infant Submarine Service. It was men like Nasmith, Horton, Laurence and Lambton, who had served in submarines since the earliest pioneer days, who brought about the final triumph of the new Branch. And it is with the exploits of these gallant commanders that the rest of this story is concerned.

CHAPTER TWO

'Incredibly Difficult Conditions'

ALTHOUGH THE British ultimatum expired at midnight 4 August, 1914, the Admiralty 'War Telegram' was issued to the ships of the Royal Navy one hour earlier, at 11 pm, and the Fleet was technically at war sixty minutes before the rest of the country; for Churchill had realized that the Germans might interpret the ultimatum as expiring at midnight European Time, one hour earlier than British GMT, and he didn't intend the Navy to get caught with its pants down.

When the war started the Royal Navy had a total of seventy-four submarines in full commission. Of these, three 'C' class boats were stationed at Gibraltar; *B.9*, *B.10*, and *B.11*, one of which was to produce the Submarine Branch's first VC, were at Malta; and the three veterans of the 1910 epic voyage to the Far East were in Hong Kong. Australia's first two submarines, *AE.1* and *AE.2* were cruising in their own home waters and the remaining 65 vessels, divided between nine flotillas, were based at home. Of these the 8th or Overseas Flotilla under Commodore Keyes consisted of eight 'D' and nine 'E' class submarines with the depot ships *Adamant* and *Maidstone* and the destroyers *Lurcher*, the Commodore's personal flag-ship, and *Firedrake*. Ten of these boats were at Harwich by 31 July, and the rest joined later in ones and twos.

Five other flotillas made up from 'B' and 'C' class boats were distributed amongst the patrol flotillas whose task was to guard the East Coast and the Straits of Dover. These were based at Dover, Chatham, Humber, Tyne and Forth. The three obsolete 'A' class flotillas were attached to local defence commands with a purely inshore role.

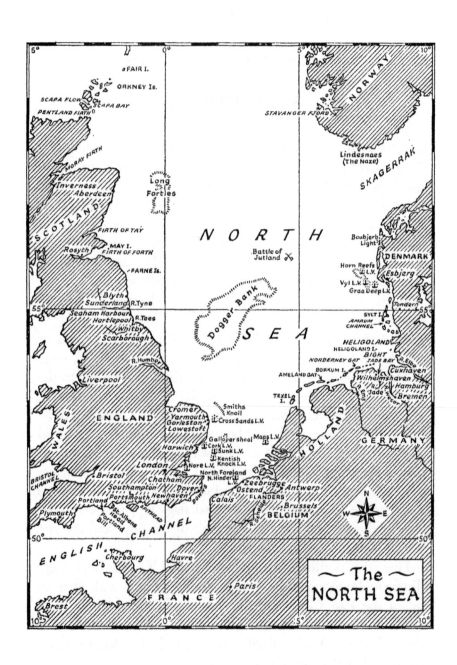

~ The ~
NORTH SEA

The war was only three hours old when the first two British submarines, both of the 8th Flotilla, set out for their patrol area. Lt-Cdr Talbot in *E.6* and Lt-Cdr Goodhart in *E.8* were towed out of the darkened harbour at Harwich by the destroyers *Amethyst* and *Ariel* and set out in the wake of a surface force of cruisers and destroyers which were steaming hard for the Heligoland Bight. Towing was adopted to ease the strain on the still unreliable diesel-engines and also to conserve oil. A further four boats of the flotilla, accompanied by Keyes in *Lurcher*, set off a little later to take up a patrol line between the Galloper and Hinder Shoals in support of *E.6* and *E.8*

It was a stirring sight as the little convoy left harbour and Keyes recorded: 'It was all very inspiring, and the *Ganges* [a training ship] and the pier and foreshore of Shotley, despite the early hour, were crowded with boys who cheered themselves hoarse as each ship passed.'

The surface ships were soon in action. Meeting up with the German minelayer *Konigin Luise* they promptly sank her with a few well-placed shells and returned to base with twenty-two wounded prisoners. The two lonely submarines were not so lucky. Deep inside enemy waters, the seas sweeping over their bows and spraying the men exposed on the bridge with white stinging foam, *E.6* and *E.8* began their dreary patrol. By day they crept along at periscope-depth, by night they surfaced to re-charge their batteries. This was their first taste of the dull routine of combat patrol.

Six days later, on 11 August, they returned to Harwich empty-handed and the weary commanders wrote up their unexciting reports. War, it seemed, was not so full of bravado and daring deeds as they had anticipated.

Meanwhile the transportation of the British Expeditionary Force across the Channel, a total of six Infantry Divisions and one Cavalry Division, had begun. By the time the main body of troops had embarked on 13 August the thirteen boats of the 8th Flotilla had been pulled back from enemy waters and were placed in a wide defensive arc eastwards of the Channel, flanked by the North Foreland and the East Dyck, to ambush any enemy surface forces sent down to shoot up the troop transports crossing the Straits to Calais.

The little 'B' and 'C' class submarines of the Dover patrol acted as close support as the heavily-laden transports pushed their way across to France.

But there was no respite for the men of the 8th Flotilla. Two days later the hardworked *E.6* and *E.8* were again detached for duties in the Heligoland Bight and the dreary routine of keeping periscope watch in heavy, rolling seas was repeated.

This time, however, they found themselves surrounded by hundreds of Dutch, Danish, and German trawlers and had to operate with the greatest care. Frequent dives were necessary to avoid the ambling fishing vessels and surfacing, even at night, was fraught with the danger of being rammed accidentally. Finally the submarine commanders called off the patrol and returned to Harwich empty-handed once again.

But Lt-Cdr Turner in *D.3* accompanied by *D.2*, *E.5* and *E.7* was having a much more exciting time. Running into a number of German destroyer patrols the submarine commanders found plenty of fast-moving targets. *D.3*, lining up for a torpedo attack, had to dive sharply as an enemy destoyer thundered in to ram and *E.5* was, at one time, in the happy position of having a German ship in the sights, both fore *and* aft. But the high-speed zig-zag movements of the enemy ships made successful attacks impossible and the submarine had to dive to avoid being rammed.

E.5 and *E.7*, on their way home on the surface, mistook the German cruiser *Rostock* for a friendly ship and were forced to crash-dive to escape destruction. Keyes had a few choice words to say about ship recognition to the two commanders when they arrived back in Harwich to make their reports!

Meanwhile in the Bight things were beginning to hot up. Lt-Cdr Ernest Leir, captain of *E.4*, played hide-and-seek with enemy destroyer patrols for several hours but neither side succeeded in their attacks. The Germans circled the area with relentless determination, knowing full well that ultimately the submarine would have to come up for air. But *E.4* stayed on the bottom for twenty-four hours, a record in underwater endurance for 1914, and the men sprawled quietly in odd corners of the submarine to conserve the precious oxygen. Heads were beginning to pound and breathing grew more shallow as the hours passed but they had no alternative but to sit it out. At last they could hold on no longer and, moving slowly to their positions, they awaited Leir's order to surface.

'Shut main vents.'

Even the effort of pulling down the levers was an agony of exertion in the oxygen-starved atmosphere and there was a long pause before the First Lieutenant reported, 'All main vents shut, sir.'

Leir moved to the periscope and swung it around in a full circle scanning the darkness for a glimpse of the enemy. All seemed clear and he nodded to his Number One.

'Surface.'

'Blow all main ballast.'

Sweating under the strain, the crew opened the valves and there was a roar of compressed air. The bows lifted slightly as the hydroplane turned and Leir unfastened the clips of the conning-tower hatch. The First Lieutenant called off the depth from the dials and as it reached 'Ten feet . . .' the Captain swung the hatch open.

There was a rush of greenish-yellow-coloured air and he had to hang on to the steel ladder until it had subsided. Then he heaved himself on to the bridge and scanned the dark surface. They were in luck. The enemy had given up at nightfall and gone home. The log laconically noted the difficulties of a long period submerged: 'Breathing nearly twice as quick but otherwise no difficulties at all.'

Leir was the humorist of the 8th Flotilla. On another patrol he surfaced in the middle of a German trawler fleet and annoyed the enemy fishermen by cruising from boat to boat demanding fresh fish for his crew. Two Naval trawlers were sent out to deal with the impudent submarine but Leir was unconcerned. Remaining on the surface he let them get close and then calmly torpedoed the leading boat after which the other departed from the scene at high speed.

The crew picked up the survivors and put them in a life-boat. Leir then towed them several miles to a German Light Vessel. Before leaving however, he selected three sailors as prisoners, taking care to 'pick the most intelligent-looking ones'.

Max Horton, commanding *E.9* used to play auction bridge with his fellow officers while his submarine rested on the bottom of the North Sea to avoid enemy patrols. And in a letter home early in the war he boasted of winning 4s 11½d during one patrol.

But war had its more serious side. Lt-Cdr Herbert, the hero of the *A.4* accident and now captain of the submarine *D.5*, sighted the *Rostock* in the Bight, screened by three destroyers. Unlike the unhappy captains of *E.5* and *E.7* he recognized the four-funnelled German cruiser immediately and dived to attack. The electric-motors hummed softly as she turned towards the enemy. It was a tricky operation. The sea was flat calm and the spray from the periscope could be easily spotted by the German look-outs. In addition the submarine had to be eased through the destroyer-screen before launching her torpedoes.

Herbert was a perfectionist and he handled the submarine with the delicacy of an artist as he steered her past the destroyers and snatched a quick glimpse through the periscope at the great cruiser. It was enough to tell him all he needed to know and he gave the course and angle of deflection ready for his attack. There was a tense silence inside the submarine and then:

'Fire One! . . . Fire Two . . . !'

D.5 shuddered slightly as the torpedoes fired and Herbert settled down, counting off the seconds, waiting for the explosion. But it never came. Herbert's aim had in fact been correct, but both torpedoes had run deep and had passed directly beneath the *Rostock*'s hull without touching her. The reason was simple. The explosive warhead weighed 40 lbs more than the practice head used in peace-time and the extra weight made the torpedo run deeper with the same valve-settings. It was simple and it was obvious—but the boffins at the Admiralty did not realize the difference in performance for several months and missed targets were a feature of submarine attacks in the early months of the war.

Commodore Keyes was now able to turn his attention to the all-absorbing task of preparing a sweep of the Bight using submarines in co-operation with surface ships of Commodore Tyrwhitt's Harwich Force. Keyes' plan was based on the information about German patrol movements obtained by the submarines of the 8th Flotilla during their sorties into the Bight. With this knowledge he and Tyrwhitt claimed that a strike-force of light cruisers and destroyers could 'roll up' the enemy patrols and gain a quick and much-needed victory. Submerged submarines were to be the bait used to draw the German ships out into the Bight and, with luck, they would also be in a position to torpedo any heavy enemy units that came out to support their light craft.

It was a scheme which particularly appealed to Churchill's imagination and in his view the idea of taking the war into Germany's home waters out-weighed any technical difficulties that might arise. Here was the perfect ambush. A decoy to bring the enemy out; then the rush of the cavalry to decimate them and cut off their retreat. And the submarines, the snipers, lying in wait to pick off the unwary German ships hastening to the rescue.

There was only one snag. The Chief of Staff vetoed Keyes' suggestion of bringing some of the Grand Fleet battle-cruisers south to support the light-cruisers, so the Commodore had to proceed on the assumption that the Grand Fleet were not assisting.

Now that he had the Admiralty's concurrence Keyes finished preparing his plans and in the early hours of 28 August the surface ships headed out from Harwich into the North Sea led by the *Arethusa* flying Tyrwhitt's pennant.

The submarines had left on the previous night, as with their slower speed they would take longer to reach their stations. *E.4*, with Ernest Leir in command, *E.5* and *E.9* were assigned an inner patrol-line north and south of Heligoland; *E.6*, *E.7* and *E.8* formed an outer line forty miles to the north-west; while *D.2* and *D.8* were sent to the mouth of the Ems River with instructions to torpedo enemy units returning to their bases after the action. Keyes himself went to sea in the destroyer *Lurcher*, which was the only way, with the chronic and short-range wireless communications then prevailing, by which the Commodore could keep in touch with his flock and receive and relay direct orders from the Admiralty.

Fortunately the Battle of the Heligoland Bight, as it was named, proved a resounding British victory. But it bore little resemblance to the set-piece action envisaged in Keyes' and Tyrwhitt's original plans.

Heavy mist cut down visibility and the action, when joined, was piece-meal and sporadic. Ships would appear out of the fog, fire a few salvoes, and then vanish back into the murk. The submarines took no part in the battle, being too slow to keep up with the destroyers and light cruisers; the Harwich Force was almost trapped, and only the welcome but unexpected arrival of Beatty's battle-cruisers 'like elephants walking through a pack of pi-dogs' saved the day.

The fact that the battle was won obscured the defects of Keyes' and Tyrwhitt's plan and the chaotic state of the Royal Navy's communications. The victory served to confirm the theory that co-operation with surface ships was a practicable possibility despite all the indications to the contrary.

Only one boat, *E.4* with the redoubtable Ernest Leir aboard, took any real part in the action, and even that was a passive one. Creeping beneath the surface at periscope-depth, Leir watched the destroyers of the 3rd and 5th Divisions hammer the German torpedo-boat *V.187* into a shattered blazing wreck and relayed an exciting blow-by-blow account of the action to *E.4*'s crew. As the *V.187* began to sink Leir decided to remain in the vicinity to watch developments. One of the British destroyers, *Defender*, hoisted out two of her boats to help pick up the survivors but as they were being rowed towards the sinking torpedo-boat a German cruiser suddenly appeared out of the mist.

The enemy opened fire on *Defender* and, abandoning her boats, she wheeled away with shells bursting all around her. Leir tried to swing *E.4* into an attacking position but within seconds the German cruiser and British destroyer had disappeared, leaving behind the two ship's boats.

Abandoned only a few miles from the enemy coast the men in the *Defender*'s boats were already resigned to seeing the war out in a prison camp when the ungainly hull of the *E.4* came to the surface a few yards away.

There was no time to be lost. Leir threw back the conning-tower hatch and the submarine's crew ran on to the hull-casing to help the sailors aboard. A British officer and nine ratings were heaved to safety together with three unwounded Germans. There was no more room left on *E.4* for the remaining enemy sailors but Leir gave them some water, biscuits and a compass and told them the course to steer for Heligoland. The two English lifeboats with their German occupants pulled slowly away into the mist and *E.4* slid quietly to periscope-depth and made her way back to Harwich.

Talbot, in *E.6*, also had his moment, although not quite in the manner intended, for faulty staff-work had left both Keyes and Tyrwhitt in ignorance of the last minute decision to send the Grand Fleet battle-cruisers and attendant light cruisers into the Bight to support the Harwich Force. Similarly, Beatty and Goodenough, in command of the cruisers coming down from the North, had no details of the submarine dispositions. It was inevitable, therefore, that when Goodenough, one of the outstanding cruiser Commodores of the war, sighted a submarine on the surface he assumed it to be a U-boat and altered course to ram at high speed.

'Suddenly everyone was electrified to see a periscope on the starboard bow, distant 500 yards,' Commander (later Sir Stephen) King-Hall, at that time serving as a junior officer on Goodenough's flagship *Southampton*, related some years afterwards. 'The helm was put hard over, the ship heeled, and we prepared to ram her. The submarine made a steep dive and went down at such an angle that her tail nearly came out of the water. A few seconds later we thundered over the place where she had been.'

Talbot's reactions saved *E.6* and her crew from an untimely end. And his quick thinking also saved *Southampton* for, in the split second she appeared in the periscope lens, he identified her as friendly and refrained from firing his torpedoes.

The First Light Cruiser Squadron swung west with *Lurcher* trailing behind and within minutes they sighted Beatty's battle-cruisers.

In his Official Despatch Beatty admitted that the lack of precise information about the British submarines was a considerable problem for he appreciated that mistaken identity was by no means impossible in the difficult conditions of a naval action. Even Churchill commenting on the battle admitted, 'Very little, however, turned out as had been planned . . . nor was Admiral Beatty aware of the areas in which the British submarines were working.' But, the Commodore claimed 'the submarines had proved, under incredibly difficult conditions, that they could be trusted to work in co-operation with surface craft and take care of themselves.' He omitted to point out that the 'incredibly difficult conditions' were due, in part, to his own planning.

When the excitement of the action had died away and, in Churchill's words, 'except for furtive movements by individual submarines and minelayers, not a dog stirred,' the men of the 8th Flotilla continued their dull but dangerous routine patrols deep inside the enemy's home waters.

On 10 September Leir fought a duel with two U-boats fifteen miles out from Heligoland, and was lucky to escape without damage. It began when Leir spotted the *U-23* coming to the surface about 1½ miles away. It was too good an opportunity to miss and *E.4* slid quietly to periscope-depth to begin stalking her quarry. As the U-boat centred in the cross-sights of the periscope Leir gave the order to fire.

According to Keyes the torpedo passed underneath the enemy submarine because Leir 'was rather too close when he fired.' With the knowledge now available about the erratic depth-keeping qualities of the British war torpedoes it seems more likely that it was a technical fault rather than a human error. Leir, however, was undismayed by his bad luck and in his report noted that the torpedo probably passed underneath his target, 'judging by the gesticulations on her bridge.'

A few minutes later he realized that the Germans were signalling and, swinging the periscope in the direction of their flashing morse-lamp he sighted a second submarine following behind *U-23*. Almost immediately she opened fire on *E.4*'s periscope as Leir prepared for a second attack and his aim was spoiled by the great fountains of water that deluged his lens as the shells exploded. The second torpedo also missed, but it had done the trick. Thoroughly demoralized by Leir's perseverance both enemy submarines turned tail and fled.

Lt-Cdr Brodie in *D.8* was also involved in an abortive duel with a U-boat which ended in stale-mate. 'Neither of us knew what to do,' Brodie complained when he returned to base.

But it was Max Horton, the man who had commanded the

salvaged *A.1* ten years earlier and who had later penetrated the
defences of the Firth of Forth in *D.6* during the 1912
manœuvres, who scored the first major victory for the 8th
Flotilla. *E.9*, his new command, had spent the night resting on
the bottom of the Bight six miles SSW of Heligoland and at
dawn on 13 September, 1914, he brought her up to the surface
ready for another patrol at periscope-depth. The weather was
thick and it was raining hard although the sea itself was fairly
smooth. After a quick look around Horton took *E.9* down to
seventy feet and at 7.15 am he brought her up to twenty feet
for another check through the periscope. A quarry was in sight.
Yard by yard Horton stalked his target with the patient skill of
the born hunter. Two miles away the crew of the German
cruiser *Hela* went about their duties unaware of the lurking
menace closing in on them. *E.9*'s log takes up the story of the
historic attack:

7.28 am Position 600 yards abeam of cruiser (two funnels).
Submarine very lively diving. Fired both bow torpedoes at her starboard side at intervals of about
15 seconds.

7.29 am Heard single loud explosion. Submarine at 70 feet,
course parallel to cruiser.

7.32 am Rose to 22 feet, observed cruiser between waves;
appeared to have stopped and to have list to starboard. Splashes from shot on our port side and ahead
of the cruiser. Turned periscope to see where shots
were coming from, but submarine was very deep,
and only observed wisps of smoke and mast very
close. Dived to 70 feet to pick up trim.

8.35 am 20 feet; sighted trawlers where cruiser had been, 4 or
5 in number in a cluster. Horizon slightly misty, one
trawler, one cable (600 feet) on beam. Dived 70 feet.

E.9 was now no longer the hunter, she was the quarry.
Throughout the rest of the day Horton and his men waited,

listening to the roar of the German destroyers criss-crossing the sea above them. It was fortunate that the depth-charge had not been developed in 1914 or the British submarine would have been lying on the bottom of the Bight, a shattered wreck. Twice Horton came up to periscope-depth and twice he had to dive again as the enemy destroyers came in to ram. Not until nine o'clock in the evening was *E.9* able to come to the surface to recharge her weakened batteries and two hours later she was taken back to the bottom for her night's rest.

But even his victory over the *Hela* failed to disturb Horton's routine and the next day found his periscope poking into Heligoland harbour scouting for more targets. He found only a few trawlers bobbing gently at their buoys.

Although 13 September was a lucky day for Max Horton and the crew of *E.9* it was a day of ill-omen for *AE.1*—the first Allied submarine to be lost on active service, *AE.1* was the Royal Australian Navy's first submarine, an identical twin, in fact, to Horton's *E.9*, and with other warships of the Dominion's fledgling fleet, she was sent to patrol off German New Guinea in search of the enemy cruiser *Geier*.

With the destroyer *Parramatta* in company the submarine set off towards Cape Gazelle but, although the surface-ship returned some hours later, the *AE.1* was never seen again. Her commander, two officers, and crew of thirty-two seamen perished by some unseen hand in the Bismarck Sea.

From 14 to 21 September the North Sea area was swept by tremendous storms which forced the patrolling submarines to seek shelter on the bottom. Keyes wrote, 'Even when cruising at a depth of 60 feet the submarines were rolling considerably and pumping, i.e. vertically moving, about 20 feet.'

Horton's log of the *E.9* for the 14th read: 'Midnight. Very heavy seas. Bent stanchions and splash-plate. Endeavoured to rest on the bottom but disturbance continued to such a depth, i.e. 120 feet, that the submarine, despite 8 tons negative buoyancy, bumped.'

While the storm raged in the North Sea an equally fierce storm was sweeping the German Naval High Command. The threat of British submarines operating in their coastal waters was causing great concern and, following the sinking of the *Hela* by Max Horton, orders were issued for the High Sea Fleet to carry out its exercises in the safer, land-locked waters of the Baltic. It was clear that the constant harrying of the 8th Flotilla was beginning to tell.

The patrols continued—fair weather or foul. A near disaster to *E.6*, still under command of Lt-Cdr Talbot, had the unexpected result of locating a newly-laid German minefield. *E.6* was diving when the incident occurred and, as her bows angled down, the crew heard 'something clatter along the ship's side and go clear.' Talbot was puzzled by the sound and he brought her cautiously back to the surface. Throwing back the hatch he began a tour of inspection. He located the cause in a few moments. A mine was lying on the hydroplane with its mooring cable jammed between the pivoting mechanism and the hull!

Although the horns of the mine were pointing away from the submarine's steel hull it was a difficult and dangerous task to lift the heavy cylinder clear without detonating it. As an additional hazard, *E.6* was surfaced only a few miles away from the German coast. Concentrating on the immediate danger of being blown sky-high by the mine, the crew went to work to free the tangled cable and, after an hour's tense labour, the heavy metal cylinder slid into the sea.

On 30 September Horton took *E.9* to the mouth of the West Ems in search of more targets. He found a German destroyer patrol and demonstrated his skill by coming up to periscope-depth in the centre of the formation so that he could observe, and later report, their tactics.

So impressed was Keyes with Horton's report that he immediately called up Tyrwhitt to suggest another sweep with surface ships and submarines and hoping to rouse the Admiralty into action Keyes wrote a plea which concluded: 'I submit that our [surface] inactivity in the Heligoland Bight, can but be encouraging to an enemy, which must necessarily be elated at its recent success.' (This success referred to the sinking of the three cruisers *Aboukir*, *Hogue*, and *Cressy* by the German *U-29*.) But Churchill had more pressing problems to attend to and Keyes' plan was pigeon-holed.

By now even the submarines of the Dover Patrol were beginning to see action and, on 2 October the veteran *B.3* was attacked by a marauding U-boat off the South Goodwins. Fortunately the enemy's aim was poor and the *B.3* lived to tell the tale.

Then, four days later, Max Kennedy Horton and *E.9* struck again; frustrated in his efforts to bag a battleship Horton set his torpedoes to run shallow and switched his search to destroyers. It was a premeditated gamble for few submarine commanders were sufficiently skilful to score a hit on these small fast-moving vessels. But his luck was in and, on the last day of the patrol, he sighted the German destroyer *S.116* and sent her to the bottom with a torpedo amidships.

'To hit a destroyer always requires maximum luck,' Horton wrote to a friend later. 'She went up beautifully, and when I had a chance of a good look round about five minutes after-wards, all that was to be seen was about fifteen feet of bow sticking up vertically out of the water.' Keyes wrote, 'To get one of those wriggling destroyers is like shooting snipe with a rifle,' and *E.9* began a submarine tradition when she returned to harbour by flying the 'Jolly Roger' to celebrate her victory— a pretty compliment to their Commodore.

Horton became a national hero and his photograph was on the front pages of every newspaper and magazine in the land. His DSO was warmly welcomed by the British public who badly needed something to cheer about in those dark days of the war.

The day after the loss of the *S.116* the Germans stopped the movement of all merchant shipping from Lubeck for twenty-four hours and it was evident that their High Command was becoming thoroughly rattled by constant submarine patrols in coastal waters.

The German C-in-C, Admiral von Ingenohl, made no secret of his thoughts on the situation: 'Submarines have entirely altered conditions in our operational bases in the German Bight; in this confined area we are exposed to continual danger and continual observation, which we have no means of avoiding.'

Although from an enemy hand it was an honourable citation to the bravery and tenacity of the men who manned the 8th Submarine Flotilla.

CHAPTER THREE

'Confusion and Lost Opportunities'

UNAWARE OF von Ingenohl's pessimistic memorandum, but sensing that the German High Command was perturbed by the activities of the 8th Flotilla, Keyes sent his submarine patrols even deeper into the enemy's inshore waters. A special reconnaissance operation was mounted during October, 1914, the ultimate purpose of which was known to only a handful of staff officers.

Lt-Cdr Boyle in *D.3* left Harwich, in company with Cochrane in *D.1*, and penetrated further east than any previous patrol in his search for information on German shipping movements in the Skagerrak. And Lt-Cdr Benning, commanding *E.5* which was engaged in the same task, even surfaced alongside the Vyl Shoal and Graa Deep Lightships where, with the impudence of youth, he bribed their captains to supply information in exchange for tins of hot soup from the submarine's galley.

The knowledge gleaned from these extensive patrols was carefully collated by the Staff Officers on *Maidstone* and there were trips to the Admiralty for top-secret conferences on the forthcoming operation. Finally, on the morning of 17 October, the *E.1*, *E.9* and *E.11* were ready to leave Harwich for the Baltic. The events that followed are told in the next chapter.

Meanwhile Ernest Leir and the hard-worked *E.4* were still hunting the enemy and, on 8 October, a white hospital-ship was sighted. The submarine commander examined her carefully through the periscope but she carried the correct international markings and she was flying a large Red Cross flag. Still, there was something about her that made Leir suspicious and he brought *E.4* to the surface for a closer examination.

The unexpected appearance of the submarine resulted in the 'hospital ship' hauling down her Red Cross and putting on a burst of speed. *E.4* gave chase but the submarine was too slow to catch up and the ship entered the Western Ems. One more vital piece of information was reported back to Keyes— the enemy were using look-out vessels disguised as hospital-ships.

Both sides were now sending submarines in search of sub-marines, on the maxim of setting a thief to catch a thief. Later in the war this form of ambush brought many successes to both the British and the Germans, but in 1914 the tactics involved were still in their infancy and most attacks proved abortive. On 9 October a U-boat came to the surface only fifty yards from the *E.10* but the range was too close to fire and both submarines slunk away.

Eight days later the Overseas Flotilla suffered their first casualty in a similar underwater ambush. *E.3*, on a routine patrol off the mouth of the River Ems, was sighted by the *U-27*. Before the alarm could be sounded a torpedo sent the British vessel to the bottom of the sea.

The naval war was going badly and, despite the success of the submarines and Beatty's battle-cruisers in the Heligoland battle, the public was restive. They had been led to expect an overwhelming naval victory in the opening days of the war but, instead, they heard only of disasters and losses.

In the Mediterranean, during the first crucial hours of the war, the German battle-cruiser *Goeben*, and her cruiser consort *Breslau* had slipped through the Navy's fingers and gained sanctuary in Turkey—a feat which materially accelerated that country's entry into the war. On 27 October, 1914, there was a fresh disaster when the super-dreadnought *Audacious* struck a mine in the Irish Sea and sank with heavy loss of life. Five days later, off the coast of Chile, the cruisers *Good Hope* and *Monmouth* were sent to the bottom by the German Admiral von

Spee at the Battle of Coronel, in the Royal Navy's first defeat
for over one hundred years.

In the midst of these disasters it was decided to call back
Fisher. And so, on 30 October, 1914, at the age of seventy-four,
Jacky Fisher returned to the Admiralty to take command of the
Royal Navy in time of war. The crowning point of a lifetime
of service.

Shortly after Fisher's return, Churchill minuted the new
First Sea Lord: 'Please propose without delay the largest
possible programme of submarine building to be delivered in
from twelve to twenty-four months from the present time.'

Fisher had crossed swords before with Winston Churchill
and felt that the current shortage of submarines was due in no
small part to the First Lord and his mercurial mentality. 'If that
young man who writes minutes in red ink thinks he is going to
run the Submarine Service, he is mistaken!' he told a friend.
He also had no high opinion of Keyes. 'There never was such a
mistake as putting Keyes in charge of the submarines', he complained, and added, '[he] had not the faintest idea of how to
employ them.' Faced with the certain antagonism of Fisher it
was clear that Keyes could consider his days numbered as Flag
Officer (Submarines).

On 3 November Fisher laid his programme before a special
meeting at the Admiralty: '[I] am convinced,' he said, 'that
twenty submarines can be commenced at once, and that the
first batch of these should be delivered in nine months, and the
remainder at short intervals, completing the lot in eleven or
twelve months.' And then with a typical theatrical gesture he
hammered the table with his fist and threatened to commit
hara-kari if the boats were not completed in the stipulated nine
months, adding, 'If anyone thwarts me, *he* had better commit
hara-kari too!'

As a result of the conference an order was placed for six of
the new 'H' class submarines. These were to be built by the
Fore River Yard in the United States—the first time in modern

history that ships for the Royal Navy were to be constructed abroad. Fisher intended to get around the problem of American neutrality by having the completed and unarmed boats sailed to Canada and having the guns and torpedo-tubes fitted in a Canadian dockyard. However, when they were ready, the United States Government refused to release them and they did not finally join the Navy for operational service until 1917.

On the same day as the meeting at the Admiralty the German High Command sent Admiral Hipper with three of his battle-cruisers to bombard Yarmouth, the first of the so-called 'terror raids' against the virtually undefended East Coast.

As the enemy closed in on Yarmouth the submarines *D.3*, *D.5*, and *E.10* were lying at their moorings in Gorleston, a small harbour three miles down the coast. The heavy rumble of gunfire close at hand brought the submarine officers on deck and Godfrey Herbert of *D.5* called across to Lt-Cdr Fraser, captain of *E.10*, suggesting that they should go out and investigate.

D.5 led the pack, running northwards at full-speed on the surface, with her look-outs straining their eyes ahead for a first glimpse of the German squadron. They were unaware that the enemy had scattered floating mines in their wake and they failed to see the mine in their path. A sudden violent explosion ripped the stern of the boat and *D.5*'s hull plates were torn apart as one of the detonating-horns touched her side. She went to the bottom in less than a minute leaving her commander and the other six men who had been on the bridge at the time struggling in the icy sea. By the time the trawlers *Homeland* and *Faithful* arrived on the scene only Godfrey Herbert and two of the men were still alive. Herbert had now survived two disasters and, unbeknown to him, a third dramatic escape from a stricken submarine lay ahead.

Later in the month a double tragedy struck at her sister ship *D.2*. On 23 November while the submarine was running on the surface in heavy seas, a wave washed her commanding-officer, Lt-Cdr Jameson, overboard. The traditional shout went up and Lt Oakley, D.2's second-in-command, dashed to the conning-tower to take over. The submarine swung around and the men leaning over the conning-tower combing stared out through the gale-driven rain for their captain. But they knew that it was impossible for anyone to survive in those wild seas and, after two hours, the search was called off. Oakley brought the submarine back to Harwich and reported the sad news of Jameson's loss to his Flotilla Commander on *Maidstone*.

The very next day D.2 left Harwich for another patrol and, as the submarine glided slowly past *Maidstone* her new commanding-officer, Lt-Cdr Head, raised his hand in salute. *D.2* was never seen again. She vanished somewhere in the North Sea and no evidence was found to indicate her fate. It was as if the sea, thwarted by its solitary victim a few days earlier, had avenged itself on the entire crew.

On 16 December the German battle-cruisers struck at the East Coast again, this time selecting Scarborough, Whitby, and Hartlepool as their targets. Once it was known that the German fleet was at sea in strength the Admiralty ordered Keyes to hold eight submarines of the 8th Flotilla in readiness to spread out on a line thirty miles NNW of Terschelling through which the enemy ships were expected to pass. Keyes disapproved of the plan and submitted an alternative but before anything could be agreed the submarines had already been ordered to sea by the Admiralty.

The Commodore left immediately in *Lurcher* and headed out into the North Sea in the hope of controlling his scattered flock. Admiralty signals were, as usual, ambiguous and unhelpful. When Keyes requested details of the British ships and their probable dispositions—vital information if our submarines were not to attack our own forces, as the Battle of Heligoland Bight had shown only too clearly—his message went unanswered.

E.10, *E.15*, the French steam-powered *Archimede* with Godfrey Herbert on board, and *E.11* commanded by Nasmith, were drawn up on a patrol line west of Heligoland. Later Nasmith was detached and sent to the area of the Elbe and Weser.

It was a day of missed opportunities and fumbled signals. The battle-cruisers made fleeting contact with the enemy but the action was broken off because of a misunderstanding and, due mainly to a faulty Admiralty appreciation of the German's probable course, the High Sea Fleet eluded the waiting *E.10*, *E.15* and *Archimede*.

Only *E.11* remained to avenge the German raid. At 7.30 am on the 17th the enemy destroyer screen was sighted, followed half-an-hour later by the Battle Squadrons. They steamed on unaware that a British submarine was lying in wait a few miles ahead.

As news of the approaching fleet spread through *E.11* the crew closed up to their action stations. Nasmith came up to periscope-depth and began to line his sights on one of the approaching battleships. But just as the cross-wires came on target the enemy changed course and the chance was gone.

Nasmith thought quickly and rapped out an order to port the helm. There was no time for a calculated attack and he fired his starboard tube in a snapshot. His aim was true but, as so often before, the heavy war-head took the torpedo too deep and it passed harmlessly under the battleship's hull.

Glancing quickly through the periscope Nasmith saw the armoured bows of a battleship coming straight at him and, to avoid being rammed, he gave the order to dive. *E.11* plunged down too sharply, lost her trim, and wallowed to the surface like a demented porpoise in full view of the enemy lookouts. Sirens roared and flag-signals fluttered as the German ships scattered wildly from the unexpected menace. It was impossible to catch them now and Nasmith realized sadly that the opportunity had gone; the delicately-balanced trim of the submarine had robbed him of the fruits of a much-deserved victory.

But *E.11*'s adventures were not yet over. Nasmith turned the submarine towards the German coast and began a vain search for the fleeing warships. Soon he was in the shoaling waters of the Jade River and he conned the boat through the shallow depths like an experienced river-pilot. But the treacherous currents proved too much even for Nasmith and, with a sudden lurch, *E.11* ran aground on a mudbank almost within sight of the enemy coast. Fortunately the tide was rising and it would only be a matter of time till they floated off but, even so, the commanding officer and his crew spent several anxious hours waiting for their boat to go clear. As it was, they only escaped detection by a German minesweeping patrol by minutes.

It had been a disappointing venture for the men of the 8th Flotilla but they had done all they could to avenge the German terror raid. Even the tiny obsolescent *C.9* had contributed her mite. She had been lying inside Hartlepool harbour when the German battle-cruisers arrived and, as the enemy ships formed up ready for the bombardment, she started up her engines and slipped her moorings.

It was low water and in order to cross the harbour-bar Lt Dering knew that he would have to bring his boat to the surface in full view of the Germans' eleven-inch guns. The bar was covered by only a few feet of water and it was quite impossible for the submarine to remain submerged as she passed over it. But, to Dering, the danger was as nothing compared to this unexpected opportunity of attacking the enemy's ships and, as he approached the bar, he brought *C.9* to the surface.

The Germans reacted quickly and a salvo sent great geysers of water cascading over the submarine as she sailed defiantly out of the harbour. She held her course unwaveringly as a second salvo fell even closer and then, clear of the bar, Dering took her down and steered for an attacking position. But the enemy battle-cruisers were not willing to face the threat of a submarine's torpedoes and, warned of her presence as she crossed the bar, they withdrew at high speed, three mighty Goliaths fleeing from a single David.

Despite Keyes' strictures on everyone concerned, there is no doubt that Dering's gallant sortie cut short the merciless shelling of Hartlepool and saved many civilian lives.

Even then the adventures of the 8th Flotilla were not over. The French *Archimede*, having been on the patrol line which had missed the Germans, stayed off Heligoland for the remainder of the day and, after resting on the bottom overnight, resumed her patrol on the 17th.

That night she ran into a fierce storm and a heavy sea struck her violently amidships, bending her funnel. The damage made it impossible to retract the funnel and, in consequence, the submarine could not submerge. The storm worsened and she remained crippled and helpless on the surface in the centre of the Heligoland Bight for two days while the crew fought to save her.

Herbert, who was still on board as liaison officer, took his place in the bucket chain and helped the Frenchmen bale out the water that kept cascading down the damaged funnel. At one time things were so serious that Lt Deville, her captain, considered taking her into Dutch waters for safety even though such a course meant automatic internment but, fortunately, things began to improve and he decided to try and make for England. Limping along on the surface, with the lookouts scanning the sea for enemy patrols and the men below baling continuously, *Archimede* plugged through the waves at a steady ten knots and finally reached Harwich late in the evening of the 19th. It had been Herbert's first experience of steam-powered submarines. It was not, as we shall see later, his last.

Keyes summed up the events stemming from the

Scarborough, Whitby and Hartlepool raids: 'The enemy certainly had all the good fortune on that day of confusion and lost opportunities, and no one suffered more tormenting disappointments than the submarines.' The men of the 8th Flotilla would undoubtedly have endorsed their Commodore's views.

CHAPTER FOUR

'Live By Valour'

CHURCHILL DID not like losing the initiative and, stung to action by the German terror raids, he cast around for new ideas. One plan under consideration at the time was a full-scale invasion of Germany's Baltic coast and a sudden drive on Berlin. But it received only luke-warm support from the First Lord. The boldness and originality of the new plan when it was eventually unfolded showed Winston's imagination and flair at its best. It was a conception of warfare thirty years ahead of its time—an air raid on the Zeppelin sheds at Cuxhaven, using sea-planes of the Royal Naval Air Service, primitive aircraft-carriers, and submarines.

It was an idea breath-taking in its originality, and in its blind faith in the capabilities of the RNAS and their flimsy aircraft. Churchill hoped that an air attack on the Fatherland's door-step would provoke the High Sea Fleet into making a retaliatory sortie against the task-force lying only a few miles from the coast and he arranged with Jellicoe for the Grand Fleet to sweep south during the operation so that it would be to hand if the enemy ventured out. Even Keyes, one of Churchill's most fervent disciples, thought that Winston's optimism on this last point was a trifle touching.

Eleven submarines were to support the raid with the object of covering all lines of approach from the enemy ports while the sea-planes were being hoisted in and out of the water, ambushing any enemy units sent to attack the task-force, and to pick up any pilots who had come down in the sea. The two destroyers *Lurcher* and *Firedrake* together with *S.1* and nine other submarines left Harwich on the night of the 23 December so as to be in position by dawn on Christmas Day. *E.7* was already on patrol off Heligoland and she was ordered to join the others at a pre-arranged rendezvous.

The raid itself was a gallant failure. Although the sea was as smooth as glass two of the sea-planes failed to take off and they bobbed up and down on the swell as their seven companions lifted into the sky, circled their mother-ships once, and then formed up on course for Germany.

On reaching Cuxhaven, however, they found the ground obscured by a thick mist and they were unable to locate their prime target, the Zeppelin sheds. Skimming across the town at 300 feet the RNAS pilots searched in vain for their quarry and finally had to content themselves by dropping their puny twenty-pound bombs on the harbour itself. They did very little damage.

It was now time to return and the little Short biplanes flew out to sea to locate the waiting aircraft-carriers. Three of the aircraft succeeded in getting back to their mother-ships where they were quickly winched back on board and taken below. One lost the way completely and came down in the sea inside Dutch territorial waters where the pilot was picked up by some fishermen. The remainder failed to locate the carriers and, as the minutes ticked by, it was clear that they would have to come down in the sea. The rescue of their crews was now solely dependent on the eleven submarines of the 8th Flotilla.

E.11 was lying submerged off the Norderney Gat when Nasmith spotted the first of the sea-planes aimlessly seeking the mother-ships. Realizing that the plane's petrol tanks must be nearly empty he brought the submarine to the surface ready for the world's first attempt at air-sea rescue.

The pilot brought his machine down in a graceful curve, and taxiing it skilfully alongside *E.11*, he leaned out of the cockpit and shouted across to Nasmith that he had had only enough fuel left for a further five minutes' flying. Still annoyed with himself for failing to bag an enemy battleship after the Scarborough raid, Nasmith was determined to carry out this new operation in style and, ignoring the fact that he was surfaced deep inside enemy waters, he ordered the sea-plane to be taken in tow over the stern. While the sailors were rigging a line the sea-plane's crew clambered aboard the submarine and were taken below for a hot drink. Then, with the flimsy plane bobbing in his wake, Nasmith set off in search of the surface force. It was a cool piece of daring for, at any moment, smoke on the horizon might herald the arrival of a patrolling German destroyer. But, for half an hour, his luck held.

'Zeppelin! Two points starboard!'

Nasmith snatched up his glasses as he heard the lookout's warning shout and focused on the silver shape of a German naval airship on the eastern horizon. He was about to order the tow-line to be cut ready for diving when the two remaining British sea-planes came spluttering low over the water losing height rapidly as their fuel ran out. It was an agonizing dilemma. Should he save his own ship by diving to safety, or risk all in a gamble to rescue the men on the two sea-planes? For Nasmith there could be but one decision.

His situation was not helped when one of his officers reported that a surfaced submarine which had been trailing them some miles astern was diving. It was an evolution that strongly suggested a U-boat preparing to attack. Nasmith reached for the diving klaxon but, at the last moment, he stopped. Moving to the voice-pipe he said quietly:

'Starboard fifteen. Full ahead both . . .'

E.11 surged towards the sea-planes, losing way at exactly the right moment so that her ballast-tanks almost grazed the floats of the nearest aircraft. While the flyers were scrambling on board the submarine Nasmith called over to the pilot of the other machine telling him to swim for it. Throwing off their heavy flying-boots and gloves the two RNAS men jumped into the water and swam towards the submarine. But saving the

airmen was not enough for the perfectionist commander of
E.11 and, determined to prevent the three sea-planes from falling into the hands of the enemy, Nasmith had a machine-gun
brought up on deck and ordered the gun-crew to open fire on
the floats.

By the time the second sea-plane's crew were aboard the
Zeppelin was almost overhead and it was time to call it a day.
The diving klaxon sounded and with a final gesture of defiance
Nasmith waved his cap at the men in the airship. Then, dropping down through the conning-tower, he secured the hatch
and ordered the submarine to be taken deep to avoid the
bombing attack which must inevitably follow. But the attack
never came. When the Zeppelin captain saw *E.11* firing at the
sea-planes he mistakenly assumed that she was a U-boat and
Nasmith's cap-waving was taken as a friendly greeting!

The incredible chain of mistaken identities was not yet complete. The submarine which Nasmith had thought to be a
U-boat was, in fact, the *D.6* under Lt-Cdr Halahan also
patrolling in search of the lost sea-planes. This time the
Zeppelin made no mistake and a stick of bombs whistled
down. Fortunately *D.6* was well under the surface and the
bombs did little harm beyond giving the crew a shaking.
Halahan waited for a while and then brought his submarine up
to periscope depth to survey the scene.

Seeing that one of the Short sea-planes was still afloat *D.6*
came to the surface with the intention of rescuing the crew. In
those early days periscopes were not fitted for air-search and so,
as Halahan lifted the hatch, he was unaware that the Zeppelin
was directly overhead. The sharp crackle of its engines made
him look up and the next moment the hatch slammed shut and
D.6 tilted her bows in a crash-dive. She had just disappeared
under the surface when the German machine-guns opened fire.
It had, indeed, been a lucky day for all concerned. All, that is,
except the Germans.

On their way back to Harwich *E.11*'s crew invited the

airmen to join them in a belated Christmas dinner and, lying on the bottom of the sea-bed at twenty fathoms, the RNAS men enjoyed the unusual experience of eating turkey and plum pudding prepared in a submarine's galley.

It was the turn of the Dover Flotilla to undertake the next operation. The Admiralty were anxious to discover details of German naval activities on the Belgian coast and, to this end, *C.31* commanded by Lt Pilkington was sent to patrol off Zeebrugge with instructions to report to Harwich on completion of her mission. The submarine left Dover on 4 January but failed to report back to Keyes' headquarters as instructed. She was never seen again and was thought to have struck an enemy mine in the shoal-water off the Belgian coast.

In those early, pioneer days the complete disappearance of submarines was a commonplace event. Even today with all our advanced electronic gadgetry submarines vanish without trace, but in 1914 the odds were considerably greater. Although the boats carried wireless-sets their range was a pitiful forty miles in good atmospheric conditions and important messages were often relayed by carrier-pigeons carried in wicker-baskets on every voyage.

On 18 January the submarines *E.5*, *E.10* and *E.15* left Harwich for another patrol in the Bight. A typical mid-winter gale was sweeping the German coast and a strong current carried them six miles off course. *E.5* and *E.15*, battling through the heavy seas, staggered back to base but, after long anxious hours of waiting, *E.10* was officially posted as: 'Overdue—presumed lost.' As so often happens in submarine disasters a complete silence obscured the fate of the missing boat and it was thought that, like *C.31*, she had fallen victim to a German minefield.

But neither tragedy nor disaster could be allowed to hold up the valuable work of the 8th Flotilla and on 23 January, Keyes, flying his broad pennant in *Lurcher*, left Harwich leading eight submarines to support another sea-borne air attack on enemy bases in the Bight. On this occasion, however, the operation proved abortive and after receiving the recall signal Keyes rounded up his charges and returned to base.

Lurcher had scarcely tied up alongside the jetty when a member of the *Maidstone*'s signal staff hurried up the gang-plank carrying an Admiralty telegram. 'Four German battle-cruisers, six light cruisers, and twenty-two destroyers are sailing tonight to scout on Dogger Bank.'

The submarine base burst into life as the boats were re-fuelled and prepared for another patrol. Weary sailors brought fresh stores on board while E.R.A.s (Engine Room Artificers) checked their still-warm engines. Officers who, an hour before, had been shivering on the conning-towers of the sub-marines crowded on board the *Maidstone* for briefing. In the parlance of the day—the balloon was about to go up.

A light sea-mist which had been threatening all day thickened as the wind dropped and a clammy fog descended over the harbour. A new problem confronted the worried captains. Would they be able to see the enemy?

At dawn, *Lurcher*, *Firedrake*, *E.4*, *E.7*, *E.8* and Nasmith's *E.11* felt their way out of the harbour and headed towards the German coast yet again. And at Rosyth, and further north at Scapa, the Battle-Cruiser Fleet and the Grand Fleet were forming up for battle.

By 7 am the submarines were off the Sunk Light Vessel and, as the sun dispersed the fog, Keyes sent up a signal ordering full-speed. Fragmentary wireless messages received by *Lurcher* indicated that an action was being fought to the north and the Commodore pushed his submarines ahead in the hope of catching the enemy making for their bases. *E.4*, *E.7* and *E.8* were sent to cover the Jade and Elbe rivers and Nasmith was ordered to the Norderney Gat—an area by now well known to all concerned.

The submarines arrived on station twelve hours before the Admiralty tardily instructed Keyes to place them in the Bight and it is to Keyes' credit that he had anticipated the correct dispositions without any hard intelligence to rely on. Nevertheless, they had arrived too late. The fleeing Germans reached the safety of their home waters in daylight on the 24th. *E.11* arrived off the Norderney Gat at 6.30 pm and the other three submarines were on station by 8.30 pm but the enemy had already passed.

To Keyes the whole affair was heart-breaking. He had been in the area with *eight* submarines only a short while earlier when he had received the Admiralty's recall signal. Then, on arriving at Harwich, he was immediately ordered back to sea. Why the Admiralty War Room did not advise the Flag Officer (Submarines) by wireless while he was still at sea within striking distance of the enemy battle-cruisers has never been revealed and there can be no doubt that the recall signal was a bad error of judgement. It is interesting to note that Churchill's account of the Battle of Dogger Bank in *The World Crisis* is strangely silent on the part played by the submarines though he takes care to mention: 'Lord Fisher was quite content with the decisions which were proposed, and action was taken accordingly.'

Churchill hailed the action as a victory and so, it seemed, did everyone else. But, instead of congratulations, the Admiralty should have been examining the real reasons why the German ships had escaped. The Dogger Bank action contained a pointer to every mistake that was later to bedevil the Navy at Jutland: poor signals, tardy intelligence from the Admiralty, the design weaknesses of the battle-cruisers, the lack of initiative shown by senior subordinate admirals, and the sea fighting ability of the German Navy. Not one single lesson was learned and complacency reigned supreme.

David Beatty was disappointed by the results of the battle although he did little to rectify the underlying faults in his own command and he sent a sympathetic letter to Keyes: 'The disappointment of that day is more than I can bear to think of, everybody thinks it was a great success, when in reality it was a terrible failure . . . it was a thousand pities you had not our submarines waiting for them. I sympathize with you and your fine fellows in the submarines for all their disappointments. What has gone wrong? I hear the damned torpedoes dive too deep.'

Fisher, too, in his heart of hearts, knew that something had gone wrong and he searched for scapegoats. Checking through the battle reports in the War Room a few days later Keyes found a signal from Admiral Moore, who had taken over command when Beatty in *Lion* had fallen behind, which contained the sentences: 'Commodore (S) reports High Sea Fleet coming out. Am retiring.'

Receipt of such a signal would, naturally, clear Moore of the growing criticism of his action during the battle. The only trouble was that Keyes had never made the alleged report. Half-jokingly he remarked to one of Fisher's aides: 'I suppose your Chief holds me responsible for the failure of the Battle-Cruiser Squadron to continue the pursuit after Beatty fell out of line.'

According to Keyes' Memoirs 'he [Fisher's aide] admitted that the point had not escaped Lord Fisher's notice . . .' and, well aware of the First Sea Lord's animosity towards him, the Commodore wrote to the Secretary of the Admiralty: 'With reference to the report of my proceedings 23–25 January, I understand that a signal to the effect that the "German High Sea Fleet was at sea" was intercepted as emanating from Commodore (S). I have the honour to report that I made no such signal.' It was a bald and unambiguous statement of fact. But Fisher was not so easily baulked in his search for scapegoats, for on 3 February he had written a letter to Beatty petulantly complaining: 'Keyes . . . has made a damned mess of the submarines in the last three years.'

The Commodore already knew his number was up. Churchill, the man who had toppled Fisher from his throne in

1911, warned Keyes that something was going on and so it was no surprise when, on 8 February, he was called to the Admiralty.

Churchill formally told him that he was being relieved of his command forthwith and that he was to proceed to the Mediterranean the next day to take up an appointment as Chief-of-Staff to Rear-Admiral Carden who was commanding the Allied Squadron waiting to force the Dardanelles. Although Keyes was removed from the 8th Flotilla, he still had a further part to play in the story of the British submarine at war, as we shall see in a later chapter.

It is difficult to define Keyes' character and he remains, even today, something of an enigma. That he was a fighter and a brave fighter, is not to be denied and he was always straining at the leash to get into battle. When the submarines were engaged in Fleet operations Keyes was always well to the fore on the exposed bridge of *Lurcher* and looking for action. He did not believe in leading his men from behind.

Commander Stephen King-Hall was one of the few people who attempted an assessment of Keyes' character and his comments in his book *My Naval Life*, are illuminating:

'He was not, however, a tremendous and impressive personality like Beatty ... Roger Keyes was more feline and feminine. He was capricious and had much more intelligence and intellectual equipment than most people supposed.' Although in appearance he was the complete antithesis of the popular conception of a hard-bitten naval commander, the public found him an attractive figure and he emerged as one of the best-known personalities of the war, his name being forever linked with the great Zeebrugge raid of 1918.

Captain Hall was appointed Flag Officer (Submarines) in Keyes' place and Captain Waistell was given command of the 8th Flotilla.

Before leaving the exploits of the North Sea submarines, one last story, however, remains to be told and, appropriately enough, it features one of Keyes' own brain-children, the Laurenti-designed *S.1*.

The submarine was on a routine patrol off the Horn Reef in a calm sea and in perfect weather conditions. She was running on the surface at a steady nine knots while the look-outs on the low conning-tower scanned the horizon.

Suddenly her diesel engines misfired, ran unevenly for a few moments, and then stopped. Lt-Cdr Kellet dropped down through the hatch to investigate. *S.1*'s 650 h.p. engines were a constant source of trouble and breakdowns of this nature were by no means uncommon. But the expression on the Engineer Officer's face quickly warned Kellet that this was no ordinary trouble that could be rectified in a few minutes by a couple of E.R.A.s.

The engineer shrugged. 'Main bearings have gone, sir,' he reported. 'It's a job for the dockyard mateys. There's nothing we can do, sir.'

Kellet kept the facts to himself but he realized that the position of the *S.1* was desperate. Without her main engines she could only move on the surface by means of her electric motors and these would last only as long as the batteries. As the diesels were required for re-charging the batteries it was obvious that once they were exhausted the submarine would have no motive-power left at all. And they were hundreds of miles inside enemy-controlled waters. Unable to call for help from base with the short-range wireless they had on board there seemed only one possible course of action, to scuttle the boat as soon as an enemy surface ship came into sight and allow the crew to be taken prisoners.

But Kellet had his own ideas on survival, and they did not include scuttling one of His Majesty's submarines.

While she still had electrical power the *S.1* was fully capable of submerging and, once below the surface, she was at least hidden from searching enemy patrol-boats. An idea was gradually forming in Kellet's mind.

'Stand by to dive.'

The men went quickly to their diving-stations while the captain pulled down the conning-tower hatch and secured the clips.

'Open main vents.'

'Main vents open, sir,' reported the First Lieutenant.

'Right. Take her down to thirty feet.'

The gentle rocking motion of the submarine gradually subsided as she slid below the surface and Kellet watched the needles of the depth-gauges swing round to show thirty feet. When he was satisfied that everything was in order he told the Lieutenant to take *S.1* to the bottom. The submarine settled gently on the floor of the North Sea and remained there through the rest of the day. An hour before dusk Kellet called the twenty-man crew into the cramped control-room and explained his plan. The men looked surprised but the broad grins on their faces indicated that they approved.

When the hands of the chronometer indicated that it was dark the Commanding Officer called the crew to their surfacing stations and they followed the standard evening routine of bringing the submarine up to periscope-depth. The long red needles of the depth-gauges steadied at twenty feet and, grasping the periscope handles, Kellet took a quick sweep of the vicinity.

His luck was in. Just half a mile away, gleaming like a ghost ship in the light of the moon, a German trawler was fishing peacefully. The submarine broke surface with a minimum of disturbance and, draining the last dregs of current from the batteries, Kellet used his electric motors to bring *S.1* silently alongside the unsuspecting enemy vessel.

A boarding-party, lavishly equipped with rifles, revolvers, and cutlasses, quietly lined up on the submarine's deck and, at a signal from their captain, they clambered up over the sides of the trawler. It was all over in a few minutes. Taken completely by surprise the fishermen offered no resistance and were soon shepherded aboard the submarine as prisoners.

While two E.R.A.s who were familiar with coal-fired boilers hurried down to the trawler's engine-room a towing-cable was passed over the stern and secured to the bows of the crippled submarine. The officer in the wheel-house gave a thumb's up signal to Kellet and the captured trawler took the strain.

It was a 300 mile trip from the enemy's home-waters to the Flotilla base at Harwich but, despite numerous breakdowns of the trawler's ancient over-strained engines, Kellet and his men were not spotted by German sea or air patrols and, finally, *S.1* was towed triumphantly into Harwich harbour by her prize, the White Ensign streaming proudly from the trawler's stern. Keyes records that everyone in the 8th Flotilla had fish for supper that evening.

It was a stirring episode and exemplified the Submarine Service's determination not to be beaten by any set-back. Kellet and his men had certainly acted on the inspiration of *S.1*'s official motto: 'Live By Valour.'

CHAPTER FIVE

'Why can't they
wear Two Shirts?'

THE SUGGESTION that British submarines should be sent to operate in the Baltic first came up for consideration at a special conference held on board Jellicoe's flagship *Iron Duke* on 17 September, 1914.

The fact that the great battleship was anchored in Loch Ewe and not at Scapa Flow was, in itself, testimony to the power of the submarine threat. The dangers of U-boat attacks on the Grand Fleet's main base, which was criminally devoid of anti-submarine defences in the early stages of the war, had forced the Admiralty to move the entire force to the north-west coast of Scotland. Although the new, temporary anchorage was several hundred miles further west than the Orkneys, Jellicoe insisted that protection from submarines was of more importance than proximity to the enemy and the loss of the *Royal Oak* at Scapa during the Second World War indicates that his appreciation of strategic necessity was, as usual, correct.

Keyes claimed the credit for proposing the Baltic idea and there is no reason to suppose that he was not the originator of the plan. Various schemes on a much vaster and more ambitious basis had already been considered by the Admiralty. The then First Sea Lord, Prince Louis of Battenberg, favoured a plan which involved the assault and capture of the Island of Sylt, a proposal first mooted in 1913. Sir Arthur Wilson was more inclined to storm the island fortress of Heligoland while Fisher, still at that time without office, thought Borkum to be the best target.

This latter operation was to be a gigantic affair involving the landing of British troops on the German Baltic coast where, so

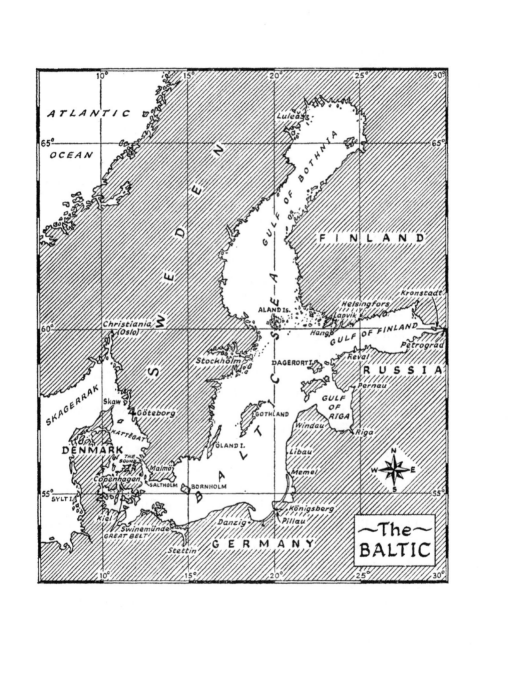

Fisher claimed, a sustained offensive for a few hundred miles would bring them to the gates of Berlin. Once installed as First Sea Lord, Fisher set the wheels in motion and Admiral Bayly was actually appointed to command the expedition.

As it was, the final operation turned out to be considerably less ambitious and very much more practical than the earlier wild schemes. It was simply to send a flotilla of submarines into the Baltic where they could operate against German shipping from Russian bases. Submarines were chosen for two reasons; firstly because they had a longer endurance and were more self-supporting than surface vessels; and secondly because they were the only type of warship capable of passing into the Baltic from the North Sea unobserved.

Jellicoe, ruminating over the idea in the solitude of his cabin on the *Iron Duke*, began to realize the value of a submarine operation in the Baltic and, just over three weeks after the Loch Ewe conference, Keyes was summoned to the Admiralty for consultations. The Commander-in-Chief began pressing Churchill for early action and, by 13 October, the Commodore (S) had received orders to put the plan into operation. Sailing was fixed for the following day for, once committed to an idea, Churchill did not believe in letting the grass grow under his feet. Keyes claimed that he had convinced the Admiralty of the necessity for the operation before Jellicoe had telegraphed his request but evidence suggests that both men had urged the Admiralty to take action at almost the same time. However, as Keyes noted, it was 'a regular case of mental telepathy.'

The flotilla of submarines mentioned in the original proposal had now been whittled down to three boats. The Commodore hand-picked his best officers. Martin Nasmith, who had already proved his worth as a submarine-commander on several occasions, was selected to go in *E.11*; Horton, after his brilliant successes against the *Hela* and *S.116*, was picked to sail in *E.9*; and Lt-Cdr Noel Laurence with *E.1* completed the trio as Senior Officer.

A conference of staff officers on *Maidstone* was attended by
the three submarine-commanders and the various problems
arising out of the Admiralty decision were carefully considered.
The major obstacle was the navigation of the Sound leading
from the Kattegat to the Baltic. Examination of the charts
showed that there was insufficient depth of water for the submarines to submerge and intelligence reports confirmed that
the Germans had very strong destroyer-patrols at the Baltic end
of the narrow passage. Once spotted from the shore the submarines would have no chance at all if the enemy surface-
patrols knew of their approach.

Horton, supported by Nasmith and Laurence, suggested that
their only hope of getting through undetected was by running
on the surface at night with the submarine trimmed as low as
possible in the water. Keyes agreed and, to ensure maximum
darkness, the operation was postponed for one day.

By dusk on 15 October the three submarines were at their
moorings at Gorleston, their crews anxiously double-checking
the equipment as zero-hour approached. A picket-boat
brought the three submarine-commanders back to their boats
after the final briefing with Keyes. A few minutes later a
shaded signal-lamp flashed from *E.11*'s bridge informing
Laurence that a serious engine defect was likely to delay
departure.

It was damnable luck for Martin Nasmith. He had been
longing for another opportunity to strike at the Germans and
was delighted when he was picked for the Baltic operation.
Now, with only minutes to go, *E.11*'s war-strained engines had
given up the ghost and it seemed that he was to be robbed of
his chance.

Laurence could not delay his departure while *E.11* was
repaired and so, with *E.9* in company, he cast off from his
buoy at precisely zero-hour, piloted the *E.1* out of Gorleston
harbour and pointed her bows towards the Skagerrak.

The next day, as the two submarines sailed across the North

DUW-E

Sea, *E.9* also developed a temporary engine-fault and fell further and further behind the Senior Officer's boat. Laurence's submarine was going well, her bows plunging into the slight swell as she pressed ahead at a steady ten knots. Rolling gently on the surface with her engines stopped *E.9* was a hive of industry as the E.R.A.s worked to repair the broken shaft and, finally, a few hours later, Horton was able to order, 'Full ahead both,' as he set off in pursuit of his companion.

Laurence reached the Skagerrak in the late afternoon, rounded the Skaw, and crept into the Kattegat, diving each time the look-outs spotted the smoke of an approaching surface ship. Then, as it was still light when he arrived off the entrance to Ore Sound, he took *E.1* down to the bottom to await nightfall.

An hour after sunset Laurence surfaced again and began the perilous passage into the Baltic. The diesel engines rumbled quietly in the darkness as he took the submarine along the tortuous channel. German 'observers' who kept a lonely vigil night after night along the shores of Sweden and Denmark failed to see the low silhouette of the submarine as she forced the Sound.

It was unexpectedly easy and, by midnight, Laurence was through. Some miles ahead in the darkness he could see the probing fingers of German searchlight-beams and he knew that an enemy surface-patrol was active. But that was one problem which could be left until daylight. The more immediate task was the evening meal which had been delayed because of their passage through the Sound. Laurence took *E.1* to the bottom and the crew settled down to their belated dinner. At dawn they would be at action stations for their first day's patrol in the Baltic.

Although *E.9*'s engine defect had been repaired quickly and Horton had reached the entrance to the Sound on the night of the 17th, he was just too late to get through during the hours of darkness. A succession of surface-ships in the Kattegat had forced the submarine to dive continuously and the time lost by their slow speed under the water meant that they were too far behind schedule to follow Laurence through as planned. And so, while *E.1* rested on the bottom at the eastern end of the Sound, her companion did likewise at the opposite western entrance to the narrows. In Horton's case it meant remaining submerged for twenty-four hours and it was half-an-hour after dusk on the 18th before *E.9* came back to the surface.

Max took her as far as Malmö without being spotted and, as he approached the shallow waters of the Flint Channel, the clutches of the diesel-engines were pulled out and the electric motors were coupled up for the next stage of their perilous passage through the Sound. Moving almost silently at slow speed on one motor *E.9* edged her way down the narrow channel while Horton and the look-outs scanned the darkness for enemy patrols. A group of searchlight-beams were sweeping the sea to the south and it seemed that there were German destroyers everywhere. As they crept forward Horton was uncomfortably aware that the enemy had been alerted and were actively searching for any British submarines trying to force the Sound.

Alone in the darkness and cut off from all contact with the outside world Horton puzzled over the reason for this unexpected activity. Had they been spotted on the surface in the Kattegat, or had enemy agents on the Danish coast learned of the plan? Whatever the reason they would have to proceed with the utmost caution.

But, in fact, it was the unfortunate Laurence who had given the game away quite unintentionally. Assuming that Horton had followed him through the Sound, Laurence brought the *E.1* up to periscope-depth at dawn on the 18th and started his first patrol in the Baltic. Just before ten o'clock a column of smoke was sighted on the horizon and *E.1* went deeper as she turned towards the approaching ships.

The next time the periscope was raised Laurence found

himself within 500 yards of the German cruiser *Victoria Luise* and the crew quickly closed up for a torpedo attack. The enemy ship was steaming on a straight course apparently unaware of the danger lurking beneath the surface and *E.1*'s captain had time to take careful aim before releasing two torpedoes at an interval of one minute. Once again the hoodoo of the heavier warheads ruined the attack and the first torpedo passed under the cruiser's armoured hull. Although the Baltic was regarded as being as safe as a German lake the look-outs on board *Victoria Luise* were alert and wide awake. Spotting the bubbling white trail of the first torpedo they yelled a warning which gave the captain time to swing the cruiser away and *E.1*'s second shot passed harmlessly across the bows. Ringing down for full-speed, and keeping a wary eye open for more torpedoes, the enemy commander turned tail and ran for safety. Disappointed by his failure, Laurence turned eastwards again and a few hours later sighted two more cruisers. But this time they were too far away and *E.1* cruised on at a steady speed for Bornholm.

Meanwhile the powerful wireless on *Victoria Luise* reported that she had been attacked by a submarine. It is interesting to note that the German High Command concluded immediately, without evidence, that the submarine was British. It *could* have been a Russian but the enemy thought otherwise and the alert went out on all channels:

'British submarines operating in Baltic!'

Urgent signals were passed to the great naval base at Kiel and, all day, groups of destroyers, torpedo-boats and trawlers left the dockyard to reinforce the patrols in the Sound. It was these newly-reinforced patrols that Horton in *E.9* was encountering.

The men on the conning-tower of *E.9* were calm but tense as the submarine swung first to port and then to starboard as Horton conned her through the shoals and narrows with all the skill of a local pilot. Suddenly the darkness ahead deepened and the straining eyes of the look-outs picked out the lean shape of a German destroyer a bare 150 yards off the starboard bow. Horton gave the order to dive and the men slid quickly down the steel ladder into the control room as *E.9* angled sharply. Horton had just slammed the hatch shut and secured the clips when the submarine lurched violently with a loud scraping noise of grinding steel. He glanced at the depth gauge. They had tried to submerge in 14 feet of water. Trapped in their steel coffin the crew waited with grim resignation for the sound of the destroyer's engines as she thundered in to ram her helpless victim. But all remained peaceful; the enemy had not seen them.

Horton could not afford to take chances and, after half an hour, he gave orders for the ballast tanks to be blown very gently. *E.9* rose slightly and Horton stopped operations every few moments while he listened carefully for a stray sound to betray the enemy he suspected was still above. Finally the submarine was trimmed so that just her conning-tower was awash and Horton very quietly raised the hatch. The destroyer was now lying a mere seventy yards away yet, incredibly, she was apparently unaware of the submarine's presence. Horton knew that this time he must take a gamble, a gamble that would put the life of every man on board *E.9* at stake. But it had to be taken.

Quietly closing the hatch, he dropped down into the control-room and told Lt Chapman, the First Officer, to take the submarine down to ten feet. At that depth he had a clear four feet beneath the keel and the tip of the conning-tower would be just below the surface. Then, with one electric-motor running at dead-slow, he took *E.9* past the enemy ship and continued eastwards down the Sound. Soon they were in deeper water and Horton was able to flood the ballast-tanks gently until the submarine was, once again, fully submerged and safe from prying enemy eyes.

They remained at periscope-depth for the remainder of the

passage and Horton sighted several enemy patrols searching for him in the distance. They had now been submerged for a long time; the air in the submarine was getting foul and already several of the crew had been sick. In addition the batteries were running low. There was nothing for it but to surface, and pray.

E.9 had been up for only two minutes when Horton picked up a German destroyer in his glasses, and she was obviously coming in for the kill. Once again the submarine went to the bottom, just in time. Moments later the destroyer roared overhead.

The brief minutes on the surface had freshened the air inside the submarine and Horton set off once again for the end of the Sound. This time there were no set-backs and finally he was running clear in the deep, smooth waters of the Baltic. *E.9* was brought to the surface the next evening to ventilate the boat and re-charge her batteries while the cook began work on a long-overdue dinner in his cramped little galley.

Next morning, in the crisp air of a frosty dawn, Horton set course for Libau (now Liepaja) where he had been ordered to rendezvous with *E.1* and *E.11*.

Laurence, meanwhile, was thirsting for blood. Coming to the surface off Danzig he surveyed the harbour through his glasses and sighted the masts of three warships. He took *E.1* down and cautiously edged his way inside the harbour. But his efforts went unrewarded. When he raised the periscope for a quick survey of the scene he found that the three warships were safely berthed inside the basin where his torpedoes could not reach. So, extricating the submarine from the harbour Laurence set off for Libau for his meeting with Horton and Nasmith.

A Russian patrol-boat met him a few miles from the entrance to the naval-base and an officer boarded *E.1* to pilot her into her new base. The Russian saluted Laurence as he was helped into the conning-tower and, with a broad grin, told him that the submarine had just sailed right through a German mine-field. Perhaps *E.1* was not quite so unlucky after all. But the other news which the Russian officer imparted, as the submarine was shepherded into harbour, was less reassuring. Apparently, the Germans were advancing rapidly along the coast and the Russians had already destroyed all the base and dock installations at Libau in readiness for evacuation. The British flotilla was to move on to Lapvik in the Gulf of Finland.

Laurence explained to the Russian staff officers on shore that he was quite willing to shift the base to Lapvik but he must first await the arrival of *E.9* and *E.11* as he had no means of telling them that the rendezvous had been changed. The Russians shrugged and left him to it. Two days later, on the 22nd, Horton's boat duly appeared on the horizon, having also passed through the minefield unscathed, and an hour later she tied up alongside *E.1*. But where was Nasmith?

Admiral von Essen who, despite his Germanic name was Commander-in-Chief of the Russian Baltic Fleet, urged Laurence to leave Libau and make for Lapvik before the German army arrived to occupy the derelict town. But the two submarine captains steadfastly refused to leave until *E.11* had joined them safely.

They waited for seven days, patrolling westwards back towards the Sound in the hope of locating Nasmith's boat broken down somewhere along the Baltic coastline. But they found nothing except a solitary German destroyer and, even then, luck was against them. Laurence moved in to attack but his torpedo missed.

Without news, and convinced that an enemy patrol had located and sunk *E.11*, Horton and Laurence had a final conference and decided, reluctantly, to leave Libau and join the Russians in the Gulf of Finland.

* * *

Martin Nasmith had been delayed for two complete days by *E.11*'s engine troubles and, by the time he sailed from Gorleston, he was uncomfortably aware that every available

German destroyer would be patrolling the Kattegat and the Sound looking for him. Alerted by the successful passage of *E.1* and *E.9*, the enemy was sure to make a determined effort to prevent any further submarines from entering the Baltic.

As expected, the Kattegat was alive with destroyers and *E.11* was harried relentlessly as she crept towards the entrance to the Sound. Twice Nasmith brought her to periscope-depth so that he could check his bearings before navigating the boat through the dangerous narrows which lay ahead, and twice waiting destroyers had forced him to crash-dive to avoid being rammed.

Ahead lay the shallow waters of the Sound where *E.11* would have to run on the surface and Nasmith knew that the enemy patrols would sink him as soon as the conning-tower emerged above the surface. He weighed up the situation carefully and decided that *E.11* would give up the attempt and turn back.

Keyes knew what it had cost Nasmith to make such a decision: 'In my opinion the moral courage displayed by Nasmith in giving up his attempt to pass through the Sound was as admirable as the bravery and enterprise which won him the Victoria Cross in the Marmora later.'

Keyes also pointed out that the German destroyer attacks were made in neutral waters and that the enemy relied on ramming tactics rather than gunfire to sink the submarine so that her loss could be put down 'to accidental collision'. In his moral indignation the Commodore failed to mention that *E.11* was also a belligerent vessel operating in neutral waters; but the British Admiralty had always tended to have one set of rules for themselves and another for the enemy!

Certainly, at the moment of decision, immersed in his steel coffin on the bed of the Kattegat, Nasmith must have felt a very lonely man. Even then, he made one final effort to break through. After re-charging the batteries he swung *E.11* eastwards again and headed for the Sound. This time his luck seemed to be in. As the submarine moved quietly across the smooth sea his keen eyes picked up the squat bulk of a conning-tower some miles ahead. Nasmith took *E.11* down and began stalking his quarry. By approaching at an angle he was able to shorten the distance to the point of interception and, at what he judged to be the right moment, he ordered the periscope to be raised, and flicked the lever so that the high-power attack lens was in position. The enemy conning-tower loomed large in the optics and, on the side in big white symbols was painted *U-3.*

There was no doubt in Nasmith's mind as he snapped out the range, depth-setting and angle of deflection to the bow tor-pedomen and, a few moments later, he gave the command to fire. *E.11* shuddered softly as the torpedo was released and her captain watched its wake streaking towards the target. Sud-denly the grin of anticipation on his face died—the torpedo had missed. Had he but known it Nasmith should have been elated by his apparent ill-fortune. *U-3* was a Danish submarine!

News of the attack quickly reached German ears and the search for the British submarine intensified. Even sea-planes were brought in to strengthen the surface patrols and it was one of these that located *E.11* on the surface re-charging her batteries. Within hours enemy destroyers were working the area like hounds with the scent of a fox in their nostrils. As he heard the roar of the German ships overhead Nasmith knew that his task was impossible and, on the 22nd, he reversed course for the last time and headed back to Gorleston.

The grip of the Russian winter had settled over the Baltic with deep, drifting snow blanketing the land and ice thicken-ing over the sea. Submarine operations would now have to enter their annual period of hibernation, according to the sea-soned experts of the Russian Baltic Fleet; but Horton had other ideas. He persuaded an ice-breaker to clear a passage out of the harbour and then set out to prove his point. It was desperately cold and, within minutes, *E.9* was encased in glare-ice like a sugared almond. Frozen slush clogged the vents and the valves seized solid. The auguries for a safe dive did not look promising but Horton was determined to find out for himself. Apart from which he wanted to test his own theories.

Running on the surface was unadulterated hell. Spray froze on the rigging wires and hung down like icicles on a fairy castle; great wedges of ice formed on the bridge, and both the periscope and the torpedo-tube caps froze immovably. Horton stationed men on the fore-casing and conning-tower to chip the ice away with hammers and one man was assigned the task of keeping the hatch free. Satisfied with what he had discovered so far Horton decided to test his theory one stage further and he ordered the men below ready for diving.

With the extra top-weight *E.9* submerged more rapidly than usual and the crew held their breaths in case the ice caused a failure in one of the many hundreds of vents and valves which governed their safety. But Horton had guessed correctly. The warmer water beneath the surface quickly melted the ice and, in a short period, *E.9* was her efficient, lethal self again.

Reluctant to lose any opportunity Horton pushed on in search of targets and on approaching Kiel Bay, he sighted an enemy destroyer. The crew closed up to their action-stations and the long, methodical hunt began. Towards the end of the afternoon *S.120* came into Horton's sights at a range of 600 yards and he gave the order to fire.

The torpedo had been set to run at a depth of eight feet but the submarine captains had still not been warned of the erratic behaviour caused by the heavier war-heads. True to form the torpedo streaked straight and true at her target and then, suddenly, plunged deep. Horton, however, did not know this and when he saw a tremendous explosion followed by a spout of water erupt under the destroyer he assumed he had scored a direct hit. In fact the torpedo had struck a mud-bank which had detonated it and the *S.120*, although severely shaken by the resultant explosion, escaped undamaged.

This new attack, right beneath their very noses, thoroughly rattled the German High Command. They were convinced that an entire British flotilla was operating in the Baltic and that it was being supported by a depot-ship hidden in a lonely inlet somewhere along the coast. Two squadrons of heavy ships which were operating in support of the army were quickly withdrawn to the safety of Swinemünde and groups of destroyers scoured the North Prussian coast for the phantom depot-ship.

The Russians seemed unimpressed by the success of the operation, and remained unconvinced that submarines could fight during the winter. Their attitude, like the weather, was decidedly frigid and the two British submarine-commanders found they were being blocked in every direction and at all levels.   ·

Horton's own personal experience of Allied co-operation gives a savage insight into the Russian approach. Both *E.1* and *E.9* had exhausted their official rum-ration and in the bitter cold of the Baltic winter, the crews needed something to warm them up when they returned from a patrol. Horton applied to the local Russian base for a supply of vodka but was curtly informed that the Imperial Navy was 'dry'. They did not add that it was only 'dry' for the lower decks, the wardrooms were usually over-flowing with champagne.

With his usual resource Horton pursued his request to higher levels until, finally, it reached the ears of the Tsar himself. But the Emperor of All the Russias, ensconced in the warmth of the Winter Palace at St Petersburg, was unconcerned by such trivialities. Surely the British Navy was there to fight, not drink? 'If they are so cold,' he remarked, 'why can't they wear two shirts?'

CHAPTER SIX

'I regard one British submarine equal to one Russian armoured cruiser'

BY WAY OF celebrating the New Year, the Admiralty were pleased to promote Max Kennedy Horton, DSO, to the rank of Commander. He was just thirty-one years of age and, in a few short months, had become Britain's leading submarine ace.

With the coming of spring, 1915, the two British submarines unleashed an orgy of destruction on German shipping in the Baltic. Yet, in accordance with International Law, every single merchant ship sunk was first boarded after due warning and the crew placed safely in life-boats.

Prince Henry of Prussia, the German C-in-C Baltic, was convinced that a complete flotilla of submarines was operating against the vital iron-ore trade from Sweden. He addressed the U-boat patrols which were operating in the Gulf of Finland: 'I consider the destruction of a Russian submarine will be a great success, but I regard the destruction of a British submarine as being at least as valuable as that of a Russian armoured cruiser.' High praise indeed.

Meanwhile offensive patrols continued without cease. Laurence was sent to search for ore-ships and Horton was ordered to find the cruiser *Prinz Adalbert* which had gone aground off Libau; but by the time *E.9* arrived the Germans had managed to drag the cruiser free. 'During this period', Horton wrote to a friend, 'we really have been busy, even more so than at the beginning of the war, 7,000 miles in two months.'

On 4 May the two British submarines were ordered to prepare themselves for new operations. Laurence and *E.1* were to
patrol the Bornholm area while Horton and *E.9* were to set
up base at Dagerort to attack the sea flank of the German
advance on Libau. But by 10 May Libau had fallen and Horton's
instructions were amended to patrol the German lines of communication between Danzig and Libau. The intelligence upon
which these new orders were based proved to be sound and,
within a few hours, *E.9* found herself in sight of three enemy
transports returning to Danzig escorted by three cruisers and a
number of destroyers.

It was a difficult target and Horton needed all his skill and
experience. Diving deep he evaded the first screen of destroyers and came up to periscope-depth to select his target.
Orders passed quickly and quietly through the submarine as
he called off the range, speed and deflection of the cruisers,
and then:

'Fire One! . . . Fire Two!'

The torpedoes streaked away but, by now, the rear ship of
the squadron was 1,000 yards off and a hit was unlikely. Even
so, *E.9* did well only to miss the target by less than 100 yards.
Disregarding the fact that the Germans had seen the tracks of
the torpedoes and were now alerted to the presence of the submarine, Horton swung his boat around and, at 200 yards, fired
his port tube at the leading transport. This time his aim was
good but, as so often, the torpedo ran deep and passed underneath the enemy ship. The German destroyers circled at high
speed. The sea was as smooth as glass and each time Horton's
periscope pushed up above the water the slim brass tube sent up
a feather of white spray. Keen-eyed look-outs on the destroyers
were quick to spot the tell-tale sign and their quick-firing guns
pumped shells at the fleeting target each time it appeared.

With supreme disdain Horton brought *E.9* about and fired
his stern tube. This time he was in luck and the torpedo struck
the transport full amidships with a shattering roar. Following

the torpedo's trail to its source the destroyers pounced for the kill but *E.9* quickly dropped to the bottom while the crew worked like galley-slaves to reload the empty tubes.

As soon as the torpedoes had been loaded Horton prepared to bring the submarine up for another attack and then, suddenly, a sharp explosion sent the crew staggering as *E.9* rocked under the impact of the shock-waves.

The Germans were using an explosive sweep which was being dragged by the destroyers and it was obvious that Horton would have to quit the scene if he were to survive. But now that his tubes were re-loaded he was determined to make one last effort. When the propeller noises of the destroyers had faded away he brought the submarine up once again and found the stricken transport swinging around into the cross-wires of his periscope. A torpedo smacked into the transport's bows and she immediately took on a heavy list. *E.9* went down to fifty feet and crawled away on her electric-motors. She was twenty miles away before Horton considered it safe to surface and make for Reval (Tallinn).

Laurence's *E.1* now had the misfortune to fracture her main motor and, as she was laid up in harbour for repairs, Horton and *E.9* were left to carry on alone. It was a busy time. Hearing that a German force was to the West of the Gulf of Riga, Horton left post-haste to find it. Intercepting a wireless message that the Russian minelayer *Yenisei* had been torpedoed by a U-boat, *E.9* swung off course and headed for the new trouble spot. They found the U-boat still in the area but, when Horton dived to attack, the enemy submarine did the same and, as Brodie had complained some months earlier in the same situation, 'neither of us knew what to do.'

A few hours later a light cruiser with four destroyers and a collier came into sight and, to Horton's amazement, the collier stopped to refuel two of the destroyers. It was a foolish action on the part of the Germans and Horton was quick to take advantage of it. Realizing that the cruiser was patrolling the stationary ships in a wide circle he decided to select her as the first target. He waited quietly for the large, sweeping circle to be completed and then, as she entered his sights, he fired his port-beam tube. Ten seconds later two torpedoes shot out of *E.9*'s bow tubes and sped towards the collier.

The first torpedo missed the cruiser but the remaining two exploded violently as they struck the collier. Somehow the destroyer alongside the collier was also hit and, by the time *E.9* left the scene, both ships had sunk and the cruiser was picking up the survivors. It is not surprising that the Germans were beginning to call the Baltic 'Horton's Sea' by this time.

For a month all was quiet. The enemy withdrew their ships from the seaward flank of their advancing armies and *E.9* found herself alone on an empty sea. There was one brief rush of activity when a German cruiser squadron was sighted some distance away but by the time the British submarine had worked herself into an attacking position the enemy had flown.

A period of fog prevented all movement for the next few days and Horton found himself navigating the shoals of the Baltic coast by means of repeated depth soundings, not the most ideal way to con a submarine through enemy-controlled waters.

By 2 July the fog was dispersing and, shortly before 3 pm, on that day Horton surfaced. Visibility was about four miles and as he scanned the eastern horizon he sighted two large warships escorted by some destroyers. They were coming up fast. The hatch slammed down and Horton threw the submarine into a dive.

'Group up. Full ahead together. Torpedomen close up.'

Moving at her maximum underwater speed *E.9* cut right across the path of the oncoming ships and swung round into the perfect textbook attack position. The caps over the torpedo-tubes opened and the tubes were flooded. All now depended on the skill of the submarine's captain.

Both bow tubes fired together with the target a mere 400 yards away and, seconds later, two violent explosions reverberated through the *E.9*'s thin steel hull. Two direct hits.

But the crew's elation was short-lived. The torpedoes had upset the submarine's delicate trim and she wallowed to the surface like a porpoise. A German destroyer was bearing down on them, the water spraying from her sharp bows as she closed in for the kill. Flooding the ballast tanks and using full-power Horton dived for safety and, by a hair's breadth, escaped destruction. It had all happened so quickly that *E.9*'s progress towards the depths was only arrested when she dug her nose into the sea-bottom at forty-five feet.

Horton described the attack in a letter to a friend: 'We hit her last Friday, 2 July, with two torpedoes, she was going pretty fast, about eighteen, with destroyers. Saw the first explosion by the foremast, fine show, debris and smoke up to the tops of the masts. I was keeping a somewhat anxious eye on a destroyer, pretty close, doing its best to ram us, dirty dog! However she failed (narrowly).'

Horton's target had been the cruiser *Prinz Adalbert*, but in actual fact she did not sink; the puny 18″ torpedoes with which the 'E' class boats were armed were too small to destroy a ship of that size; but she was badly damaged and put out of action for four crucial months.

Even the Russians were pleased with this latest exploit and, a short while later, the new Russian C-in-C (von Essen had died on 20 May) decorated Horton with the Order of St George, their highest military award.

The Admiralty had been taking note of the successes achieved by *E.1* and *E.9* and it was decided to reinforce the Baltic flotilla with some new blood. *E.8* (Lt-Cdr Goodhart), *E.13* (Lt-Cdr Layton), with *E.18* and *E.19* were ordered to the Baltic through the Kattegat and the Sound, the same hazardous route taken by Horton and Laurence, while the smaller *C.26*,

C.27, *C.32* and *C.35* were to be towed to Archangel and then sent overland to Petrograd. It was an ambitious project but their Lordships were determined to follow up the earlier successes, and to try and bolster up the sagging Russian morale.

Unfortunately things went sadly awry. In order to lighten the four little 'C' class boats for their long tow across the North Sea to Archangel it was decided to remove their batteries and ship them separately. On arrival in North Russia they were hoisted on to barges and transported to Petrograd down a maze of narrow canals and rivers. It was a tremendous task for each submarine was 143 feet long and weighed, even when stripped of torpedoes and batteries, around 200 tons. But the wholehearted efforts of the Russian canal-labourers succeeded and, finally, the four boats were lowered into the waters of the Baltic by gigantic cranes. The planning and execution had been superb. But there was one drawback—the ship carrying the batteries had been torpedoed by a U-boat and sunk in the North Sea. Without power for their electric-motors the submarines were useless hulks and it took several months for the replacement batteries to be shipped from England.

The 'E' class boats faced different and more dangerous problems. On 14 August *E.8* and *E.13* left Harwich with orders to proceed through the Sound and rendezvous with *E.9* outside Dagerort in the Gulf of Finland, and they reached the Kattegat without incident.

Goodhart in *E.8* arrived first and at three o'clock in the morning of the 18th he sighted a small convoy ahead. Not wishing to alert the enemy he took the submarine to the bottom and waited for the ships to pass. Cautiously rising to periscope-depth an hour later he was about to surface when another ship hove into view and, once again, *E.8* went deep.

When he returned to periscope-depth Goodhart found that a thick fog had conveniently settled over the area and, taking advantage of the immunity it offered, he set off for the entrance to the Sound running on the surface with his diesels. But the

DUW—F

fog thinned and as it was still daylight he decided to lie doggo on the bottom until it got dark.

Rising to the surface at dusk *E.8* was trimmed down so that only her conning-tower showed above the water and headed through the Sound at full speed. Copenhagen was now well astern and Malmö was receding into the darkness. All seemed clear for a quiet run until, an hour later, a bridge look-out on a patrolling German destroyer sighted the submarine's conning-tower. His warning shout was followed by a series of sharp orders. The engine-room telegraph was thrust to full ahead and the enemy ship swung round to ram.

Fortunately the men on *E.8* were as wide awake as their opponents and she dived rapidly at almost the same moment. But Goodhart, like Horton, found the water too shallow to escape and *E.8* hit the bottom with a resounding thump at a depth of nineteen feet. Bumping his way along the sea-bed Goodhart kept the submarine moving and succeeded in evading the destroyer only to find another enemy torpedo-boat 200 yards ahead.

In the circumstances it was impossible to dive and *E.8* was conned quietly past the German ship on her electric motors. This time she wasn't spotted but the men on the bridge had scarcely recovered their breath when a third torpedo-boat loomed out of the darkness. Once again *E.8* crash-dived, this time in only 16 feet of water, and as she hit the bottom the blades of her starboard propeller were ripped off the shaft.

By now her batteries were almost exhausted and it was obvious that the end could not be long delayed. Added to which the torque to port caused by the broken starboard propeller made steering a nightmare. For the next few desperate hours Goodhart played hide-and-seek with the hunters on the surface and, yard by yard, the crippled submarine edged closer to the deep waters of the Baltic. Each time the periscope broke surface the torpedo-boats roared in and *E.8* had to run deep again. Finally she broke through the German cordon and on the 22nd she met the veteran *E.9* for the run-in to Reval. Twenty-four hours later, with a new propeller fitted, she was again ready for operational duty.

Geoffrey Layton in *E.13* was not so lucky. In fact the unfortunate submarine lived up to the superstitions of its ill-omened number in a spectacular manner for Layton had actually succeeded in navigating the Sound, the most difficult part of the passage, when, just after 11 pm, disaster struck. The magnetic-compass failed and the submarine swung off course and embedded herself firmly on the south-eastern edge of the Saltholm flat, a notorious mudbank between Malmö and Copenhagen, *inside* Danish territorial waters.

Under International Law a belligerent warship is only permitted to remain inside neutral waters for a maximum period of twenty-four hours after which time she must be interned. Layton was well aware of this and the crew worked frantically to lighten *E.13* sufficiently to enable her to float clear of the mudbank at the next high tide. They worked all through the night and at 5 am, a Danish destroyer closed in and reminded the submarine captain of the time limit.

The Germans, too, had learned of *E.13*'s mishap and before long two enemy torpedo-boats appeared over the horizon. Their orders were apparently quite clear for, ignoring the Danish guard-ship, and the fact that they were in Danish territorial waters, one of the German vessels fired a torpedo at the stranded submarine. It struck the mud on which *E.13* was lying and although there was a mighty and spectacular explosion, it did no damage.

Determined not to be foiled of their prey the torpedo-boats closed in to 300 yards and opened fire with their guns. The submarine stood no chance against such a murderous attack at close quarters and within minutes she was a twisted flaming hulk of steel. A number of the submarine's crew were killed by the shell-fire and, realizing the hopelessness of the position, Layton gave orders to abandon ship.

The survivors leapt into the water but the Germans opened fire again. In all, fifteen men were shot or drowned. The captain of the Danish destroyer courageously put his ship between the men in the water and the enemy torpedo-boats and undoubtedly saved the lives of the remainder. Sixteen survivors were rescued including Lt-Cdr Layton. Kitted out with fresh clothing they were taken off to an internment camp and, before the war was over, were repatriated to England as shipwrecked mariners.

As Sir Julian Corbett described the incident in *The Official History of the War—Naval Operations*: 'The outrage was perpetrated in cold blood, by men well under the control of their officers, upon a helpless wreck on a neutral shore. For a cumulation of illegality it would surely be hard to match in the annals of modern naval warfare.'

By a strange coincidence *E.13*'s destruction on the mudbanks of Saltholm was avenged almost within minutes several hundred miles to the east. A strong German force of the 1st Scouting Group commanded by Admiral von Hipper had been sent to destroy the submarine base in the Gulf of Riga and, at the same time, to give support to the coastal flank of the Kaiser's army. The attempt to force the Gulf began on 18 August and, when the news was received, the two British submarines then in the port moved out to counter the attack.

The following day Laurence sighted four giant battle-cruisers travelling at high speed in line abreast with a close escort of destroyers. There was no time for elaborate manœuvring and, within ten minutes of the sighting, Laurence had sent two 18″ torpedoes towards them. It was too foggy to see the results of the attack and the escorting destroyers made it unwise to remain at periscope-depth. *E.1* went deep. Suddenly the submarine shuddered under the impact of a violent underwater explosion. One of the torpedoes had struck the battle-cruiser *Moltke*. The damage was not serious and she was still able to proceed under her own power but the sudden attack unnerved von Hipper. Abandoning the operation he signalled his four heavy ships to return to harbour.

E.1's outstanding success had defeated the powerful enemy attack on the Gulf and von Hipper's abandonment of the operation saved the base from falling into German hands at a critical time in the war. Noel Laurence was presented to the Tsar who personally decorated him with the Order of St George for saving the city of Riga.

E.18 (Lt-Cdr Halahan) and *E.19* (Lt-Cdr Cromie) had also passed safely through the Sound by this time and were a welcome addition to Laurence's fast-growing Baltic Flotilla. From now on Germany's vital iron-ore supplies from Sweden were at the mercy of the British submarines.

Goodhart's *E.8* was the first to strike and, on 5 October, she captured the steamer *Margarette* outward-bound from Königsberg and destroyed her by gunfire after putting the crew safely into the ship's boats. The submarine then moved on to Libau to take up her patrol-line but enemy activity in the approaches to the port was so intense that it was impossible to get close. It was obvious that something was in the wind and when, on the evening of the 22nd, a naval trawler began sending up flares to mark the entrance to the channel into Libau, action seemed imminent. But nothing happened that night and the first few hours of the morning passed without incident. Goodhart was just beginning to think that it was a false alarm when he sighted a large three-funnelled cruiser coming over the horizon. She was travelling at fifteen knots and was escorted by two destroyers, one on each bow, zig-zagging at speed in search of submarines. *E.8* spurted to seven-and-a-half knots, her maximum underwater speed, and then eased back to five knots in case her wake was disturbing the water on the surface.

It was a bright, clear autumn day with good sunlight and a slight SSE wind. At 9.28 am the nearest destroyer passed clear of Goodhart's periscope and nothing now stood between him and his target.

When the range had closed to 1,300 yards he fired a single torpedo. Sixty seconds later there was a terrible explosion and a volcano of burning debris erupted from the stricken warship. *E.8* went deep and eight minutes later when Goodhart came up to survey the scene the great cruiser had completely disappeared. His victim was the 9,050 ton *Prinz Adalbert* which Horton had already damaged in July. Since then she had been in dry-dock undergoing repairs and this was her first cruise. Goodhart's torpedo, by penetrating her fore-magazine, had ensured that it was also her last.

The other submarines of the Baltic Flotilla also had the bit between their teeth. On Monday, 11 October, Cromie and *E.19* had 'started to chase merchant shipping' with results that deserve to rank high in the annals of underwater warfare. At 9.40 am they intercepted the iron-ore ship *Walter Leonhardt* and, having placed the crew on board a passing Swedish vessel which they had signalled to stop, they sank her with a charge of gun-cotton. Two hours later Cromie gave chase to the Hamburg-registered *Germania* loaded with 3,000 tons of ore. She refused to stop and, in her desperate efforts to escape, ran aground. *E.19* came alongside to save the crew but they had already abandoned ship, so Cromie tried to tow her off. She proved to be too large for the straining engines of the submarine and, when *E.19* left her, she was filling with water and sinking fast. At 2 pm Cromie was chasing the *Gutrune*, another ore-carrier bound from Lulea to Hamburg. An hour later she, too, was on the bottom of the Baltic, the crew having been safely transferred to a passing neutral steamer.

But the day was not over yet. By the late afternoon *E.19* was pursuing two more steamers. The first was the Swedish ship *Nyland* en route for Rotterdam. She was allowed to continue; and ten minutes later Cromie stopped the second ship, the *Direktor Rippenhagen* loaded with magnetic-ore for Nadenheim. Having put her crew aboard another Swedish ship Cromie proceeded to sink his fourth victim. Number five, the

Nicomedia, tried to outrun the submarine but a shot across the bows soon discouraged her and the crew was placed in the ship's lifeboats before she, too, was sunk.

Cromie's regard for International Law was precise and exemplary, in sharp contrast to the sinking-on-sight policy of the German U-boats. On another occasion he stopped the Swedish ore-carrier *Nike* and found her carrying a contraband cargo to Germany. As she was a neutral ship he was forbidden to sink her but he *could* confiscate her cargo. Without further ado he sent Lt Mee aboard with two seamen to act as prize-crew and told them to take her into Reval for examination.

The result was a first-class diplomatic row for there was no British Prize Court in Reval and the Russians had no intention of upsetting a neutral neighbour; they had enough on their hands already. Sir Edward Grey intervened and intimated that the Russians could do as they liked as he didn't want an international inquiry into our Prize Court procedure which was, to say the least, a trifle arbitrary. The Russians promptly handed the ship and cargo back to the Swedes.

While he was aboard *Nike* as Prize Officer, Lieutenant Mee learned that *E.19*'s operations on 11 October had resulted in a complete standstill of all shipping engaged in the iron-ore trade and fifteen ships had to wait at Lulea while convoy protection was arranged. And the repercussions spread wider still, for the High Sea Fleet had to release two cruisers and two flotillas of destroyers for trade protection in the Baltic and 'was rendered incapable of carrying out sweeps whilst the destroyers were absent.' The Baltic plan had proved its worth.

Horton, too, had been busy and on the 18 and 19 October added four large steamers to his long list of successes. Like Cromie, he carried out his obligations under International Law to the letter. As he reported to the Admiralty: 'Due and proper warning was given in every case ... careful search of each vessel sunk was made previous to the sinking to ensure there was none of the enemy crew remaining on board. Ample time was allowed for placing personal gear, food and water in the boats and in no case was the weather unsuitable for small boats or the distance to the nearest shore more than fifteen miles . . . no casualties occurred or were reported in Sweden where enemy crews landed.'

Cromie, now apparently bored with merchant ships, began searching for more ambitious targets and on the morning of 7 November while cruising in the Western Baltic, he sighted a warship escorted by two destroyers. He shaped up to attack but an alteration of course by the enemy squadron took them out of range and they vanished. Disappointed, he continued his patrol and was rewarded, three hours later, by the sight of a light cruiser and accompanying destroyer steaming towards him. *E.19* submerged rapidly and the attack began. At 1.20 pm the periscope sights centred on their target and Cromie released his starboard torpedo at a range of 1,100 yards. It struck the cruiser near the bows and she swung into a wide circle, belching smoke, before stopping. Anxious to finish her off, Cromie avoided the destroyer, took *E.19* under the stern of the sinking ship, and sent a second torpedo into her. This time he exploded the magazine and fragments of white-hot debris hissed into the sea 200 yards away. Within three minutes the 2,650 ton *Undine* had gone to the bottom leaving the destroyer to pick up the survivors.

Winter was now closing in and *E.1* had already returned from her last patrol by the end of October. *E.8*, *E.9* and *E.19* were all back in Reval by 8 November and the last boat, *E.18*, sailed into base on the 17th. For the next few months the submarines were frozen in and operations were suspended until the spring thaw.

On 17 December, 1915, Horton and Laurence were recalled by the Admiralty in a telegram stating that they were 'urgently required for service in new submarines in home waters.' The Russians did not wish to lose such valuable officers and they attempted to stop the transfer. When this failed they urgently requested that Horton should remain at Reval as Senior Naval Officer Baltic. The Admiralty, in its wisdom, thought not. And the Second Sea Lord minuted the request: 'I understand Commander Horton is something of a pirate and not at all fitted for the position of SNO in the Baltic.' Such, it seemed, was the price of success when viewed through the conservative eyes of the Admiralty. As we have seen, Horton was anything but a pirate in his strict regard for the letter, and the spirit, of International Law.

Even the intervention of Sir George Buchanan, the British Ambassador in St Petersburg, failed to gain a reprieve. 'I learn that Commander Laurence and Commander Horton are under orders for England,' he telegraphed. 'The latter gets on particularly well with the Russians which requires special qualifications, and his experience in the Baltic is also valuable. Would it not be possible to allow him to remain.'

But their Lordships remained adamant and, on 31 December, 1915, Horton and Laurence packed their bags ready to leave. Horton travelled overland through neutral Sweden and Norway on a faked passport and arrived in Newcastle wrapped in a huge sable-coat, smoking some evil-smelling Russian cigarettes. In his case he carried the Order of Vladimir with swords, the Order of St Ann with swords and diamonds, and the Order of St George. In addition the French had made him a Chevalier of the Legion of Honour. All in all, not a bad reward for a 'pirate'.

With the coming of spring, 1916, the British flotilla sailed out into the Baltic once again in search of the enemy. But, by now, the pickings were scarce. In a desperate effort to protect their vunerable and valuable iron-ore ships the Germans had adopted the convoy system, finding the answer to the submarine threat many months before our own Admiralty, and a total of seventy torpedo-boats and armed-trawlers were now active in the Baltic.

The little 'C' class boats now joined in the fray, their

batteries having at last arrived from England, and Lt Sealy celebrated their new operational role by sinking an enemy transport in the Gulf of Riga with *C.27*. In early May, Lt-Cdr Halahan, still a relative newcomer to northern waters, located the German destroyer *V.100* and steered *E.18* to an attacking position. Despite his disadvantage in speed he succeeded in scoring a direct hit which completely blew off the enemy's bows. But she failed to sink and, by superb seamanship, the crew managed to get their crippled ship safely back to base.

The following day *E.18* vanished without trace and no clue to the fate of Halahan and his crew has ever been found. It seems probable that they fell victim to an enemy minefield.

Sad though the loss of *E.18* was, this was the Germans' only real success against the Baltic submarines throughout the whole of this campaign. *E.13* had been sunk before she had arrived in the Baltic and *C.32* was lost through accidental causes. It was a balance sheet of which the Royal Navy had every reason to be proud.

Patrols continued throughout the summer months but targets were becoming scarcer, and the submarine crews were uncomfortably aware of a strange, uneasy rumbling in their rear as the seeds of revolution took root amongst the Russian sailors.

Summer passed, and then autumn. Once again winter ensured that the submarines remained in their frozen harbours and, finally, the fateful year of 1917 began. Patrols restarted but for most of the time the submarine commanders found themselves staring at an empty sea. The German convoy system was tightly efficient and even the experienced veterans of the Baltic Flotilla were denied success. The happy-hunting days of Horton, Laurence and Cromie had gone.

In October Lt Downie found himself facing a large section of the German fleet which was taking part in a combined operation with the army. *C.26* moved in to attack but, as she was closing the range, she grounded in 20 feet of water.

Downie, try as he might, could not get her off so he was left with no alternative but to get clear by surfacing.

As soon as the Germans sighted her the destroyers swooped and the submarine made a dash for deeper water where she could submerge. She was fortunately well beneath the waves by the time the hunters arrived over the spot and, after circling around for an hour, they were recalled to join the fleet.

Unshaken by his narrow escape Downie prepared for a second attack but, when C.26 came to periscope-depth again there were ships on all sides and sea-planes overhead. At first Downie tried a high-speed run but as the destroyers closed in and shaped course to ram he changed his mind and gave orders to dive.

At this critical moment the diving-rudders jammed and the little submarine appeared to be doomed. Downie, however, preferred to face the dangers of the deep to annihilation by the enemy and, with her tanks flooded, C.26 plunged down out of control and smacked hard against the sea bottom at twenty feet.

This time the Germans used depth-charges, a relatively new invention at that period of the war, and the submarine rocked under the hammer-blows of their explosive charges. Downie and his men sat tight and, by some act of Providence, the hull was not damaged. The enemy prowled overhead for several hours but finally withdrew and C.26 crept thankfully away to fight another day.

Downie and his crew had another lucky escape shortly afterwards, when, three miles from the enemy shore, the petrol tanks caught fire. Sir John Durston's misgivings about petrol engines in submarines some fifteen years earlier had, once again, proved to be well-founded. The crew scrambled on deck and the hatch was closed in an effort to starve the flames of oxygen. It was a bitterly cold day and the men had had no time to grab warm clothing when the fire started. Standing exposed on the narrow wind-swept deck of the submarine, they were half-dead from exposure before the fire burned itself out and they were able to get below again. But they managed to get *C.26* back to Reval by using the electric motors.

On 24 October her sister ship, *C.32*, stranded on a mudbank in the Gulf of Riga, had to be abandoned and blown up by her crew. But far worse was to come.

The Bolshevik Revolution erupted on 6 November, 1917, and, in the turmoil that followed, the Baltic Fleet supported the Soviet against the legitimate Provisional Government. By the 17th an armistice had been signed with the Germans and one of the terms of the document specified the surrender of the British submarines.

Cromie, now Senior Naval Officer Baltic, refused to accept the armistice and the flotilla moved northwards to Helsingfors (Helsinki) where the bulk of the Russian fleet was based. On their arrival they found complete chaos. Many of the senior officers had been executed or murdered and the allegiance of the Fleet seemed open to doubt. Rear-Admiral Stchasny was in nominal command, more by reason of seniority than appointment, and he tried to move the ships to Kronstadt to avoid internment.

For days no one knew what was happening. Seamen Soviets were in control of many of the ships and boat-loads of Russian sailors circled the British submarines calling on the crews to join the Revolution. At other times the guns of the Russian warships pointed menacingly at their erstwhile allies as if threatening to blow them out of the water if they dared to move. It was a tense and difficult time and Cromie's task was not made easier by the fact that, for days on end, he could not establish radio contact with London.

Finally Stchasny gathered his mutinous collection of ships together and left Helsingfors. The Baltic Flotilla could, for the moment, breathe again.

With Russia in chaos the German army continued to advance along the coast. In April the enemy landed at Hangö and it was now clear that resistance could not continue much longer. Surrender seemed inevitable.

But Cromie would not consider such an inglorious fate for the gallant flotilla. Using all his authority, backed up by a considerable amount of bluff, he forced a Russian ice-breaker to clear a passage out of the harbour. *E.1, E.8, E.9, E.19, C.26, C.27* and *C.35*, formed up in line ahead and followed the smoke-belching ice-breaker into the Baltic, their White Ensigns streaming bravely in the breeze.

On reaching deep water a number of explosive charges were primed in each boat and the crews taken off by a waiting tug. Minutes later the fuses detonated and a series of explosions echoed from the snow-covered hills surrounding the barren bay. Defiant to the last the veteran survivors of the Baltic Flotilla settled slowly in the water and disappeared for ever.

The crews of the scuttled submarines returned to England but Commander Cromie stayed behind and was appointed Naval Attaché to the British Embassy in Petrograd. And it was here that he died, a fighter to the last, defending the building single-handed against a mob of looters.

CHAPTER SEVEN

'This Very Gallant
Enterprise'

WHEN THE *Goeben* and *Breslau* escaped to Constantinople in
August, 1914, Churchill and the Admiralty knew that war
with the Ottoman Empire was inevitable. As the First Lord
said himself, when the *Goeben* 'entered the Dardanelles . . . the
Curse descended irrevocably upon Turkey and the East.'

In August, 1914, the Turkish Navy was no more than a
collection of rusting, derelict hulks but the situation changed
dramatically when the Kaiser presented the battle-cruiser and
its consort to his prospective allies. Naturally, the gift had
strings attached. Admiral Souchon, the German Squadron's
commander, was immediately appointed Commander-in-
Chief of the Ottoman Navy by the grateful Sultan while the
Kaiser's sailors were distributed amongst the Turkish ships to
instruct their crews, raise morale, and prepare them for war
service.

Flying the crescent ensign of the Sublime Porte, and now
rejoicing in the names of *Jawus Sultan Selim* and *Midilli*, the
two ex-German warships posed a new and unpredictable
threat to British naval power in the Eastern Mediterranean.
Throughout September, the Turkish army under its German
officers mobilized and organized itself for the coming conflict
while Souchon and his men worked miracles to instill sea-
worthiness and efficiency into the neglected Turkish Navy.

By the middle of the month the situation was extremely
tense. Churchill, ever eager for battle, telegraphed Vice-
Admiral Carden in Malta: 'Assume command of squadron off
Dardanelles; your *sole duty* is to sink *Goeben* and *Breslau* no
matter what flag they fly if they come out of the Dardanelles.

We are not at war with the Turks but Admiral Souchon is now C-in-C of Turkish Navy and Germans are largely controlling it.'

As the battle-cruisers *Indomitable* and *Indefatigable* steamed out into the Mediterranean no one paid much attention to the little group of submarines that followed the fleet out to sea. Yet a young lieutenant commanding one of them was, in a few months' time, to win the Navy's first Victoria Cross. *B.9*, *B.10* and *B.11* had joined the local defence flotilla at Malta in 1910 when it was decided to send submarines to Britain's overseas' bases. Built in 1906, they were now obsolete and worn out and the sight of the incongruous little flotilla seemed a slightly comic anti-climax as they wallowed out of the harbour in the wake of the powerful battle-cruisers.

Even in 1914 they were almost museum pieces. Displacing 280 tons on the surface, their narrow steel hulls only 135 feet in length, they relied on the treacherous and still primitive petrol engine for their motive power. But in their bows they carried two eighteen-inch torpedo-tubes and these, as events subsequently proved, were sufficient to convert them from obsolescent old tubs into the lethal equals of any battleship which might cross their path.

A submarine base was set up at Mudros on the island of Lemnos and the old depot ship *Hindu Kush* acted as headquarters and accommodation vessel. Lt-Cdr Pownall was in command of the flotilla and they were soon reinforced by the arrival of three French submarines. Word was received also that the Gibraltar submarines, *B.6* and *B.7*, were on their way to join them under the command of Lt-Cdr Brodie.

Admiral Carden instituted a close blockade across the entrance to the Dardanelles but, for a few weeks, all remained quiet. And then, suddenly, on 28 October, the former *Goeben*, *Breslau* and the Turkish *Hamidieh* made a sortie from the Golden Horn and without warning bombarded the Russian Black Sea ports of Sebastopol, Novorossisk and Odessa. War had not been declared but Enver Pasha's signal to Admiral Souchon indicated that this was now only a formality: 'The Turkish Fleet is to win command of the Black Sea. The situation demands war.'

On 1 November the Ottoman Empire declared war and Carden prepared for a quick blow against Britain's new enemy. Two days later *Indomitable* and *Indefatigable*, supported by French warships, carried out a short sharp bombardment of the Dardanelles fortresses. It was a not unsuccessful raid but it warned the Turks that their defences needed to be improved and reinforced—and it was to have dire consequences later when a full-scale attempt was made to force the narrow passage of water which links the Mediterranean with the Black Sea. But that episode, and the blood bath of Gallipoli, were yet to come.

On board *Hindu Kush* Pownall and his submarine commanders, Holbrook, Warburton and Gravener, considered the possibility of sending submarines into the Dardanelles to search for targets. The low submerged endurance of the 'B' class boats made it impossible for them to pass right through the Straits into the Sea of Marmora but it was felt that some demonstration of strength in the Dardanelles itself would be worthwhile. After long, and at times heated, discussions it was agreed that, provided some form of anti-mine guards could be fitted, the plan was feasible. Accordingly, Pownall put up the proposal to Carden for approval.

The idea was supported and, in early December, instructions were received from the flagship to go ahead.

Tubular steel guards were duly designed and fitted over the many projections which studded the sides of the submarines. Now the mine-cables would be pushed clear and no longer snag round the hydroplanes or other protuberances. And then came the big argument. Which of the six submarine captains, three British and three French, would be selected for the first mission.

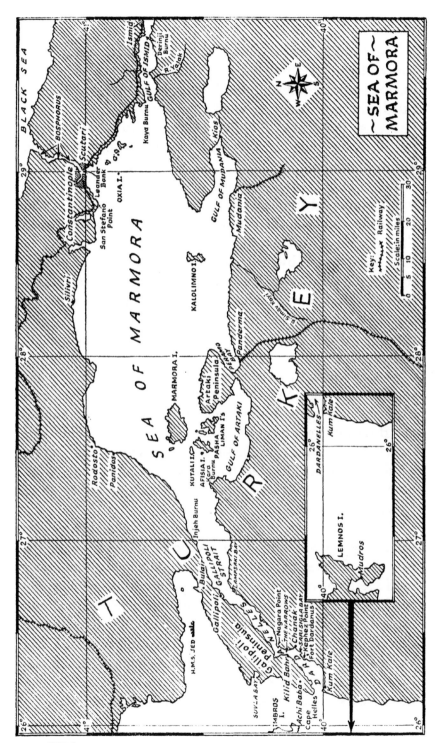

~SEA OF~
MARMORA

Key:
railway
Scale: miles
0 5 10 20 30

BLACK SEA

BOSPHORUS
Scutari
Constantinople
Leander Bank
San Stefano Point
OXIA I.
Silivri
Rodosto
Panidos

Kava Burnu GULF OF ISMID Derinji Burnu
R. Simon Kuli

GULF OF MUDANIA Kios
Mudania
Panderma

SEA OF MARMORA

KALOLIMNO I.

MARMORA I.

Artaki Peninsula
Artaki
PASHA LIMAN I.
GULF OF ARTAKI
KUTALI I.
AFISIA I.
Kara Burnu

T U R K E Y

Injeh Burnu
Bulair
GALLIPOLI STRAIT
Gallipoli
H.M.S. JED
Gallipoli Peninsula
KAMPSTAL BAY
SUVLA BAY
TIMBROS I.
Achi Baba
Cape Helles
Kum Kale
Nagara Point
THE NARROWS
Chanak
SARI SIGLA BAY
Kephez Point
Fort Dardanus
DARDANELLES

Kilid Bahr

DARDANELLES
Kum Kale
LEMNOS I.
Mudros

DUW-G

The decision, when it was made, was finally based upon various technical considerations. The British boats were most suitable which eliminated the French, and *B.11* had just been fitted with new batteries, which disposed of Warburton and Gravener. In addition Norman Holbrook had already penetrated several miles into Turkish waters in pursuit of two enemy gunboats.

In December, 1914, the only obstacle blocking the Straits was a barrier of five rows of moored mines; but the Turks could also count on the natural vagaries of the current to aid their defences. At about ten fathoms there was a stratum of fresh water which, by reason of its different density, made submarine depth-keeping extremely difficult and this, plus a strong adverse current, constituted a dangerous natural hazard for submarine-commanders. And, by fighting the swiftly-running current, the power of the batteries would be quickly exhausted.

At 4.15 am on 13 December Holbrook was running on the surface three miles from the entrance to the Straits. Powerful Turkish searchlights were sweeping the narrow waters ahead and *B.11* submerged to wait for dawn. As soon as the lights were switched off she came to the surface again and crept to within a mile of Cape Helles before trimming down and diving. From now on they were at the mercy of Turkish guns if they dared to return to the surface.

Moving at two knots and keeping a depth of eighty feet the submarine crawled into the Dardanelles and headed for the first row of mines. For half-an-hour everything went smoothly until a series of vibrations made it apparent that something had worked loose. Holbrook decided to risk being spotted and came to the surface to inspect the hull. The trouble was quickly located; the forward port hydroplane-guard had twisted itself around into a hook shape; a couple of strong seamen wrenched it clear and threw it over the side. *B.11* slid quietly back under the surface and continued on her way.

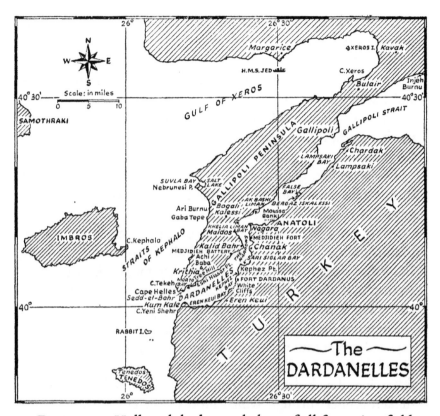

By 9.40 am Holbrook had passed clear of all five mine-fields and rising to periscope-depth he began to survey the scene. Luck, it seemed, was with him for, anchored off his starboard beam, was a large two-funnelled warship with the Turkish ensign fluttering from its mainmast.

The current was strong and the Lieutenant had to use full-power to swing *B.11*'s bows around and close the target. But the new batteries held their charge well and soon the submarine was only 800 yards away from her adversary. The torpedomen in the bows grinned at each other as the order came down to flood the tubes and all was quiet as Holbrook made the necessary corrections to course so that his sights were lined up full-square on the target.

'Stand by . . .'

Every man in the submarine held his breath as the seconds ticked away.

'Fire both!'

B.11 lurched as the torpedoes were expelled from their tubes and Holbrook watched the twin wakes speeding straight for the enemy. Then a sudden eddy in the current swung the submarine sideways, the periscope dipped under the water, and the coxswain swore as he brought her level again.

The shuddering thump of the torpedo exploding echoed through the submarine and, by the time Holbrook was able to get a clear sight in his periscope, the warship was settling by the stern with an enormous cloud of thickening, black smoke mushrooming from her shattered hull. Sharp spurts of flame along her sides indicated, however, that the Turkish gunners were still at their posts and a hail of shells churned the water into a white froth as they spotted *B.11*'s periscope.

They were still serving the guns when the cruiser *Messudieh* capsized ten minutes later trapping them inside the armour-plated hull. But Allah looked kindly on his sailors and the following day holes were cut in the upturned keel of the sunken cruiser through which most of the crew were able to climb to safety.

Holbrook had little time to savour his victory. The shore-batteries were remarkably accurate, no doubt due to the instruction of their German officers, and, after one last look at his victim, he took the submarine down and swung her around so that her bows were pointing towards the exit to the Straits.

But the tribulations of the little *B.11* were only just beginning. As she steadied on her new course Lt Winn, her First Officer, reported that the compass lens was fogged. The 'B' class submarines were so old that they still carried their compasses mounted on deck where they were viewed through a system of lenses when running submerged. They were now navigating blind.

Without a compass the safety of the submarine rested solely

on the skill of Lt Norman Holbrook. And, to make matters worse, the current had driven *B.11* to the west which, according to the charts, meant there was the additional hazards of passing through an area of shoal-waters. If, as he assumed, they had sunk the *Messudieh* in Sari Siglar Bay they would be running into the shallows at any moment. Almost as confirmation of his fears the submarine bumped violently as she grazed the bottom. Holbrook immediately ordered full-speed in the hope of keeping clear. She scraped off the bottom and then lurched on to another patch of mud.

Unlike the more modern submarines *B.11*'s conning-tower was not sealed off from the hull and, as the commander stood in the control-room, he suddenly realized that sunlight was streaming in through the circular-glass ports in its base. That meant one thing. The conning-tower was sticking up above the surface.

It did not take the Turkish shore batteries long to spot it and, once again, the submarine was subjected to a deluge of shells which threw up great spouts of water as they exploded in the sea only yards from the exposed conning-tower.

Inside *B.11* the electric-motors were pushed to their limits and the control dials flickered alarmingly as the propellers churned at maximum revolutions. The ancient hull groaned and creaked under the strain of full-power but the effort succeeded and slowly but perceptibly the submarine slid off the mudbank. Taking up position in the conning-tower Holbrook peered out through the tiny glass ports and calmly conned the boat through the shallow waters. But his vision was limited and they were virtually running blind. For half-an-hour the submarine bumped and thumped along the bottom before she reached deep water and could slip gently down under the surface once again.

After a short interval Holbrook judged it safe enough to raise the periscope and he sighed with relief as he sighted an area of open water to starboard. They were through the

Straits. An hour later *B.11* came to the surface and the hatch was thrown open to allow the accumulation of poisonous air to escape from the confined hull. They had, in fact, been submerged for so long that it took over half-an-hour for sufficient oxygen to get into the boat to enable the petrol-engines to be started. A destroyer moved into position and the tiny submarine was triumphantly escorted back to Mudros.

She was given a great welcome and the crews of the other ships in harbour lined the rails to cheer her as she cruised past. Holbrook's sensational success was soon in every British newspaper. Even the enemy admitted that his victory was well-earned. And who was better able to judge the tremendous obstacles, man-made and natural, that *B.11* had surmounted in the course of her historic attack?

Lt Holbrook was awarded the Victoria Cross and Lt Winn the DSO. Everyone else aboard was suitably decorated. It was, indeed, a great day for the infant Submarine Service.

Admiral Carden was greatly impressed by *B.11*'s achievements and he immediately requested the Admiralty to send out some 'E' class boats which, with their longer submerged endurance, would be capable of going through the Dardanelles into the Sea of Marmora. But, for the moment, his request fell on deaf ears. The valuable 'E' class boats could not be spared for operations in 'side show' theatres of war.

The Middle East was, however, growing in importance and, when the Russians asked the British Government for assistance, Lord Kitchener asked the Admiralty to make a demonstration against the Turkish defences in the Straits. It must be a purely naval operation, Kitchener pointed out, as he had no troops to spare for a land campaign. Churchill himself had visions of attacking Constantinople which, as he correctly pointed out, would result in the collapse of the Ottoman Empire. But he had only a hazy conception of the effort required and was of the opinion that such a feat could be accomplished by naval forces only.

Fisher did not like the idea. His own experience against the forts at Alexandria in the 'eighties had convinced him that ships could not tackle land-based guns with any degree of success. Apart from which he was reluctant to give up his beloved Baltic project for which preparations were already in hand. Finally, for reasons best known to himself, he agreed to support Churchill's plan *provided* the admiral in command on the spot considered it to be desirable. His proviso proved to be a convenient avenue of escape in due course as we shall see.

The decision to bombard the Dardanelles fortresses and to force a passage to Constantinople was taken on 28 January. A few days later Roger Keyes arrived at Mudros to act as Chief-of-Staff to Carden. By this time, also, the Gibraltar submarines under Lt-Cdr C. G. Brodie had arrived and Keyes at once took them under his wing. Pownall was given command of the two flotillas and Brodie was added to Carden's staff where, with Keyes as his Chief, control of the submarine force now lay.

The bombardment of the Outer Forts began on 19 February but the consequences of this abortive operation are outside the scope of this book. It must suffice to say that although the bombardment was successful there was no follow-up. Churchill took the sanguine view that we were in sight of success and, as he wrote later: 'Not to persevere, that was the crime.'

Carden's resignation some days later (he was succeeded by Admiral de Robeck) was as much caused by a breakdown in his health as by opposition to the plan. But Fisher seized on it to argue that the admiral 'on the spot' no longer had any faith in the operation. Then, amid theatrical tantrums, the old First Sea Lord used this as the excuse for tendering his own resignation. But it was only an excuse. The true reason for Fisher's resignation was his age-old antagonism to any plan that Churchill supported.

One result of the increased naval pressure on the Dardanelles was the decision to send seven 'E' class boats to the Mediterranean and to transfer the only Australian submarine, *AE.2*, to Mudros.

By 29 March the first three boats were in the Bay of Biscay on the first leg of their long passage to the Middle East. Escorted by the depot-ship *Adamant*, *E.11* (Lt-Cdr Martin Nasmith), *E.14* (Lt-Cdr Courtney Boyle) and *E.15* (Lt-Cdr T. S. Brodie, twin brother of C. G. Brodie on Keyes' staff) headed for Gibraltar. All three commanders, as we have already seen, were seasoned veterans of the 8th Flotilla and all were eager to have a crack at 'Johnny Turk'.

The little convoy arrived safely at Gibraltar but, before leaving again the next evening, *E.11* was found to have trouble with a stiff clutch. Remembering his disappointment over the Baltic operation when engine-trouble had robbed him of an opportunity for glory, Nasmith refused to stay behind and insisted on following the others to Malta.

Despite nearly running out of fuel *E.11* entered Grand Harbour with her companions after an altercation with the Harbour Master who had refused entry the previous evening and had left them to spend an uncomfortable night in a small inlet further up the coast. The three submarines tied up alongside *Egmont*, an old wooden man o' war serving as a depot ship, and Nasmith went on board *Adamant* to report to the Flotilla leader, Cdr Somerville.

His news was not good. *E.11*'s clutch was now so stiff that it took two men to engage it and, in addition, the armature of the port motor had shorted. An examination by dockyard experts found that a main-shaft had cracked and a replacement would have to be shipped from Portsmouth. Nasmith knew bitter disappointment for the third time in his career as the two remaining submarines sailed without him the following morning.

Also at Malta was the Australian boat *AE.2* which was being repaired following an incident with some unyielding rocks off the entrance to Mudros harbour, an accident which her skipper, Lt-Cdr Stoker, said wryly had caused 'a distinct loss of popularity with the Admiral.' He and Nasmith spent many hours in the wardroom discussing methods of forcing the Dardanelles and *AE.2*'s captain was eager to hear of the technical advances made by the men of the 8th Flotilla.

But as he sat quietly talking to Stoker, Nasmith was fretting to get away and he kept thinking of Boyle and Brodie, now many miles ahead and approaching their new base at Mudros. When the armature was repaired he decided to take a chance and leave for Mudros immediately despite the cracked shaft. He gave instructions that the replacement shaft was to be shipped on to Lemnos when it arrived from Portsmouth and, in typical style, he gambled on the engineers of the repair-ship *Reliant* at Mudros having the right equipment to carry out the work of stripping the submarine's engine.

Early on the 15th *E.11* left Malta, passed through the boom-defence gate, and set course to the east once again. Their luck held and, three days later, Nasmith brought her in sight of the Island of Lemnos and guided her into the tiny, overcrowded harbour at Mudros.

Mooring alongside *Adamant* he shut off the engines, handed over to his second-in-command, D'Oyly Hughes, and climbed quickly up the companion-way to the deck of the depot-ship. He sensed that something was wrong and realized that only Boyle's *E.14* was tied up alongside. Somerville met him at the rails and told him the bad news.

Brodie had left Mudros at dawn on the 17th in an attempt to be first into the Sea of Marmora and three RNAS seaplanes had been sent up to follow him into the Dardanelles. His twin brother flew as passenger in one of the planes piloted by Cdr Samson, an officer who had gained prominence early in the war by forming an RNAS armoured-car squadron during the defence of Ostend. Then came disaster.

E.15 had submerged ready for her run under the lines of

moored mines when the treacherous current swept her ashore on Kephez Point directly under the guns of Fort Dardanus. The Turks opened fire immediately and, as they ranged on the stricken submarine, her captain tried to get her off the mud by running full-speed astern. The propellers threshed the murky water into a froth but *E.15* was immovably stuck.

A Turkish torpedo-boat was closing in and, as Brodie opened the hatch to the conning-tower, the first shell exploded against the hull killing him instantly. As the gunners found the range more hits were scored and one shot pierced the hull amidships, exploding in the battery-compartment. Sea water rushed in through the torn steel plates and, as it reached the acid from the shattered batteries, a dense cloud of chlorine gas spread through the boat.

Struggling blindly through the swirling, yellow fumes the crew scrambled up on deck to surrender and, as they were taken ashore, the torpedo-boat hooked a rope over the submarine's stern in an effort to haul her off. The RNAS seaplanes swooped in low and their bombs drove the Turkish ship away but it was very clear that the enemy intended to salvage their unexpected prize as soon as they could. Brodie's brother and Cdr Samson flew back to Lemnos with news of the disaster and a hurried conference was called on board *Hindu Kush*. It was there decided that at all costs the submarine must be destroyed to prevent the Turks laying their hands on it. Lt Birch was summoned and Pownall told him to take *B.6* into the narrows and torpedo the wrecked *E.15*.

Within an hour the little 'B' class veteran was chugging out of Mudros on her mission of destruction. The Turks were waiting for her and a hail of shells swept the sea as Birch approached Kephez Point. With quiet determination the young lieutenant brought his boat in as close as he dared and fired—but both torpedoes missed.

The flotilla staff now decided to await nightfall and the destroyers *Scorpion* and *Grampus* were given orders to blow

E.15 out of the water. They sailed at dusk with Brodie's brother on the bridge of the *Scorpion*; her captain, incidentally, was Lt-Cdr A. B. Cunningham, at that time an up-and-coming young officer. In the Second World War he was better known as Admiral Andrew Cunningham, the victor of Matapan and vanquisher of the Italian Fleet.

Searchlights probed the darkened waters and both destroyers were soon caught in their beams. Shore-batteries opened up from both sides of the Narrows and, although Cunningham ventured as far as he dared, the two ships had to withdraw with their mission uncompleted.

The sea-planes made a further attempt next morning without success and then Holbrook was sent in with *B.11* for another torpedo attack. He managed to reach Kephez Point but heavy mist made it impossible to locate the stranded submarine and, after coming under a barrage of Turkish shells, Holbrook too had to return empty-handed.

The battleships were now given a chance to show what they could do and, when the mist lifted, *Triumph* and *Majestic* steamed in to administer the *coup de grâce* to *E.15*. But the enemy had no intention of losing their prize and, as the ships moved in, the batteries opened up with a murderous crossfire from both shores. It was suicide to go closer than 12,000 yards and, at that range, the battleship's big guns were too inaccurate. A signal flag fluttered from *Triumph*'s halyards and they turned away.

The situation was now becoming serious. The Turks had moved more guns into position to cover their salvage operations and an RNAS sea-plane reported that two tugs were trying to re-float the submarine. De Robeck's staff met on board the flagship and got down to their fifth attempt to solve the problem. This time a cutting-out expedition was proposed, almost certainly by Keyes who had had personal experience of similar operations in the China campaign, and the Admiral gave his approval.

The plan was simple and straightforward. Two picket-boats, each fitted with two fourteen-inch torpedoes and dropping gear, would go in under cover of darkness. With their small size it was probable that the Turks would not spot them until it was too late. And, if they were seen, they were handy enough to wriggle out of trouble.

Volunteers were called for, and obtained without difficulty, and *Triumph* and *Majestic* supplied one picket-boat each. Command of the expedition was given to Lt-Cdr Robinson who embarked in *Triumph*'s boat.

The element of surprise upon which the operation depended was quickly lost when enemy searchlights on shore picked up the two boats. Almost at once the guns opened fire but Robinson pushed on to complete his mission regardless of the shells exploding all around his little squadron.

An enemy searchlight, mounted close to the submarine as a defence against night attacks, flashed on and blinded the *Triumph*'s helmsman as the picket-boat ran in, and the first torpedo missed. Robinson immediately swung around in a wide circle and came in again—so close that the Turkish gunners were firing over open sights. Suddenly a stray searchlight beam illuminated the submarine and Claude Godwin, the lieutenant in charge of *Majestic*'s boat, fired both of his torpedoes at two hundred yards range.

There was a tremendous explosion and *E.15* seemed to leap off the mud as her hull erupted in flame. Realizing that the attack had been a success Robinson signalled Godwin to withdraw but, as *Majestic*'s picket-boat swung around, she was hit full square by a six-inch shell.

With complete disregard for danger Robinson ran alongside his stricken companion and, with shells bursting only yards away, his men hauled the *Majestic*'s crew to safety. Then, dangerously overloaded, *Triumph*'s picket-boat pulled clear and headed out towards the entrance and the open sea beyond.

Despite the tremendous fire to which they had been subjected the volunteers from the two battleships had suffered only one casualty—a sailor from the *Majestic* who later died of his wounds. Robinson was promoted to Commander for his daring leadership and was later awarded the VC for an earlier incident at Kum Kale. The men who manned the picket-boats all received decorations for what Keyes described as 'this very gallant enterprise.'

So *E.15* was now completely destroyed with her secrets safe. But was she? De Robeck's staff wanted confirmation and as the RNAS sea-planes could not get close enough, it was decided to send *B.6* into the Narrows again 'to examine her at close range.' Brodie immediately requested permission to go with the submarine, and approval was given.

The next morning, the 19th, *B.6* left Mudros under command of Lt MacArthur and, running deep, crept in towards Kephez Point. The first part of the passage was accomplished without incident and, apparently, the Turkish gunners were unaware of their presence as they approached at a depth of eighty feet.

MacArthur brought *B.6* to periscope-depth but, as the little submarine climbed towards the surface, she was thrust sideways as if a giant's hands were dragging her towards the shore. Trapped by the same treacherous current which had driven *E.15* to her death, the young submarine-commander gave his electric-motors full boost in an effort to fight clear, but their puny power was insufficient to fight the current and there was a sharp grating sound as *B.6* grounded only one hundred yards away from the shattered *E.15*. Her conning-tower and superstructure were in full view of the enemy shore-batteries, and delighted at their good fortune, the Turkish gunners immediately opened up on their new target. All now seemed set for a tragic repeat of the previous disaster.

Brodie, however, was beginning to understand the art of submarine-handling in these difficult waters and he guessed, correctly, the cause of his brother's death: the normal reaction of a submarine commander when he found himself stranded was to blow the tanks so that the lightened submarine would float clear. *But*, by lightening the boat, he was offering himself as hostage to the current.

Shells were exploding all around *B.6* as he calmly explained his theory to MacArthur and the young lieutenant nodded his agreement. Then, as if he was on an unhurried peacetime exercise, MacArthur gave the submarine *negative* buoyancy and ordered full-speed astern. The boat slid gently off the mud, backed out into the current, and then bumped her way along the sea-bed until she reached open water.

Back at base and apparently unperturbed by his narrow escape Brodie reported that *E.15* was on her beam ends and completely wrecked. The combined efforts of the submarines, the sea-planes, and the big ships had finally achieved success.

The Germans were greatly impressed by the Navy's efforts to destroy the unfortunate submarine and one officer in Constantinople was heard to say: 'I take my hat off to the British Navy.' The Turks, too, demonstrated their admiration. When Djevad Pasha learned that the *E.15*'s dead had been hurriedly buried in the sands on the beach he had them re-interred in the British cemetery and gave orders that they were to have a Christian burial.

The executive decision to send an 'E' class submarine through the Dardanelles into the Sea of Marmora had been taken by Keyes himself at a conference of the Submarine Staff on 14 April. The men had discussed how such an operation could be carried out and then Keyes had asked each officer, one by one, whether they thought it could be done. Somerville, Pownall and C. G. Brodie all said 'No'. Boyle of *E.14* also gave a negative reply but Theodore Brodie, commander of *E.15* gave a confident 'Yes!' Keyes immediately jumped to his feet saying: 'Well, it's got to be tried, and you shall do it.' This first attempt, as has been seen, ended in disaster.

Lt-Cdr Stoker had now rejoined the flotilla from Malta and, as always, was pulling every string to be selected for the second attempt. But, for the moment, there was an embargo on any further submarines endangering themselves in the Narrows and, in addition, last-minute preparations were in hand for landing troops on the peninsula for a land offensive against the Turkish capital.

On 23 April Stoker received a signal telling him to report to Keyes on board the flagship. The Commodore informed him that if he thought he could get through the Dardanelles he might try. Admiral de Robeck, who had succeeded Carden as naval C-in-C, was sceptical about the operation but agreed that it should be tried once more and Stoker returned to *AE.2* with a broad grin on his face.

The Australian submarine left the next day but a broken hydroplane shaft forced her to return within a few hours and Stoker fretted impatiently as the *Reliant*'s engineers worked to replace the damaged part. The task was completed by midnight and *AE.2* received the Admiral's permission to make a second attempt.

The next day was 25 April, 1915—a date which was to be written in blood in the history of the Great War—the day on which the first landings were made on the beaches of Gallipoli, the day when the bloodbath of the Dardanelles *really* began.

At 3 am the Australian submarine stood to sea. Lieutenants Haggard and Pitt-Carey joined Stoker on the tiny bridge and, in the darkness, they could see the vast armada of two hundred ships forming up ready for the assault on the heavily-defended Turkish coast. On board one of the landing-ships was Pownall, the submarine flotilla's commander, who had volunteered to act as Naval Beachmaster for the landing at Cape Helles. Like thousands of others he never returned; he was killed when an enemy shell struck the leading boat before it had even reached the beach.

When the landings began at 5.15 am Stoker was already

running below the surface and had entered the field of moored mines that blocked the narrow entrance to the Straits. The crew could hear their steel mooring-cables scraping down the sides of the submarine but fortunately they ran clear and *AE.2* passed safely through the minefield.

In accordance with Keyes' instructions Stoker came up to periscope-depth off Chanak to search for the minelayers. There were none to be seen but, as he prepared to dive again, he spotted a Turkish gunboat steaming slowly towards him. A torpedo was fired and the ship came to a stop with smoke pouring from its shattered bows. Other gunboats dashed to the scene and started firing at the stalk of the periscope, so after a final check to see that his victim was sinking, Stoker took the submarine down to seventy feet.

She bounced up again as she hit the fresh water layer and the current whirled her against the shore. The crew heard her bottom-plates grate on the shingle as she grounded under the guns of Anatoli Mejideh but Stoker's prompt juggling with the engines pulled her off before the Turkish soldiers realized what had happened. Running at full-power to combat the current, her batteries were being rapidly exhausted, but Stoker had no alternative.

In an attempt to avoid the current he took her across to the European side of the channel but, running into shoal-water, she grounded again. Once more the propellers churned to full-power and the submarine slid back into deeper water. By now the Turks were thoroughly alert so Stoker went down to thirty feet and lay on the bottom while torpedo-boats prowled above,

By nightfall the Turks had tired of the search and *AE.2* started her motors again as the crew closed up for surfacing.

'Bring her to twenty feet.'

The hydroplane operators swung their wheels to 'rise' and the bows tilted as Haggard called off the readings on the depth-gauge.

'Thirty feet, sir. Twenty-five feet. Twenty feet, and horizontal.'

'Right, hold her there, Number One.'

Stoker grasped the handles of the periscope and viewed the area with one quick sweep. It was still dark and the sea was completely empty.

'Take her up, Mr Haggard.'

There was a sharp hiss of compressed air as the main tanks were blown and, at a signal from the lieutenant, Stoker pulled the clips of the hatch and swung it open.

The cool night air smelt sweet and fresh after the stale, oxygen-starved atmosphere inside the submarine, and the Commander took a deep draught into his lungs. Pitt-Carey joined him on the bridge and, as the look-outs clambered up the steel ladder, they scanned the surface for any sign of the enemy. Satisfied that all the Turkish torpedo-boats had gone home for the night Stoker called down the voice-pipe:

'Clutch in—starboard diesel. Start charging. All hands stand down for dinner.'

Having re-charged the batteries, now almost exhausted after the battle with the current, and with all hands having snatched a hasty meal, *AE.2* was ready to push on again. By 9 am on the 26th Stoker was in the Sea of Marmora and he sent a wireless signal back to Mudros reporting his success. It came at an opportune moment.

The Admiral and the Naval Staff on board *Queen Elizabeth* were aghast at the terrible casualties suffered on the beaches and, for a while, evacuation was considered. De Robeck, Thursby and Keyes were in conference with some of the Generals when Stoker's signal was brought in. Realizing the importance of *AE.2*'s achievement, Keyes read the signal aloud to the officers gathered around the table, and went on: 'It is an omen—an Australian submarine has done the finest feat in submarine history and is going to torpedo all the ships bringing reinforcements, supplies and ammunition to Gallipoli.'

DUW—H

Cheered by this good news and by Keyes' highly optimistic forecast, the Generals decided to hang on. The Commanding Officer in the field, General Birdwood, was told 'There is nothing for it but to dig yourselves right in and stick it out . . .' —easy words to write in the peaceful surroundings of a great battleship. And the troops, decimated by Turkish machine-guns and blown to atoms by high-explosive shells, did as they were ordered. From now on the murderous and hopeless campaign of Gallipoli was to drain the life-blood of the Australian and New Zealand divisions which formed the bulk of the Allied invasion forces.

Yet the vital decision to 'stick it out' which resulted in a final casualty list of 25,279 killed, 75,191 wounded, and 12,451 missing, was largely made because one solitary submarine had forced its way through the Dardanelles into the Sea of Marmora.

Such, indeed, was the power of the 'Damned un-English weapon' by the spring of 1915.

CHAPTER EIGHT

'Go and run amuck in the Marmora'

IT WAS Courtney Boyle's turn next and, the following day, he was called on board *Queen Elizabeth* to receive his orders from Keyes. Less than twenty-four hours after Stoker's signal had been received the second British submarine was nosing its way into the enemy-controlled Strait.

The escorting destroyers swung away to starboard at precisely 3 am on the morning of the 27th and *E.14* pushed on alone into the glare of the Turkish searchlights. An hour later the gun battery at Suandere opened up and Boyle took the submarine down ready for her attempt to force the Dardanelles. For the next twenty hours they would be running submerged —assuming, of course, that they did not fall foul of the minefields, get rammed by an enemy torpedo-boat, or find themselves swept ashore by the current like the unfortunate *E.15*.

But Boyle had his own ideas about the tactics to be adopted and, once clear of Suandere, he trimmed the submarine so that the conning-tower was awash, and rumbled through the darkness on his diesels. He roared past Chanak at full-speed, moving so fast, in fact, that the Turkish gunners allowed too little deflection and completely missed him, and burst through the Narrows without incident.

There were a number of patrol-ships ahead so Boyle switched to his electric motors and dived out of sight. Crawling forward against the current *E.14* edged her way towards an unsuspecting Turkish gunboat and the torpedomen closed up, flooding the tubes ready for the Captain's order to fire.

Boyle stood with his eyes glued to the periscope during the last tense moments of the run-in; he gave the order and the torpedo streaked away. There was a gush of water from the stricken gunboat and then a remarkable thing happened—something seemed to close over the periscope lens completely blocking out the light. For a few seconds Boyle thought a fragment of steel from the gunboat had smashed the lens, until he remembered having seen a small Turkish fishing-boat in close proximity as he had fired at his target. The fisherman, having seen the brass tube of the periscope sticking out of the water, had grabbed it with both arms and grasped it firmly as if to prevent it getting away. His body was completely obscuring the lens and, as he hung on for grim death, the submarine was towing his boat along the surface.

When Boyle realized what had happened he grinned and ordered, 'Down periscope.' The tube slid beneath the water leaving the fisherman empty-handed and bemused!

The next part of the passage was not so amusing. As *E.14* passed Gallipoli the Turks instigated a full-scale hunt for the submarine and Boyle had to remain submerged for nearly forty-eight hours while destroyers, torpedo-boats, and gun-boats, threshed overhead. By the time he reached the open waters of the Marmora his motors were dangerously over-heated and the batteries nearly exhausted so he surfaced to re-charge and cool off.

During the afternoon the look-outs sighted smoke approaching from the east and *E.14* dived. The smoke came from two large transports escorted by three destroyers and, despite the glass-smooth sea, Boyle turned to attack. Moving underneath the escorting destroyers he fired one torpedo and scored a direct hit on the leading transport. Evading the destroyers he came up to periscope-depth and saw the transport making for the shore with yellow smoke billowing from her hull.

That night *E.14* rendezvoused with *AE.2* and, leaning over the edges of their conning-towers, the two captains compared notes. Stoker, it seemed, was out of luck. He had attacked several ships, including a Turkish battleship, but on each occasion his torpedoes had run too deep and missed. Now he was down to his last torpedo and prospects were not very encouraging. Boyle tried to cheer him up and then the two boats drew slowly apart having arranged to meet again the following night. But it was not to be.

The next day *AE.2* was diving in Atarki Bay when she lost her trim in a patch of dense water and bobbed to the surface. The Turkish torpedo-boat *Sultan Hissar* was only a mile away and, as she saw the bows of the submarine thrust to the surface, she swung in to ram. Stoker ordered the forward tanks to be flooded in an effort to regain trim ready for diving but *AE.2* failed to respond.

Then, suddenly, as the *Sultan Hissar* was almost upon her, she plunged down at a steep angle as the weight of water in her forward tanks upset the submarine's delicate trim. When the depth-gauges swept past the 100 feet calibration Stoker put the engines astern and told Haggard to blow the forward tanks.

But *AE.2* was behaving like an untrained horse and, once again, she shot to the surface. The Turkish gun-boat was waiting and, as the submarine appeared, her guns opened fire. Three shells holed the pressure-hull and she could no longer escape by diving. Stoker was now faced with the decision that every captain dreads. Ordering the crew on deck, he and Haggard quickly opened all the valves, and as the submarine slid beneath the surface for the last time the enemy ship circled around picking the sailors up out of the water. Stoker, Haggard, Pitt-Carey and seventeen seamen were taken prisoner; nine other members of the crew were never seen again.

Keyes heard of *AE.2*'s loss when the Germans announced the news, but he did not allow it to upset his plans. On the same day he confirmed another attempt to force the Narrows, this time by the French submarine *Joule* under the command of Lt Dupetit-Thouars de Saint-George. She left on 1 May but struck a mine and was lost with all hands, the second French submarine to be lost during these operations, the other being the *Saphir* which had run aground off Nagara Point some weeks before. So far, of the five submarines which had attempted to enter the Sea of Marmora, only one, *E.14*, had survived. Yet, despite these daunting odds, Nasmith was still eager to try.

E.11 was now lying alongside *Reliant* with her hull-plates removed so that the engineers could get the broken shaft out. For the time being, at least, Nasmith's hopes of action had to be deferred and he spent his time going over the charts with D'Oyly Hughes and Brown as they discussed the best way to navigate the Narrows.

Then, one morning, *E.11*'s captain created a minor mystery by arranging for a launch to take him across to the neighbouring island of Tenedos. Once there, he sought out Cdr Samson who was in charge of the RNAS station and asked whether he could be taken over the Dardanelles in one of his sea-planes. It was a novel and startling idea but, aware of Nasmith's reputation as a perfectionist, Samson quickly agreed. Lt Bell-Davies, who was himself to win the VC at a later stage of the campaign, was selected as the pilot and the submarine captain was bundled into the observer's cockpit of an ancient Maurice Farman biplane.

It proved impossible to locate the Turkish mine-fields from the air but the submarine commander was able to note all the important landmarks including the lighthouses which he would be using to fix *E.11*'s position. Nothing, unfortunately, was learned of the enemy defences but Nasmith had enjoyed a bird's-eye view of the Narrows and this, he felt sure, would be even more valuable than the Admiralty charts.

Boyle, meanwhile, was hemmed in by the Turks and, each time he surfaced, torpedo-boats swooped to attack. By 1 May he was thoroughly tired of acting as the quarry and decided to turn the tables on his pursuers. He circled around the enemy patrol-boats and came up to periscope-depth on what the Turks fondly imagined was their disengaged side. A single torpedo streaked through the water and the minelaying-gunboat *Paykisevkei* was rent asunder by a violent explosion. Within a minute she had disappeared from sight.

The other vessels turned to attack and Boyle fired another torpedo. A fault in the gyro-mechanism caused it to circle and, relieved of the immediate threat, a Turkish gun-boat raced in to ram. *E.14* dodged away like a matador teasing a bull and a third torpedo sped through the water. The sea was glassy-smooth and the trail of bubbles marking its course were spotted by the enemy look-outs in time to swing away—but Boyle's determination had damped their ardour. From then on they hunted him with more caution than valour and once again *E.14* was free to roam in search of targets. Unfortunately the little inland sea was deserted. Terrified of risking ships and troops in the face of the marauding submarines the Turks were sending their reinforcements overland by rail and road.

This state of affairs persisted until 5 May when a single transport ventured out escorted by a destroyer. The sea was calm and Boyle had to exercise all his skill to reach an attacking position without being sighted. But although he scored a direct hit on the transport the torpedo failed to explode and the little convoy steamed on unaware of their good fortune.

Alarums and excursions followed daily as more and more Turkish ships were caught out of harbour. One transport sighted *E.14* approaching and ran for shelter to Constantinople. Others when stopped and searched were found to contain only refugees and were allowed to proceed.

10 May brought better luck when, after an early morning brush with a destroyer, Boyle came across two large transports escorted by a single destroyer. His first torpedo missed the leading ship but the second hit the 5,000 ton *Gul Djemal*. There was a spectacular explosion and the stricken transport hauled off course in an effort to beach herself. Eye-witnesses on the island of Kalolimno later reported that she sank taking 6,000 troops and an artillery battery to the bottom with her.

On the same day *Reliant*'s workshops finished *E.11*'s new shaft and it was carefully lowered into the submarine's engine-room. It was a delicate, exacting job and it was two days before the shaft was in position.

While Nasmith took his boat out to sea for diving-trials and a general work-up, Boyle continued his one-man blockade of the Turkish shipping in the Marmora. His last torpedo had been used to sink the *Gul Djemal* and one of his two periscopes was unserviceable following a direct hit by an enemy shell. But his crew still had a store of rifles and, so far as he was concerned, *E.14* was therefore operational. He continued to patrol and, when possible, board and inspect passing ships. On one occasion, by outrageous bluff, he forced a small steamer to beach herself to escape his obviously hostile intentions.

On 17 May Keyes, acting for de Robeck, wirelessed Boyle to return and warned Nasmith to be ready to take his place. The return passage through the Narrows proved fairly quiet and, aided by the current, *E.14* was able to achieve a good speed. Meeting up with a Turkish patrol vessel she followed her through the Chanak minefield safely but had to dive sharply when the shore-batteries opened fire. Keeping deep, the submarine nosed through the minefield off Kephez Point, and finally surfaced triumphantly alongside a French battleship anchored at Cape Helles.

Lt-Cdr Courtney Boyle was the first submarine captain to return from the Sea of Marmora in one piece and it was of men like him that Churchill wrote: 'the Naval History of Britain contains no page more wonderful than that which records the prowess of her submarines at the Dardanelles.' For his efforts Boyle was immediately promoted to Commander and awarded the Victoria Cross—the second officer of the Submarine Service to win this coveted honour.

On the evening of the 18th Admiral de Robeck held a dinner party aboard *Lord Nelson* to which both Boyle and Nasmith were invited. In the company of such top-brass as Admiral

Wester Wemyss, General Sir Ian Hamilton, General Braith-waite, and Roger Keyes, Boyle was called upon to give a short talk on his experiences in the Marmora. After dinner Keyes took Nasmith to one side for a final briefing. He explained that *E.14* was going back to Malta for a re-fit and that he wanted *E.11* to stay in the Sea of Marmora until Boyle returned to relieve him. His parting words were: 'Well then, go and run amuck in the Marmora.' Which was precisely what Nasmith intended to do.

Nasmith and *E.11* set out from the harbour at Kephalo at 1.10 am on 19 May. The destroyer *Grasshopper*, with Brodie on the bridge, followed astern. At 3.10 they glided past the trawler patrol and four miles up the straits *Grasshopper* turned away, her signal-lamp flashing a final message of good luck. *E.11* was on her own and, from now on, every man's hand would be against her.

By 3.50 she was abreast of Achi Baba and Nasmith took her down to eighty feet ready to run the gauntlet of the Turkish minefield. *E.11* crept up the steep-sided gorge at three knots while hands stood down for cocoa. There was an ominous scraping sound as the first mine-cable brushed along the side of the submarine's hull. The mooring-rope brushed clear and the crew sighed with relief. Then a second cable dragged taut as *E.11*'s steel plates rasped against it—then it, too, was clear. Each line of mines presented a fresh threat but the submarine threaded her way through like a shuttle in a loom until, finally, Nasmith ordered:

'Up periscope.'

They were off Kephez already. Well ahead of their schedule thanks to a reverse current which was giving them a surface velocity one knot greater than the engine revolutions suggested. Nasmith navigated around Kilid Bahr and headed for Nagara Point.

Once into the deeper water he took *E.11* down again and drove steadily upstream until, at 5.30 as dawn tinged the night sky, he came up for another sweep with the periscope. This time the Turks spotted him. The field-guns ranged along the cliffs opened fire and the sea boiled and frothed as the shells exploded. A sharp clang echoed through the submarine and Nasmith knew that the shells were getting dangerously close. The periscope slid down and *E.11* sought protection again deep under the surface.

Every few miles Nasmith took a quick bearing through the periscope and called off the various landmarks and angles to the second officer, Brown, who was plotting the chart. His trip in the old Farman biplane was now paying dividends and he had no difficulty in picking out the various lighthouses against the hills. By 9.30 he was in sight of Gallipoli itself and, after a quick check of his bearings, he took the submarine down to negotiate the final line of mines.

E.11 reached the open waters of the Marmora by the early afternoon and Nasmith took her down to rest on the bottom until nightfall. The men fell out, the rum ration was issued, and they settled down to a long wait while D'Oyly Hughes carefully inspected the hull for leaks with the aid of a small hand-torch. Inside the cramped interior of the submarine the air was foul from the long period spent underwater. Breathing was an effort and the faces of the crew were grey with oxygen starvation. Most settled down for a nap, their heads resting against the steel walls of the boat which were now streaming with condensation. Nobody spoke and nobody moved. They just waited.

The order to surface was given at 9 pm and Nasmith, aware of the physical strain involved, cautioned everyone to proceed in slow motion. *E.11* lifted off the sea-bed, floated quietly upwards, and emerged into the cool night air like some ancient dragon surfacing from its underwater lair. As the look-outs took up their positions the port diesel was started up to charge the batteries and the fresh night air was drawn into the hull.

But their rest did not remain undisturbed for long. Twice a patrolling destroyer caused them to break the charge and dive rapidly but, apparently, on neither occasion were they spotted. As soon as things had quietened down a coded signal was drafted announcing their arrival and was transmitted to the destroyer *Jed* which was acting as the radio-link to the flotilla base at Mudros. No acknowledgement was heard and it was increasingly apparent that they were not being received.

At 4 am Nasmith could wait no longer, for it was already growing light and the submarine might be spotted from the shore at any time. He gave orders to dive and *E.11* began her first day's patrol near the north-eastern entrance to the Dardanelles. For the first time since they had left their base Nasmith came off watch and, as he relaxed in his tiny cabin, his other officers, Brown and D'Oyly Hughes took turn at the periscope.

There was no shipping activity and, by the afternoon, *E.11* had shifted her position to a point twelve miles off the town of Rodosto. Still it was quiet and Nasmith took the opportunity to surface and charge the batteries. Then, with the calm aplomb for which he was to become famous, he ordered, 'Hands to bathe.'

Deep inside an enemy sea, ringed on all sides by hostile patrols, and with the ever-present danger of a destroyer coming up over the horizon, he allowed his men to have a swim, three at a time for ten minutes each, that they might relax after the strain and exhaustion of their passage through the Dardanelles.

They spent a quiet night on the surface, carried out a brief and unproductive dawn patrol, followed at 6 am by another bathing session. Then *E.11* moved on to more serious business.

The first target proved disappointing, a two-masted sailing vessel. A boarding-party was sent across to inspect her but her cargo consisted only of small logs, hardly contraband even if it was intended to warm the feet of some Turkish soldiers around a camp fire. Suddenly Nasmith had an idea. He sent a man up the tall foremast to act as look-out—a far loftier and more satisfactory position than the low conning-tower of the submarine—and ordered D'Oyly Hughes to hoist the sails. Then, using the sailing-ship as a screen, he set off in search of new targets.

His ruse, however, brought no success and, in the evening, he cut the Turkish boat free and allowed her captain to go. Once again the submarine spent the night on the surface charging her batteries while the wireless-operator continued his fruitless efforts to make contact with base.

In the early hours of 23 May *E.11* was making for the Turkish capital of Constantinople. Nasmith carefully scouted the approaches to the harbour, noted the routes taken by the various boats moving in and out for future reference, and searched for targets. At last his luck was in for, as he swept his periscope round, he sighted a Turkish torpedo-gunboat anchored off the entrance to the harbour. It was a sitting target and his first shot, ranged at 700 yards, struck amidships. The *Pelenk-i-Dria* began to list to starboard but, despite the shock of the surprise attack, her crew manned the guns and opened fire in return. *E.11*'s slender periscope was the only visible target yet, with their second shot, the Turkish gunners scored an incredible direct hit that plugged a neat round hole right through it. Then the bows of the gunboat lifted into the air and she sank, slowly and gracefully, stern first.

Fortunately the construction of the damaged periscope prevented the sea from gushing down the shattered tube but the fluke shot meant that the submarine was now reduced to one serviceable periscope. Not wanting to face an attack in such a condition Nasmith left the Turkish capital behind with more haste than decorum and made for the Island of Kalolimno where he could carry out temporary repairs.

Once safely anchored the crew set about removing the damaged periscope, plugged the hole securely, and carried out general minor repairs while the torpedo-men reloaded their empty tube. With his usual punctilious regard for naval tradition Nasmith carried out the customary Sunday 'captain's inspection' and then the hands were called to prayer. Once the service was over they could all relax and Nasmith was delighted to find a present from D'Oyly and Brown lying on the wardroom table—a box of cigars and several bottles of beer. It was a gesture that meant a lot for, many months before when they were on patrol in the North Sea, *E.11*'s commander had sworn not to smoke or drink until he had sunk an enemy warship. And with his usual strength of mind he had kept his pledge—even at the dinner-party on board the *Lord Nelson* the night before he sailed.

The rest of the day passed with bathing and Swedish drill and then it was time to try and get off their arrival signal again. Nasmith guided the submarine into her wireless billet on the north side of the Marmora and, handing over the duties of watch-officer to Brown, he went below to snatch a brief rest. At 2 am it was reported that they had at last succeeded in making contact with the *Jed*—the fault had been located, apparently, in *E.11*'s aerial.

The signal which Nasmith handed to the wireless operator for transmission was an interesting example of his advanced approach to the problems of undersea warfare, an approach which was several decades ahead of its time. After a brief action and intelligence report he informed base of the damaged periscope. The signal ended with a request for a replacement which, he added, could be flown out to him. And this, it should be remembered, was in 1915.

With such a far-seeing appreciation of the flexibility of air-power, which he had already demonstrated by his preliminary scouting flight over the Dardanelles with Bell-Davies, it is small wonder that Martin Nasmith was one of the outstanding submarine captains of the 1914–18 War.

Blue sparks spluttered from the aerial as the signals passed to and fro and Brown sat decoding the messages before passing them across to his captain. One report interested him and caused some momentary concern; a small U-boat was believed to be operating in the Marmora. He would have to make sure his look-outs were wide awake. By 5 am the wireless masts had been neatly stowed away and the submarine was ready to resume her patrol.

Just an hour later *E.11* intercepted a small steamer, the *Nagara*, and Nasmith ordered her captain to stop for inspection. There was a panic aboard the Turkish ship. Bedlam broke out on deck and there was a mad rush for the lifeboats. Many, impatient of delay, leapt overboard and swam for it. In the midst of the confusion an American passenger came to the rails and, calling across to the officers grouped in the conning-tower, introduced himself as Raymond Gram Swing of the *Chicago Herald*. He informed Nasmith that the *Nagara* was carrying a detachment of Marines, field guns, and Krupp ammunition. He followed this up by asking, in true reporter style, for a story.

There was no time for a leisurely chat and Nasmith cut him short, warning him to get into one of the lifeboats as he intended to blow the boat up. He found time, however, to pass over the false information that there were eleven British submarines operating in the Marmora. Once the crew, and Mr Swing, were safely in the boats Nasmith sent a boarding-party across to place explosive charges on the steamer. Five minutes later the *Nagara* was blown sky high.

But *E.11* had already dived. As the boarding-party were being helped back into the submarine the look-outs had sighted another steamer approaching and Nasmith was anxious to increase his score.

The sudden explosion had, however, warned the Turkish captain of the unknown danger ahead and he immediately turned his boat around and headed back to Rodosto. Nasmith surfaced and gave chase but the steamer was faster and she reached the wooden pier in safety. The speed with which the crew abandoned ship and the indecent haste of their disembarkation suggested that the steamer was carrying munitions.

E.11 bumped the sea bottom as she closed the range but Nasmith was not going to be deterred. When he considered he was close enough a torpedo was fired. There was a mighty explosion which not only destroyed the ship but also demolished half the pier as well. It was abundantly obvious that she had indeed been carrying a cargo of high explosives.

The submarine went astern, found deeper water under her screws, and began to swing her bows away from the shore. Then Nasmith saw a third ship, a paddle-steamer, approaching the harbour. Her decks were piled high with barbed-wire destined for use at the front and there could be no doubt that she was a legitimate target. One torpedo and she, too, would go to the bottom.

But the captain of the paddle-steamer had other ideas. Refusing to obey *E.11*'s signal to stop, he crammed on speed, and shaped to ram. The klaxon on the submarine's bridge screamed as Nasmith yelled 'Full ahead both,' down the voice-pipe. White foam erupted from the stern as the propellers bit fiercely into the water and the aggressive paddle-boat only missed by inches.

The two antagonists drew apart and the Turkish ship started to make for the shore, zig-zagging wildly in an effort to escape any torpedoes following in her wake. Nasmith brought *E.11*'s best shots up into the conning-tower and a volley of rifle-fire cracked out across the waves. The enemy helmsman abandoned the wheel and the paddle-steamer veered wildly off course. *E.11* closed again. The action was hot and Nasmith later admitted his admiration for the courage of the Turkish captain.

The Turk's wheel was under control again and she swung round to ram with the desperation of a cornered rat baring its teeth to a terrier. Another volley of rifle-fire dissuaded her at the last moment and the paddle-boat's skipper steered for the beach. She hit the sandy shore at full-power and stuck fast, her paddle-wheels still churning at top speed, as her crew tumbled over the side and ran for cover.

She was too small to waste a torpedo on so Nasmith ordered D'Oyly Hughes to board and finish her off with explosive charges. As *E.11*'s First Officer and two of the submarine's sailors were about to begin their task of destruction a troop of fifty Turkish cavalrymen appeared on the cliff-top. Dismounting quickly, they spread out amongst the bushes, and opened fire with their carbines. *E.11* answered back with her rifles and a ding-dong battle ensued while Nasmith ordered the boarding-party to return. Once everyone was safe on board Nasmith ran the engines slow-astern and gently backed away out of range, but not before he had collected a Turkish bullet through his cap.

He made one last effort to destroy the stranded paddle-boat but the torpedo missed and, giving his gallant little adversary best, he returned to the middle of the Marmora well content with a good day's work.

Martin Nasmith had always been determined to take a British submarine into Constantinople harbour and he had mentioned his ambition to several people before he left Mudros. Always ahead of his time, he knew the value of psychological warfare and he astutely realized the immense propaganda effect of such a feat. It was the equivalent of a German U-boat appearing inside the Pool of London and he was prepared to accept almost any risk to carry out the operation.

By the next morning, 25 May, the submarine was abreast of Oxia Island as she ran in for the final approach. A small steamboat passed in front of them, a uniformed Pasha seated in the stern, but the official and the crew were all, by good luck, looking in the opposite direction. There was plenty of small-boat traffic about and Nasmith only allowed himself a brief glimpse through the periscope as he edged closer.

Nasmith swept deep inside the harbour searching for targets. A large transport, the name *Stamboul* clearly visible on her bow, was lying alongside the arsenal and she was selected as the

1. 'A Damned un-English Weapon' – Holland No. 3 passing HMS *Victory*, Portsmouth Harbour.

2. Reginald Bacon. The Royal Navy's first Inspecting Captain of Submarines.

3. Roger Keyes, Commodore (S) from 1910 to 1915.

4. Martin Nasmith and the crew of *A*.4 (1907).

5. No place for claustrophobia. Interior of an 'E'-class submarine.

6. Cromie's *E.*19 returns to Libau after a marauding cruise in the Baltic.

7. Out of wireless range. A carrier pigeon takes back a vital mesage.

8. A flurry of 'E' class submarines lying alongside their depot ship.

9. Norman Holbrook – the first submarine VC – with the victorious crew of *B.11* after sinking the Turkish battleship *Messudiyah*.

10. Martin Nasmith, VC, third from left, with D'Oyly Hughes, to his left, and the veteran crew of *E.11* – 'The scourge of the Marmora'.

11. The business end. Bow torpedo compartment of an 'E' class submarine.

12. At speed! A submarine on surface trials. *Lord Keyes*.

13. Close quarters!

14. Caught on the surface. *C.25* under attack from German seaplanes in a
    tragic action which cost the lives of her skipper and five of her crew.

15. 'K' for Killer! *K.6* a survivor of the May Island disaster.

16. *En route* for Zeebrugge. The explosive-filled *C*.3 under tow. The davits and escape boats on either side of the conning-tower are clearly visible.

17. Dick Sandford, VC, command of *C*.3.

18. Success! The hole blown by *C*.3 in Zeebrugge viaduct.

first target. Nasmith brought *E.11* into position, called off the range, deflection and depth-setting to the men in the bow torpedo-compartment and, as his sights came on, jabbed the firing button.

The first torpedo ran wild, leapt into the air like a drunken porpoise, and then sank. Nasmith fired the starboard bow tube, This time he scored a direct hit but the enemy had spotted him. A Brennan torpedo, a controlled harbour-defence weapon, sped towards the hull of the half-submerged submarine. *E.11*'s captain swung to starboard and went deep as the enemy shore-batteries opened up.

Constantinople harbour was a maze of strange and powerful currents, many uncharted by the Admiralty cartographers. As *E.11* plunged down she was caught in one of the currents and the helmsman had to fight to hold her level. One moment she was wallowing towards the surface, the next dropping like a stone to the harbour-bottom. Her bows swung like a barn-door in the wind and Nasmith had to use all his skill in trying to control the unmanageable boat.

She grounded on Old Seraglio Point but a rapid surge of power from the engines pulled her off and the faces of the men inside the submarine were glistening with sweat as they opened the valves, swung the wheels, and pulled the switches, in obedience to the steady stream of orders from the control-room. But, finally, they made it and *E.11* was safely heading out of the harbour for the open sea again.

Reviewing the charts and log with D'Oyly Hughes as they slipped quietly away Nasmith concluded that they had, in fact, grounded on the Leander Bank and not on the western side of the harbour as he had at first thought. More alarming, however, was his revelation that the torpedo they had evaded was not a controlled Brennan torpedo fired by the Turks but their own port-bow torpedo. After running wild it had circled round and made straight for the submarine like a homing-pigeon making for its roost.

DUW–I

The next day Nasmith gave his tired crew a rest. While the sailors slept or carried on with various personal odd jobs, Brown and D'Oyly Hughes joined their skipper in the wardroom to discuss the next operation. They had five torpedoes left, and the captain wanted a ship for each one.

By dawn *E.11* was once again on combat patrol and, as she cruised the empty Marmora, the torpedo crews were busy adjusting their charges so that, instead of sinking after an unsuccessful attack, the seventeen foot cylinders would float on the surface where they could be recovered and used again. D'Oyly Hughes had been building a small raft fitted with a dummy periscope constructed from a broom-handle and an old tin. This, he claimed, would make an excellent decoy. Nasmith was more doubtful. But the scheme was put to the test a few hours later.

The daily ritual of 'Hands to bathe' was in progress when a Turkish sea-plane suddenly swooped out of the sun and made a surprise attack on the unwary submarine, one of the very few occasions when Nasmith allowed himself to be caught on the hop. The klaxon screamed and, as the swimmers scrambled on board, the aircraft started its dive. As *E.11* slid gently under the surface and vanished from sight the sea-plane closed in to attack. Three bombs whistled down and exploded harmlessly some distance away and, by the time the submarine surfaced, the enemy had vanished into the blue as suddenly as he had appeared. D'Oyly Hughes naturally claimed that the Turkish pilot had attacked his decoy raft in error and, although Nasmith and Brown pulled his leg, they had a feeling that the First Lieutenant's toy had probably proved to be *E.11*'s salvation.

The early hours of 27 May found the submarine cruising on the surface. A dark shape was sighted in the distance and was soon recognized as the battleship *Barbarossa* which had previously eluded them during their passage up the Dardanelles. Nasmith tried to attack on the surface but was spotted at the last moment by an escorting destroyer and had to dive hurriedly to avoid being rammed. *Barbarossa* had escaped for a second time.

The rest of the day was quiet except for a chance encounter with an armed yacht which Nasmith evaded by diving and, later that night, *E.11* made her routine wireless contact with *Jed*. There was nothing much to report and the submarine captain received a glowing account of the panic in Constantinople following his attack on the harbour. There was only one black spot. Keyes sent a message to say that no spare periscope was available so Nasmith's flirtation with air-power came to naught.

But next day started brightly at 6.30 with the sighting of a convoy which consisted of one large steamer, four smaller ones, and a single destroyer escort. *E.11* dived beneath the warship and fired one torpedo scoring a direct hit on the large steamer which sank inside one minute. The destroyer opened fire on the submarine's periscope but she proved easy to evade and the British boat crept away under the surface.

One down—four to go.

By noon the magnet of Constantinople was exerting its influence over Nasmith again and he was patrolling off Oxia Island where he could watch the entrance to the harbour. A large ship came out, its decks crowded with passengers, and the submarine captain took her to be a military transport. Closing to 1,000 yards he fired his starboard beam tube and waited for the explosion. But it never came. Nasmith's annoyance changed to sudden heart-felt relief when he realized that the people crowding the decks were civilians including women and children being evacuated from the Turkish capital. For once in his life he was glad that a torpedo had misfired.

Once the ship had passed out of sight the hunt began for the errant torpedo. They found it bobbing gently in the swell and Nasmith dived over the side to remove the firing-pin and detonator. Everyone held their breath as he worked away the sensitive parts from the war-head and then he signalled for the torpedo to be hoisted back on board again.

Although they were lying exposed on the surface close to the Turkish capital, the fore-hatch was opened, and the long, steel cylinder was lowered inboard where the torpedo technicians could examine and correct the fault in its gyro-mechanism. But it was an operation fraught with danger for if the submarine should be discovered by the enemy with the hatch open, it would be impossible to escape by diving.

Nasmith considered the problem that evening with his two young officers and, after discussion, it was agreed to try a different method of recovery in future. The torpedo would be drawn into the flooded tube nose-first aided by a swimmer outside. Then, after pumping the chamber dry, it would be pulled back into the boat, swung around, and inserted back into the tube the correct way round. It would be a tiring, back-breaking operation for the eighteen-inch torpedo was no lightweight but it had one great advantage over the previous method. The boat would be fully capable of diving at all stages and most of the work could be carried out submerged.

As *E.11* continued her search for targets the shattering effect of Nasmith's raid on Constantinople was becoming apparent. The German Naval Historian wrote of this period: 'The activity of hostile submarines was a constant and heavy anxiety, and if communications by sea had been completely severed the army would have been faced with catastrophe.'[1]

An air-reconnaissance report from Samson's sea-planes—it is quite amazing how advanced was the tactical organization of the Marmora submarine operations—and transmitted by wireless from the *Jed* indicated a concentration of shipping in the northern entrance to the Gallipoli Straits. Nasmith immediately altered course westwards to investigate.

One merchant ship was sighted but *E.11* was experiencing difficulty with her depth-keeping controls and an unexpected

[1] *Der Krieg zur Zee, 1914-1918.* Chapter XV.

dip of the bows robbed Nasmith of a chance to attack. The enemy fled at top-speed when she spotted the submarine and the remainder of the day was a complete blank except for the appearance of two destroyers which were lured away from their main target by D'Oyly Hughes' decoy raft and periscope.

By 31 May the submarine was off Panderma and, at 8 am, found a large liner anchored outside the town embarking troops from a number of small boats. She was a sitting target and, as Nasmith fired the port bow tube, he knew he could not miss. The torpedo struck the port side in the area of the engine-room and the liner took an immediate list. A tug bustled out from Panderma to tow her ashore but Nasmith decided not to waste another torpedo; she was sufficiently damaged to be out of action for several months and that was what counted.

Two down . . . three to go.

That evening *E.11* was probing the narrow Gulf of Ismid. The sea was quiet and empty of ships and Nasmith took the opportunity to scout along the shore. At this point the railway ran close to the sea and the men in the submarine cursed their lack of a gun as they watched a Turkish troop train clanking towards the front. A small iron bridge was located a little further up the coast and D'Oyly Hughes proposed a daring plan to land and blow it up with an explosive charge. Nasmith considered it to be too risky but the idea stuck in his mind as we shall see later.

In the early hours of the next morning *E.11* was surfaced and charging her batteries while the operator sat in his tiny wireless cabinet exchanging signals with *Jed*. One message reported that the Turks had started moving their ships out of Constantinople again.

2 June found the submarine on patrol in the north-east sector of the Marmora and, at 8.10 am, a supply ship escorted by a destroyer was sighted. *E.11* slipped below the surface while the warship passed and then came up to chase the other

vessel. It took twenty minutes to overhaul her but it was worth it. At 9.40 Nasmith fired a torpedo from the starboard-bow tube and the enemy ship, apparently loaded with munitions, sank within three minutes.

Three down—two to go.

His next attack, however, proved abortive. A small steamer was sighted just before noon but the torpedo missed and the Turkish boat dropped anchor near Panidos after which her crew rapidly abandoned ship. *E.11* surfaced to put a demolition crew on board but heavy rifle fire from the shore drove them off and, after several attempts to board, Nasmith finally withdrew. He was annoyed at missing the steamer, but the thing that really made him angry was the loss of his last-but-one torpedo.

A few hours later he fired his last torpedo at a despatch vessel and had the chagrin to see that also miss. This time there was no rifle fire from the shore so, once the enemy ships had passed over the horizon, Nasmith surfaced to recover the torpedo.

Now it was D'Oyly's turn and, diving over the side with a spanner tied around his neck, the First Lieutenant set about removing the firing-pistol. When it was safe he was joined by six seamen and, while Nasmith trimmed *E.11* lower in the water and flooded the stern-tube, they carefully shunted the torpedo nose-first into the circular opening.

The whole procedure worked perfectly. The torpedo was brought back into the submarine, transported through the hull by means of a small trolley slung from an overhead rail, and gently inserted into the port-bow tube after the working-party had checked it and re-fitted the firing-pistol. Throughout the operation, *E.11* was resting safely on the bottom immune from attack by enemy patrols.

The score-board now read: Three down, one lost, and one to go. The important question was, would the last torpedo, after all the trouble it had caused so far, bring further success?

Nasmith was quite convinced that it would. The rest of the crew just kept their fingers crossed.

E.11's engines were now beginning to show signs of strain and an intermediate shaft was found to be cracked. In addition the armature of the port motor was earthing badly and there was a grave risk of fire if the sparks ignited. Clearly the patrol was near its end but Nasmith refused to make for home until he received the recall signal from base.

By evening the defects had worsened and, establishing contact with *Jed* at 8 pm the submarine commander reluctantly asked for permission to return. No reply was received to the request and Nasmith had to spend the next day fruitlessly patrolling the empty Marmora. Returning to the wireless billet the following evening he again failed to obtain any instructions so he sent a signal reporting his Estimated Time of Arrival off Cape Helles the next day.

At 3.40 am the wireless masts were stowed for the last time and *E.11* steered for the entrance to the Straits. By 9.30 the submarine had passed safely under the Gallipoli minefield and was proceeding downstream at a depth of thirty feet. Nasmith, still determined not to waste his last torpedo, swung from the European side of the Narrows to the Asiatic side as he probed every bay and anchorage for targets. But the small steamers and dhows were of little military value and he held on in the hope of bigger and better things. By the time he reached Chanak it was becoming obvious that there were no Turkish ships further south, and without a word of explanation to his officers or crew, he swung *E.11* round in a wide circle and turned back towards the Marmora.

Reaching the Moussa Bank he found a large transport at anchor and fired his last torpedo at a range of three hundred yards. It was, deservedly, a direct hit and as the transport began to settle in the water Nasmith reversed course for the second time and headed for the open sea.

There was the usual struggle with the current off Kilid Bahr and then, ominously, the submarine listed to port and started to drag on the steering. The movement seemed inexplicable and Nasmith took a quick peep through the periscope to see what was causing the trouble. He almost wished he hadn't.

The mooring cable of a mine had caught in the port hydroplane and it was being towed alongside the submarine's thin-plated hull. In fact it was only the pressure of water created by *E.11*'s momentum which was keeping the deadly horns away from the boat and, if they dared to slow down, it would swing in against them.

Nasmith had taken in all this at a glance. And, at the same time, he resolved not to tell the crew what had happened. Even D'Oyly Hughes was kept in ignorance of the peril they were in for this was the sort of crisis where only the captain can bear the full responsibility.

E.11 was approaching the Kephez minefield and Nasmith took her down to eighty feet to pass beneath it. The rasping scrape of the mooring wires as they echoed down the submarine's sides sent cold shivers down the spines of the listening crew but the suspense for Nasmith was ten times greater. He, and only he, knew that they were dragging their own mine along with them. At any moment one of its horns might snag a passing cable and then . . .

Somehow they got through and at 3.50 pm Nasmith trimmed the submarine to run just below the surface as Cape Helles came into sight through the periscope. For the first time the crew discovered they were trailing a mine and Nasmith told them quietly that they had, in fact, been towing it along for several hours. At the moment it was floating ominously just above the foredeck so that any attempt to surface would bring it into contact with the hull with the inevitable resulting detonation.

But Nasmith was not beaten. Keeping the bows underwater he ran the engines full-astern. There was a tense pause as the propeller bit into the sea and then, as *E.11* surged backwards, the mooring-cable slipped free from the hydroplane and the mine slid into the depths.

A White Ensign was streamed from the conning-tower to act as a recognition signal and the destroyer *Grampus*, which had been watching the submarine's strange evolutions from a distance, closed in. Her sailors were lining the rails and cheering as she swung around to escort the *E.11* back to Kephalo and Nasmith brought his own men up to the conning-tower to return the compliment.

The legend of the *E.11* had preceded her for the British propaganda machine had made excellent use of her exploits as soon as her nightly signals were received and there was a gala air in the crowded harbour as the rust-streaked submarine nosed towards her berth.

Martin Nasmith's first foray against the Turk was over. There were more to follow.

CHAPTER NINE

'A gun would be
of great value'

ON THE FOLLOWING evening Nasmith was invited on board
the flagship for what was becoming the traditional dinner with
Admiral de Robeck at the end of a patrol. Roger Keyes, of
course, was present and so too was Courtney Boyle who had
been chosen to take Nasmith's place in the Marmora with *E.14*.
During the meal *E.11*'s captain related the details of his epic
patrol and 'had so thoroughly enjoyed himself, [he] was
obviously looking forward to his next trip.'

He took the opportunity of telling Boyle his theory about
the deadly currents in the Dardanelles, and with the aid of
pencil and paper he explained how the top surface, down to
about sixty feet, consisted of fresh water sweeping down from
the land-locked Marmora to the sea. He then demonstrated
that a similar belt of *salt* water, running below that level, was
continually moving *upstream*. This theory, of course, helped to
explain the strange antics of the submarines when they dived in
the Straits and the knowledge which Nasmith passed on
undoubtedly helped Boyle on his next trip.

De Robeck had already telegraphed the Admiralty asking
them to submit Nasmith's name to the King for the Victoria
Cross and, apparently, General Sir Ian Hamilton made it
known that, if Their Lordships refused to do so, then he would
make an independent request 'in the name of the Army of
Gallipoli' for the award to be granted. In fact there was no
opposition from Whitehall and Martin Nasmith joined
Holbrook and Boyle as the Royal Navy's third submarine VC.
He was also specially promoted to Commander for his
exploits against the Turks. His score of one gunboat, two

transports, two ammunition ships, and two supply steamers sunk, plus a third transport forced ashore was, indeed, an outstanding achievement and he set a high standard to the men who were to follow him into the Marmora.

A few days later *E.11* was towed out bound for Malta—her engines too weak to stand the strain of an open-sea voyage—for a refit and overhaul. The dockyard at Valletta was waiting to receive her and, much to Nasmith's delight, they had been instructed to fit a twelve-pounder gun in front of the conning-tower.

E.14 now standing-by for her second patrol in the Marmora, had also been fitted with a gun although in her case it was a smaller six-pounder quick-firer and Courtney Boyle had high hopes of success as he waited for the signal to leave.

Hopes, too, were high on the flagship for the new First Lord, Arthur Balfour, had promised to send two more 'E' class submarines and four of the very latest 'H' class boats to Gallipoli to reinforce the Marmora flotilla.

On 10 June *E.14* was under starter's orders and Boyle, a man of whom Keyes has written, 'I never came across anyone more completely oblivious of danger', stood on the conning-tower at the salute as she cleared the harbour and set course for the Dardanelles.

The trip through the Narrows was tense but unexciting and, aided by Nasmith's theory on the two contra-currents and the density layers, Boyle had no trouble in taking his boat through the minefields. Even the shore batteries gave him little difficulty and, well within bogey time, he was running free into the Marmora.

It was soon apparent that the submarine threat had swept the Turks off the water and Boyle found himself patrolling an empty sea. His only luck came off Panderma where he found a large steamer lying inshore being off-loaded by lighters and other small boats. A single torpedo quickly disposed of her and Boyle decided that his target was probably the transport which

Nasmith had torpedoed and driven ashore earlier. To avoid using the sea-route to Gallipoli the Turks were sending their troop reinforcements to Rodosto by train from where they had a three-day route march to the front. Only supplies were still being sent across the water and they, in the main, were being shipped in sailing dhows which kept close inshore to avoid attack. So, deprived of more worthwhile targets, Courtney Boyle decided to make use of his gun and destroy the dhows.

It was a slow and tedious process. With due regard for International Law *E.14* stopped each little boat and ensured the safety of its crew before blowing it out of the water with a few six-pounder shells. In some cases Boyle took the Turkish sailors aboard the submarine when they had no boat in which to escape and then transferred them to another enemy ship later in the day. On one occasion the crew of a dhow dived overboard in panic when they saw *E.14* approaching. The British sailors fished them out of the water and Boyle gave them a meal before dumping them back on their little sailing-boat which he allowed to escape unscathed. The inshore traffic was increasing daily so he sent an urgent wireless message back to the Admiral for a second submarine to be sent up in support.

Earlier on her patrol the submarine had come up with a brigantine which had been ordered to stop. The sea was too rough to run alongside with a boarding-party and Lt Lawrence, RNR, volunteered to swim across. Once on board he found her well-laden with supplies and, using some paraffin and matches from one of the cabins, he set it on fire before diving back into the sea to return to the submarine. The crew of the Turkish ship were too demoralized to retaliate and they just sat watching in a small boat as the brigantine went up in flames.

On 18 June *E.12* under the command of Lt-Cdr Bruce, left Imbros to join Boyle in the Marmora. This was Bruce's first trip up the Dardanelles and, like all the previous submarine captains before him, he had a tremendous struggle with the current. In addition the Turks had stretched a steel-mesh net across the narrowest part of the Straits since *E.14*'s second passage and, unaware of its existence, *E.12* ran full tilt into it.

A line of indicator buoys marked the position of the net and a flotilla of patrol boats cruised along its length on guard. When the buoys began jerking beneath the surface it meant that a submarine was trapped and they eagerly waited for it to surface and finish it off with their guns. Bruce, however, had guessed what the trap was and so long as he remained submerged he knew he was safe for, fortunately, at that stage of the war the depth-charge had not been developed.

He ordered the submarine to go slow-astern but the net retained its grip and he realized that only brute force was going to extricate him which would mean running the battery dangerously low. But there was no alternative and he sent *E.12* full ahead. A few strands of wire snapped and the boat was again brought to a standstill with her propellers whirling. Once more he ordered slow-astern—followed quickly by another surging thrust forward under full-power. He repeated these see-sawing tactics a number of times until, at last, the remaining steel wires parted and *E.12* burst through. But the effort had put a serious strain on her electric motors and they were beginning to run hot. From now on Bruce had the continual worry of a breakdown to contend with for, if the electrics failed, the submarine would be unable to operate under water.

Bruce rendezvoused with Boyle on the 21st and spent the next two days working on his electric motors in an effort to rectify the damage caused by overstraining them earlier. When *E.12* was ready for duty Boyle sent her into the eastern sector of the Marmora while his own *E.14* patrolled the western end of the inland sea. Two days later Bruce sighted his first target, two steamers towing five small sailing vessels. Coming to the surface, he ordered them to stop but, although one steamer obeyed, the other carried on. The stationary vessel looked innocent enough. No guns were visible and the crew were assembling on deck in their life-belts with the obvious intention of abandoning ship. But it was all a little *too* innocent.

Bruce brought the submarine alongside with its gun ready for action and his best marksmen drawn up with rifles. The First Officer, Lt Fox, climbed on board followed by two sailors ready to carry out a routine inspection of the ship's papers and cargo. If she was found to be carrying war materials their orders were to open the sea-cocks and sink her.

Suddenly someone on board the Turkish steamer hurled a bomb at the submarine. It hit the steel fore-deck with a resounding clatter but failed to explode and bounced off the exposed ballast tanks into the water. The bomb attack was apparently a signal for, within seconds, a small naval-gun was unmasked aft and a line of rifles appeared along the upper-deck. Then all hell was let loose.

The two boats were only ten yards apart and both crews slammed it out at point-blank range. The dhows which the steamer had been towing joined in the battle and their occupants tried to foul the submarine's propellers with lengths of rope. Lt Fox and his boarding-party were trapped on the steamer's deck in a murderous cross-fire but, somehow, they managed to fight their way to the side, dive over and swim back to the waiting *E.12*. As soon as they were safely back aboard, Bruce quickly drew away from the decoy-ship. Then, when he judged he was out of range of Turkish small-arms, he circled round and ordered his gun-crew to open fire. The two dhows were quickly battered to pieces and, after fifteen minutes, a shell penetrated the steamer's magazine and she blew up and sank.

Having disposed of one adversary Bruce set off on a long stern chase in pursuit of the other Turkish boat which had failed to stop at the beginning of the action. When he started firing at her the steamer slipped the three dhows she was towing and made for the coast at maximum speed. *E.12* followed, throwing shells as fast as her crew could reload the gun, but they were now too close to the shore for comfort and Bruce abandoned the chase. His quarry was well on fire and it was quite obvious that she would have to be beached. The high-speed dash had made the engines run hot again and, while the E.R.A.s worked to locate and rectify the damage, *E.12* continued her patrol through the Gulf of Ismid.

Bruce forced another steamer ashore but by this time one of his engines was completely out of action and it was clear that the submarine was crippled. By luck he met up with Boyle in *E.14* who passed over a message from Kephalo ordering *E.12* to return to base for repairs. It was sad to leave the Marmora after such a short run but there was no alternative and, after a brief chat with Cdr Boyle, Bruce took his crippled boat back towards the Dardanelles.

There was the usual struggle with the current in the Narrows, a struggle intensified on this occasion by the lack of engine-power but *E.12* won through and crawled into the harbour at Kephalo on the evening of the 28th with one engine dead and the other misfiring badly.

Next into the Marmora was *E.7* commanded by Lt-Cdr Cochrane, great-grandson of Lord Dundonald, the famous naval hero, whose captain and crew were hardened veterans of the famous 8th Flotilla at Harwich. With typical abandon he burst through the steel anti-submarine net at full speed only to discovered a new Turkish delight. Two fixed torpedo-tubes had now been mounted on the shore upstream of the net arranged to fire as soon as the buoys dipped beneath the sur-face under the weight of a trapped submarine.

It was at this precise moment that *E.7* came up to periscope-depth for a quick sweep and the crew claimed forever after-wards that the enemy torpedoes passed directly between their two periscope standards! Be that as it may, it was certainly a narrow escape, and it meant that there was now one more hazard for the submarine captains to overcome in future trips up the Narrows.

Cochrane had more than his share of troubles on *E.7*'s first patrol. Dardanelles fever, an unpleasant form of depressive dysentery, had been brought aboard the boat by one man and in the confined space of a submarine it was not long before nearly all the crew, including Cochrane himself, had been struck down. But, despite high fever and the other discomforts of dysentery, they stuck at their posts and remained on patrol.

They met Cdr Boyle and *E.14* off Kalolimno Island on the night of 1 July and, after exchanging information, the two captains separated, Boyle returning through the Straits to Kephalo and Cochrane pushing up towards Rodosto for his first day's patrol. He found a steamer and five dhows moored alongside the pier and, ever resourceful, entered the harbour on the surface relying on his deck-gun to put down any opposition from shore-batteries. Two of the dhows were set on fire while the other three cut their mooring-ropes and ran for the beach. It was now time to deal with the steamer and Lt Halifax went across with a boarding-party to place demolition charges in the holds. What should have been a routine operation turned to disaster when one of the charges exploded prematurely. Halifax and an able seaman were severely burned by the blast and had to be carried back aboard *E.7* as the steamer sank. Both men were unfit for duty for the remainder of the patrol and by now the submarine's interior bore more resemblance to a hospital than an operational warship.

But Cochrane—now commanding the only British submarine in the Marmora—kept up the pressure and in the next ten days destroyed two brigantines, two small steamers, and several dhows. By 10 July he was inside the harbour of Mudania where he located the 3,000 ton ammunition ship *Biga* loading explosives and shells for the front. One torpedo was enough to despatch her and the resulting explosion was so great that it was likely that the ammunition dump had blown up as well.

Cochrane excused his inactivity in his report by observing:

'As both available officers and several of the crew were suffering from the prevelant fever, and the telegraphist had developed dysentery, not much work could be done!

By the 15th Cochrane was probing the entrance to Constantinople, following in Nasmith's able footsteps. Like *E.11* he found himself caught in the swirling current and, before he could take corrective action, *E.7* was firmly grounded on a sand-bank on the Leander Bank. By a stroke of good fortune the submarine's bows were pointing directly at the Imperial Arsenal and Cochrane decided to add to the Turk's confusion by firing a torpedo at it. There was a violent explosion but *E.7*'s captain was too busy getting his boat off the sand-bank to investigate the result of his impudence.

Fighting against the current he headed out of the Bosphorous but when level with the Zeitun powder-mills in the western suburbs of the city he took the submarine to the bottom to await nightfall. Just before midnight *E.7* came to the surface, her gun-crew raced along the narrow deck, and she began bombarding the explosive factory. Her tiny six-pounder shells caused little material damage but they tore Turkish morale to shreds. Wild rumours spread through the city that British surface units had forced the Dardanelles, all work stopped, and many of the panic-stricken inhabitants fled into the countryside.

The next morning, as Constantinople was fading astern in the shimmering heat haze, Cochrane sighted a destroyer towing a German submarine. They were beyond the range of his torpedoes and he had to let them pass. The submarine was the *UB-15* and, thanks to her lucky escape, she lived to sink the *E.20* later in the Marmora campaign. But the sighting boded ill for the future. From now on British submarine-commanders could no longer assume that a passing periscope was friendly.

Cochrane next headed for the eastern side of the Marmora where he originated a new phase in offensive operations against the Turks. Near Kava Burnu the main railway line ran through a cutting well within gun-range of the shore. *E.7* came to the surface, located the cutting, and began bombarding the line with her six-pounder. By hitting the walls of the cutting with high-explosive shells the submarine captain was able to dislodge a large amount of earth and, within a few minutes, the line was effectively blocked. He then moved up the coast to Derinji but the ship-yard there proved disappointingly empty and he cruised back to Kava Burnu. Cochrane's luck was in. A troop-train steaming down the line had found the cutting blocked, and came to an unpremeditated stop a few hundred yards away. Once again the gun-crew raced into action and the shells screamed in. Three ammunition trucks were hit and exploded and *E.7* then departed silently. The operational area was changed to the Mudania Gulf where some more successes were enjoyed against various small steamers and dhows and, after three days, the submarine returned to the Gulf of Ismid where she shot up another troop train and shelled a viaduct.

On 21 July Cochrane was ordered to rendezvous with Boyle who was coming up to the Marmora for his third patrol. He had been in the inland sea for twenty-four days and, in that time, had destroyed five steamers and twelve sailing vessels—not to mention totally disrupting the military railway time-table.

Courtney Boyle and his veteran *E.14* passed back through the Dardanelles without undue difficulty although, at one point, a mine mooring-cable turned the submarine eight points off course before her engines dragged her clear. Boyle had also spotted yet another obstacle being prepared off Nagara, a strong net extending to a depth of nearly eighty feet, but he dived safely below it and was able to warn Cochrane of this new obstruction when they next met at their appointed rendezvous to exchange information.

E.7 set off on her return trip home in fine style. Running with the tide and driving at full-speed she smashed through the new nets at the first attempt. But the exit from the Marmora was never easy and shortly afterwards the hydroplanes snagged two mine moorings and the submarine pivoted around to face upstream again while Cochrane fought to extricate his boat. After running his electric motors at maximum power for thirty minutes he broke free, swung *E.7* back in the right direction, and headed again for the entrance. The submarine had been continuously submerged for eleven hours and, with the additional strain caused by her struggle with the mooring-cables, her batteries were almost exhausted by the time she surfaced and set course for base. As Keyes wrote: '[Cochrane] had worthily upheld his ancestor's reputation for conducting war offensively.'

By now the British submarines had proved so successful in forcing the Dardanelles that many people were beginning to think the dangers of the passage were over-rated. A rude awakening lay ahead, however, for on the 25th, the day after *E.7* returned to base, the French submarine *Mariotte* set out to join Boyle in the Marmora. She was caught in a net, forced to surface, and then shelled mercilessly by the Turkish batteries at Chanak. Unable to submerge the French captain could only scuttle his ship and surrender.

Cochrane's new tactics encouraged the Commander-in-Chief to increase the naval offensive against the Turks and he gave orders that in future two submarines were to operate together in the Marmora in place of the previous single-boat patrols. Boyle was already there with *E.14*. Who could best be sent to join him? There could be only one answer. Commander Martin Nasmith, VC, had just returned to Imbros after *E.11*'s refit at Malta, with his famous submarine now fitted with a powerful twelve-pounder gun. The Naval Staff did not take long in coming to a decision and, on 5 August, 1915, *E.11* left harbour for her second patrol in the Marmora. Her destroyer escort took up station at 1.30 am as she left Kephalo and, as they approached Suandere, signal-lamps flashed last minute farewells. The destroyers wheeled away, and *E.11* slid down into the depths.

Nasmith encountered a new obstruction almost immediately. Something seemed to be holding the submarine at twenty feet and he brought her cautiously back to the surface to investigate. The rushing turbulence caused by blowing the tanks for surfacing dislodged the obstruction and a quick examination revealed no damage. Looking astern Nasmith could see a line of buoys apparently supporting a wire hawser designed, so it seemed, to snare a submarine's periscope and bend it. As they had passed it safely *E.11*'s commander merely shrugged, closed the hatch, and took his boat down in readiness for the next hazard—the minefields.

As usual the mine mooring-cables brushed down the side of the submarine with an ominous grating sound and, despite their experience on the first patrol, a tense silence descended over the boat as the men listened to the wires scraping against the thin plates of their underwater coffin.

Bump!

Every man heard the metallic clang of a mine striking the hull. But there was no explosion. Some prayed, some chewed their lips, some just waited—there would be no second chance.

Bump!

The contact was more violent this time and seemed to be in the midships section. Yet there was still no detonation, no sudden bursting of riven plates, no roaring invasion of rushing waters engulfing their tomb. Could a miracle happen twice?

'That was a near one,' breathed an unidentified voice. No one answered. Somewhere deep inside the engine compartment a hoarse cockney voice chuckled: 'And that was a bad bloody egg Johnny Turk laid that time.' The laughter eased the tension. There were no more heart-stopping bumps. *E.11* was through the minefield.

The fact that so many British submarines actually bumped against the Dardanelles mines without exploding them is a frequent source of surprise. The explanation is, however, simple. The Germans had supplied the Turkish Government with a whole range of naval armaments including a consignment of the pre-war 'Carbonite' moored mine. It was a highly efficient weapon and the Allies lost several battleships in the Dardanelles as a result of it. But the mine was designed for use against surface vessels and, for this reason, the detonating horns were all set in the upper part. When running submerged the submarine normally made contact with the underside of the mine and thus did not touch the horns. Even if the submarine snagged the mooring cable in its hydroplanes the mine was usually drawn downwards so that only the base came into contact with the hull.

At least three Allied submarines were sunk by the 'Carbonite' mines in the Dardanelles. But it seems almost certain that the boats were either running on the surface or, by sheer chance, the mine was drawn down at an angle. Providing the submarine ran through the minefields at a good depth there was every probability that she could break through unscathed.

After ninety minutes *E.11* was safely round Nagara Point and Nasmith dived to 110 feet to slide beneath the new obstruction which Boyle had reported to Cochrane. Since then, however, the Turks had extended it and the submarine ran full tilt into a steel mesh and found herself promptly hoisted to ninety feet. Nasmith reversed engines and backed cautiously away.

'Group up. Full ahead.'

E.11 surged forward, gathering speed as her propellers churned the water. A sharp crack echoed through the hull as the steel strands parted and, with the exertion of no further effort, *E.11* slid safely through the gap she had ripped.

Coming to periscope-depth off Ak Bashi Liman, Nasmith searched the inlets and bays for likely targets. Turkish battleships often lurked in this area but today, alas, there were none. As he swung the periscope further round Nasmith suddenly spotted a large three-masted transport and D'Oyly Hughes passed his order forward to flood the bow-tubes. Thrusting against the current *E.11* was skilfully coaxed into the perfect firing position

'Starboard tube stand by.'

The order was repeated back and, a moment later, the torpedo hissed into the water. Nasmith was counting the seconds off as he estimated the range:

'Five—four—three—two—one . . .'

The concussion of a tremendous underwater explosion rocked the submarine as the torpedo struck home and a cheerful thumbs up passed down the boat from bow to stern. First blood to the captain—and they weren't even through the Straits yet. It was still only 7 am.

E.11 slid into the depths and purred northwards up the Narrows, her course changing every now and again in response to Nasmith's quiet instructions to the helmsman. Soon the white-walled houses of Gallipoli were sliding past and, thirty minutes later, it was safe to surface. But it was not all plain-sailing. She was located by a Turkish gunboat during the afternoon and a cat-and-mouse hunt lasted for several hours before Nasmith was able to evade his tormentor. The night was spent on the surface re-charging batteries and there was a nasty moment when, at dawn, an enemy sea-plane switched off its engine and glided down to attack. Two bombs were dropped. Fortunately they missed.

On the afternoon of 6 August the two VC commanders made their rendezvous. The mighty marauders of the Marmora were to operate together for the first time and, to an impartial observer, the outlook for the Turks must have looked distinctly unpromising.

CHAPTER TEN

'A Revolver and
a very sharp Bayonet'

'SMOKE, BEARING Green Three—Five!'

Nasmith and Boyle were closeted in the cramped wardroom of *E.14* discussing their plans when the look-out's alarm came down the voice-pipe and, scattering the charts to one side, both officers dashed for the conning-tower. A faint wisp of smoke curled over the distant horizon and the two commanders knew that the enemy ship could not yet see the low silhouettes of the submarines. Nasmith jumped across to *E.11* shouting an order to D'Oyly Hughes to start the motors as he clambered up the steel ladder, while Courtney Boyle sent *E.14*'s crew to their diving stations. Within minutes both submarines were swinging in a wide circle towards the enemy and, in a flurry of white frothing water, they slid gently beneath the surface.

The *Berc-i-Satvet*, a torpedo-gunboat of 775 tons, built in 1907 and armed with two four-inch guns, was unaware of the submarines and she looked a splendid sight as she plumed through the water at a steady fifteen knots. Her course was taking her to the north and Nasmith was in the most advantageous position. By cutting corners the two submarines kept up the chase and, finally, at 4.30 pm off the ancient port of Silivri, *E.11* sent a torpedo plunging straight into her amidships. There was a loud explosion, black smoke billowed from the gaping wound, and the *Berc-i-Satvet* heeled around with a heavy list as her captain steered for the shore. He ran her aground successfully and Nasmith fired a second torpedo to finish her off. Unfortunately he was less successful this time and the submarines had to leave the enemy high and dry on the beach with a gaping hole in her side, but still capable of being salvaged.

As dusk closed in *E.11* and *E.14* turned towards the Straits and spent the night surfaced re-charging their batteries. At dawn they moved along the coast to a point near Bulair where they could see the military road leading to Gallipoli. Nasmith pushed on further east and the two submarines submerged to periscope-depth to watch the vital highway along which the Turks were sending their troops and supplies to the front. Soon after 11 am a cloud of dust moved slowly down the road and, as it came nearer, Nasmith could pick out a column of enemy troops marching along in full equipment.

'Stand by to surface—Gun-crew stand by.'

'Shut main vent.'

'Main vents closed, sir.'

'Surface.'

'Blow all main ballast. Hydroplanes to rise.'

Nasmith stood by the conning-tower hatch as *E.11* rose towards the surface. D'Oyly Hughes called off the decreasing depth and the commander slipped the hatch clips ready to throw it open. 'Gun-crew close up—stop blowing.'

Nasmith threw back the hatch and pushed out through the tiny aperture followed by Kircaldy, the gun-layer, and the rest of the gun-crew. The tampion plugging the barrel was removed and a stream of sharp orders came from the conning-tower:

'Bearing Green Three-o—Range o-two-o—deflection zero —with H.E., load.'

'Gun ready.' Kircaldy yelled.

'Ready to open fire, sir,' D'Oyly Hughes reported. Nasmith nodded.

'When you're ready, Number One.'

There was a sharp whip-lash crack as the twelve-pounder fired. The gun-crew quickly slid another shell into the breech. A cloud of brown dust erupted alongside the road as the first shell exploded, the horses of the officers reared in fright, and the soldiers scattered wildly as they heard the second shot whistling down. By the time five rounds had been fired the road was empty except for the dead and dying; the Turkish troops had vanished behind any available cover. Nasmith ordered the fire to cease, the gun-crew went below, and *E.11* slid down to periscope-depth again. Confused and shaken, the enemy soldiers straggled into a ragged column and resumed their march.

Thirty minutes later a second column appeared and, coming to the surface, *E.11* gave a repeat performance. This time the enemy tried to keep on the move and Nasmith followed them down the coast firing each time a party was sighted running from cover to cover. They reached *E.14*'s beat and Boyle joined in the fun with his six-pounder. For the next hour the Turkish infantrymen cowered behind scrub and boulders as the two submarines deluged them with high-explosive shells and only the arrival of a field-gun detachment saved them from further punishment. Nasmith discreetly withdrew.

Despite the shelling the bulk of the column had maintained discipline and kept marching 'at high speed' throughout the savage bombardment. But their steadfastness had only increased their casualty rate.

At 4.40 am next morning, the 8th, *E.11* was lying some five miles off Gallipoli preparing for her dawn patrol. Smoke was sighted in the distance and, as it drew closer, was seen to be coming from a large ship escorted by a destroyer. Nasmith dived and waited patiently for his quarry to approach and excitement mounted when it was realized that the large ship was none other than *E.11*'s old adversary the battleship *Hairredin Barbarossa*. She had escaped them on two previous occasions. Would this be a case of third time lucky?

The attack went off without a hitch. Everything functioned perfectly and Nasmith's torpedo struck her amidships. The battleship took on a heavy list immediately but, despite the danger of being drowned at their posts, her gunners opened fire on the periscope as the great ship staggered for the shore.

Their gallant efforts were to no avail. The fires started by the torpedo spread to the magazine and, at 5.20 am, *Barbarossa* was rent asunder by a tremendous explosion. 10,060 tons of Krupp steel and four eleven-inch guns had gone to the bottom of the Marmora and fifty per cent of Turkey's battleship strength had been destroyed by a single well-aimed torpedo.

Having disposed of the big ship Nasmith turned his attention to the destroyer. He edged the submarine into position and loosed off a torpedo but it ran deep and passed beneath the target. A second enemy destroyer arrived on the scene to join in the hunt and, deciding that the odds were too great, *E.11* dived to eighty feet and crept away. Meanwhile Boyle and *E.14* were improving on the score. A 5,000 ton transport was located off Dohan Aslan and a well-placed torpedo sent her limping for the shore. Boyle surfaced to finish off his victim by shell-fire and a short while later Nasmith joined him. By the time they turned away the Turkish troopship was ablaze from stem to stern.

The following day found the two submarines playing their old game along the railway line but, by now, the Turks had moved up a number of field-guns and both commanders agreed that this rather spoilt the fun.

Boyle received his recall signal a few days later and, after a final chat with Nasmith, he set off on his return passage down the Narrows. The way back was not without the usual incidents. They managed to burst through the Nagara net in twenty seconds but narrowly missed destruction by a torpedo fired from the shore. Later *E.14*'s propellers fouled the cables of an electric-contact-mine but, by turning on full power, she was able to rip herself clear. Boyle arrived off Suvla Bay at 5 pm and, later that day, tied up alongside the depot ship *Triad*. Only then was it learned that Lt Stanley, the second-in-command, had been ill for the previous sixteen days with a fever that hovered between 102 and 104 degrees.

Nasmith, too, was having troubles. The mounting of the

twelve-pounder had been stressed with such violence during the shelling of the transport that Kircaldy, the gun-layer, had been tossed overboard, fortunately without ill-effects. Repairs could only be effected from the submarine's own resources and *E.11* found a quiet anchorage to lick her wounds. Neither Nasmith nor D'Oyly Hughes knew enough about gun-mountings to see how it could be put right, but fortunately one of the crew came to the rescue. The solution was dramatic but practical. The upper part of the mounting was cut away with a hammer and cold-chisel and the gun was remounted on the lower part. It was a bodge job and the gun would have to be handled carefully but it did the trick and, twenty-four hours later, *E.11* was back on patrol.

At San Stefano Nasmith had an abortive fight with a destroyer but succeeded in burning five small sailing vessels. Moving on to Mudania he shelled the railway station but had to withdraw quickly when Turkish shore-batteries opened up in reply. This time he was shadowed by an enemy sea-plane and, repeating his North Sea gesture when attacked by the Zeppelin, he waved goodbye to the pilot before closing the hatch and diving to safety.

That night he established wireless contact with the sloop *Aster* and received orders to meet Lt-Cdr Stocks who was coming up to join him in *E.2*.

Stocks had an adventurous trip up the Dardanelles and emerged with a length of three-and-a-half-inch wire wound around his twelve-pounder deck-gun. The Turks were now using depth-bombs (a primitive form of depth-charge with a pointed nose and without a hydrostatic valve to control detonation at a pre-set depth) and Nasmith listened with interest as the young officer described the effects of these terrifying new underwater weapons. In fact they had done Stocks a good turn for they had blown a hole in the net defence through which the submarine was able to wriggle like an eel.

By the time she reached her rendezvous *E.2* had already

chalked up her first victim—an armed steamer which she had torpedoed off the entrance to the Gulf of Artaki. More important, she had brought a fresh supply of twelve-pounder ammunition and *E.11* was able to replenish her shell-racks before leaving for the Bosphorus.

When he arrived off Constantinople Nasmith found a collier tied up alongside the Haidar Pasha pier while a group of Turkish officials huddled together to discuss unloading the cargo. *E.11* solved their problems with a single torpedo which blew the collier out of the water and distributed her cargo over a fairly large area.

The same evening *E.11* met up with *E.2* and they set off together for San Stefano where Nasmith had his first brush with an enemy 'Q' ship. A small steamer was sighted a few miles ahead and both submarines closed on the surface with the intention of destroying it by gun-fire. *E.2*'s gun, however, was quickly out of action when the mounting collapsed as a result of the damage she had suffered on her journey up the Dardanelles, and *E.11* shortened the range as she took over the attack. Nasmith scored two direct hits on the steamer which stung her into unmasking her true identity. Deckhouses collapsed and screens fell aside to reveal a formidable battery of quick-firers and both submarines found themselves under heavy fire. It was a dangerous situation for a single hit on either *E.2* or *E.11* would prevent them from diving and, trapped in the land-locked sea, they knew they stood no chance of survival. There was only one thing for it and both submarines quickly slid beneath the surface and scuttled away for safety. Prudence was also an important facet of a submarine commander's character.

That night Nasmith renewed his attack on the railway and *E.11* surfaced to bombard a viaduct. But the Turkish shore-batteries had been reinforced and their return fire was so hot that Nasmith had to withdraw after lobbing only fifteen rounds at the bridge. Clearly the railway was now heavily

defended and further attempts at bombardment seemed likely
to end in failure.

As they sat in the wardroom discussing the problem D'Oyly
Hughes renewed his earlier suggestion for a one-man raid. His
plan was to land on the beach near the viaduct with a sack
of gun-cotton, blow up the viaduct, and then swim back to
the submarine which would be lying off-shore to pick him
up. Nasmith thought it over and, after much persuasion,
agreed to try it. But, he insisted, they must give the area a
wide berth for a few days so that the Turks would relax their
vigilance.

E.11 therefore cruised back to Constantinople, moved along
Artaki Bay and then, doubling back, stopped in the lee of
Kalolimno Island on the afternoon of the 20th while prepara-
tions were made for the raid.

A small raft was constructed from empty casks with boards
lashed to the sides and across the tops while D'Oyly Hughes
gathered together his personal requirements—sixteen pounds
of gun-cotton, a revolver, a very sharp bayonet for silently
despatching any sentries found en route, an electric hand-torch
for signalling, and a whistle which he could blow as he swam
back, so the submarine could locate him in the darkness. It was
a daring scheme and one which called for great personal
courage. Nasmith was still none too happy about the project
and he told D'Oyly to blow up the railway line instead of the
viaduct which he felt was likely to be too well guarded.

Shortly after two o'clock Hughes climbed down the con-
ing-tower and dropped into the water. Pushing the raft ahead
of him, he swam towards the shore and reached the pebble
beach without trouble. But luck was against him. The cliffs
rose sheer from the water's edge and it was quite clear that they
were completely unscaleable although from the submarine's
conning-tower they had appeared to be an easy climb. Fortunately it was a dark night and it was unlikely that the coast-
watcher had spotted him so D'Oyly pushed his little raft back

into the water and swam down the shore-line searching for a more promising landing place.

He located a small beach a quarter of a mile further down, pushed the raft carefully up the sand clear of the water, put on his uniform, draped the revolver, whistle, torch and bayonet from his belt, and picked up the tin of explosive. It was a stiff climb up the cliffs and by the time he had reached the top he was very short of breath. The landing had been made in a small cove some half a mile east of Eski Hissar village and, although the railway was not in sight, he knew that it was only a short distance inland and that the viaduct was to the right. After a brief rest to regain his breath he set off on his march.

It was a pitch-black night. The area was silent as a grave. Revolver in hand D'Oyly made his way through the irregular scrub keeping a sharp look-out for guards and sentries. After five minutes the line was still not in sight so changing direction slightly, he crept cautiously across a field. After half-an-hour he located the railway line and then turned thankfully to the right so as to follow it down to the viaduct.

Suddenly he heard voices and 'froze' as his ears tried to discover their direction. When he felt tolerably certain he crept forward and slipped the safety-catch of his Webley revolver ready for instant action. He found three Turkish pickets sitting together chatting volubly, their minds and attention far away from their task of guarding the railway line and, skirting past them in true Red Indian fashion, he set off across country in search of the viaduct. He soon found himself in an agricultural district criss-crossed by low stone walls and dotted with small farmhouses. Carefully heaving himself over one of the walls he trod on a chicken and all hell was let loose. An aggressive rooster attacked him, feathers whirled and screams of protest shattered the silence. D'Oyly hopped back over the wall and continued his stealthy approach to the viaduct. Crawling through a hedge he suddenly saw the gaunt steel girders framed against the night sky; but further exploration proved disappointing. There was a sizeable body of Turkish labourers on the viaduct and they seemed to be working to repair the damage inflicted by *E.11*'s shells a few days earlier. A fire was burning brightly in the camp and the puffing of a steam-locomotive echoed down the line. D'Oyly withdrew to consider the situation.

He had left the explosives a short distance away from the three pickets and he decided to return there, gather up his belongings, and blow the track itself as Nasmith had ordered. Creeping back through the darkness, he skirted the hen-roost, made his way along the line, and found the gun-cotton still safely buried under a small heap of stones. Loaded up again he set off to find a suitable section of track under which to place his charges.

D'Oyly selected a small culvert spanning a dried-up stream; but it had one substantial disadvantage, it was only 300 yards away from the three-man picket. With the enemy so close every sound seemed magnified ten-fold. He scraped a small hole with the tip of his bayonet, and carefully slid the tin of gun-cotton under the culvert. The detonator was already in place and he pulled the tiny fuse pistol from his pocket to ignite it. The noise, he knew, was sure to attract attention but he counted on having a three-hundred yard start on the Turkish sentries. He pushed the end of the fuse gently into the barrel of the pistol and wound a piece of rag carefully round the gun to muffle the report. He took a deep breath and pulled the trigger. The sharp detonation echoed through the darkness and the picket scrambled to their feet in alarm. D'Oyly checked that the fuse was burning and then, revolver in hand, made a dash for it.

The soldiers were not far behind and, after a few hundred yards, he turned towards them and fired several shots, all of which missed. But his pursuers hesitated and, dropping to the ground, returned his fire with their rifles. It was an unpleasant moment but, at least, it widened the gap between them. A mile further on he found the long slope to the beach and, as he threw himself down the incline, there was a tremendous explosion, as the main charge detonated, reducing nearly fifty yards of track to useless scrap metal. He had now reached the water's edge and, running straight into the sea, he began swimming out to where he supposed the waiting submarine to be. Four-hundred yards out D'Oyly stopped swimming, put the whistle in his mouth, and blew several shrill blasts as he gently dog-paddled to conserve his energy. But there was no sign of *E.11*.

Realizing that the long chase had probably carried him well past the rendezvous-point and aware that he had not the strength to swim half a mile or so in search of Nasmith, D'Oyly turned back to the shore, hoping that the soldiers had not seen him. Reaching the shore, he hauled himself up on the sand, and hid beneath some scrub while he regained his breath.

Once recovered D'Oyly made his way carefully along the shore keeping under cover as much as he could until he reached the small cove where he had originally landed. Leaving the bayonet and gun on the sand, he quickly stripped off most of his clothing, and waded out into the sea again. This time the Turks had spotted him from the top of the cliffs and there was a sharp crackle of rifle-fire but, fortunately, the deceptive dawn light upset their aim and the bullets splashed into the water many yards away.

E.11's friendly bulk came slowly into view and a signal-torch flashed from the conning-tower. It was answered by a feeble blast from the waterlogged whistle and a group of sailors ran down the forecasing to drag the First Lieutenant aboard. Without losing a moment Nasmith called down for full-speed and the submarine circled away from the shore and disappeared into the dawn mist.

It had been a gallant little episode and one which was to be repeated many times in the Second World War when saboteurs were landed from submarines along the coast of

Hitler-occupied Europe. Once again Nasmith had carried out
an operation which was to set the pattern twenty years in the
future. And young D'Oyly Hughes had shown that the long
years of peace had not undermined the resilience and initiative
of the Navy's junior officers. The DSO he won for his exploit
was, indeed, very well-earned.

On 22 August *E.11* came upon a small armada of dhows in
the tow of armed tugs under the protection of a destroyer. It
was a formidable little convoy and Nasmith decided to have a
crack at it. His first two attempts ended in failure, once due to
the close proximity of the destroyer, and once when the submarine lost her trim. When he came in for a third attack the
destroyer was well in the rear so he came to the surface and
the gun-crew closed up for action.

It turned out to be a very odd affair. As soon as the two leading tugs saw the submarine they slipped their tows and scurried
wildly for the shore leaving the six dhows bobbing helplessly
on the water. Realizing that something was amiss the destroyer
steamed from the rear of the convoy and, thinking that the
enemy intended to ram, Nasmith recalled his gun-crew and
took *E.11* down again as fast as he could. The destroyer roared
overhead making a noise like an express train but, instead of
circling, she remained on course towards the two fleeing tugs. A
bevy of signals fluttered from her mast-head and one of the tugs
was sent back, reluctantly it seemed, to round up the dhows
and tow the third tug which had apparently broken down.

Nasmith surfaced again to find one tug towing the other
which, in turn, was towing a dhow. He opened fire and was
met with a heavy cannonade from the second tug, so he submerged again. Meanwhile the leading tug had slipped her tow
and was, once more, steaming hard for the shore. Catching the
scent of panic, the sailing dhow had also cut loose, hoisted her
sail, and was high-tailing it to the south.

E.11 selected the dhow as her first target and quickly sank
her. Amongst the twenty survivors dragged on board was a

German bank manager from Chanak who had been evacuating the bank's deposits to safety. The broken-down tug was despatched next and when further surface ships began steaming towards the scene of the scattered action Nasmith decided it was time to evacuate the area as well. *E.11* dipped beneath the waves and set off in search of somewhere to dump her unwanted prisoners.

The problem was solved later that afternoon when the submarine came on a small sailing-ship loaded with fruit. D'Oyly Hughes made her crew throw the cargo overboard and then shepherded the twenty survivors from the dhow on board. Then, with dire threats of what would happen if they related their adventures to the military, the little sailing vessel was sent on her way.

That evening Nasmith received a wireless signal from Mudros informing him that a group of transports had collected in the Dardanelles; so, after spending the night re-charging batteries, he set off while it was still dark in search of his new targets. Once more *E.11* nosed her way into the Straits and, in the early hours of the morning, she was near Ak Bashi Liman, a small anchorage just above Nagara.

There was a healthy concentration of shipping in the roadstead and Nasmith selected an anchored gunboat as his first target. His torpedo missed but exploded amongst the ships in the rear although with what results he could not ascertain. The gunboat and a destroyer attacked but Nasmith went deep and made for the northern shore of the Straits. At dawn he moved in again and, by 10 am, two fat transports were in his sights. Both bow tubes fired and there was a fierce double explosion as both transports went up together.

E.11 crept away silently and was soon investigating the pleasures of False Bay. A third transport was located and, after an abortive first attack, Nasmith's next torpedo tore a hole in the troopship's bottom and she began settling in the water. There was now only one torpedo left in the stern tube and it seemed a pity to waste it. The submarine moved on and found yet another transport which was quickly despatched with the last shot.

Meanwhile, Stocks in *E.2* had been busy. On the 21st he had torpedoed a 1,500-ton armed-steamer in Artaki Bay with a well-placed shot which had cut the ship clean in two. On the 22nd he sank a large steamer off Mudania pier and a few days later he followed *E.11* into the Straits to try his luck against the transports. Stocks, too, missed the gunboat but managed to get home a torpedo on a large transport anchored near Bergaz Iskalessi.

The effect of this onslaught shattered Turkish morale and as the German Official History, *Der Krieg zur See*, records of this period: 'The British submarines succeeded for the first time in raising the losses (of shipping) to a point that caused anxiety. If this destruction of tonnage had been maintained at anything like that level during the next few months the resistance of the 5th Army would have come to an end.'

By 28 August both *E.2* and *E.11* were operating together once again and they carried out a devastating bombardment of Mudania railway station with their two twelve-pounder guns. And, to use up his few remaining shells, Nasmith returned to D'Oyly's viaduct at Ismid to give it a farewell pasting.

On 3 September it was time to go home. *E.11*'s crew removed the deck-gun and took it below so that it would not snag in the net defences. Then the submarine set out on her hazardous return passage through the Dardanelles leaving Stocks to hold the fort in the Marmora until the arrival of Cochrane in *E.7*.

The trip down the Straits was free of incident and, once they had burst through the net at Nagara Point, it turned out to be a fast, easy run. *E.11* surfaced at Helles seven hours later at 9.15 am, the destroyer *Bulldog* greeted her with a blast on her siren, and the veteran submarine was escorted back to the depot-ship for a much needed rest and overhaul.

Nasmith made his customary informal report to Roger Keyes and told him that, on the return run through the Dardanelles, D'Oyly Hughes had stood in the conning-tower with the dead-lights raised so that he could obtain first-hand information about the net defence at Nagara. The young lieutenant had watched the whole operation and was able to report that the net was made of two-and-a-half-inch wires in a ten-foot mesh. But more important was his disclosure that it 'parted on impact'—which was at least some consolation to the submarine captains who had to face it in future.

E.11's second patrol had lasted twenty-nine days and she had sunk or destroyed one battleship, one gunboat, six transports, one armed steamer and twenty-three sailing vessels—not to mention messing up the railway track at Ismid and dirtying the nice white uniforms of the Turkish officials standing on the Haidar Pasha pier when Nasmith had blown up the collier *Ispahan* in Constantinople harbour.

As Keyes wrote afterwards: 'Nasmith's arrival from the Marmora . . . was like a breath of fresh air to me.'

CHAPTER ELEVEN

'Yes . . . a Toothbrush'

E.7 HAD BEEN selected to go up the Dardanelles to replace Nasmith and, on the evening before he sailed, Lt-Cdr Cochrane told Keyes his plans for the next patrol. They were highly exciting and, according to the Commodore, 'for ingenuity rivalled the most brilliant of his great-grandfather's exploits.'

The submarine left Mudros in the small hours of 4 September and, in accordance with the usual routine, was escorted to the diving position by a destroyer. After submerging Cochrane took her down to eighty feet and set course for the first minefield. They nosed their way through without any undue incidents and, after rising to periscope-depth to check his bearing, the commander headed for Nagara where the next obstruction in the obstacle race was situated.

He arrived at 7.30 am and, calling for full-power, he pointed E.7's bows towards the net. Unknown to Cochrane the Turks had recently strengthened the obstruction and it was now an extremely formidable defence system consisting of wire-rope in twelve-foot meshes which reached right down to the bottom of the sea-bed.

E.7 was running at a depth of one hundred feet and she charged into the net under full-power. There was a sharp clang as the wire ropes burst under the impact and Cochrane began forcing his boat through the gap. For a few minutes success seemed assured but, suddenly, a length of wire fouled the starboard propeller and had wound itself tightly around the shaft before the motor could be shut off.

The hum of the motors died away and the submarine rolled gently in the current, the frayed wires of the net scraping against her steel sides like branches clawing at a window in the wind. The Chief E.R.A. bustled into the control room.

'Starboard motor's burned out, sir.'

Cochrane shrugged.

'Well we'll have to make it on the other, Chief. See if your lads can fix anything.'

The engineer nodded, ducked through the narrow opening of the bulkhead door, and went back to the motor-compartment. Cochrane moved over to the chart, studied it intensely for a few seconds, and then straightened up.

'It's now or never, Number One. Full ahead port.'

'Full ahead port, sir.'

E.7 vibrated gently as the power surged into the motor and she shifted slightly. It was impossible to tell which way she was moving except by means of the compass. Suddenly the needle swung 90 degrees and the grating sound of the net came, this time, from aft. The submarine had swung broadside and was now lying with her full length against the net trapped at both bow and stern! At 8.30 am there was a violent explosion. The Turks had dropped their first depth charge.

A line of marker-buoys floated on the surface above the net and the enemy were patrolling in small boats. Each time the submarine tried to wriggle free the buoys dragged beneath the water and it was a simple matter to locate her position with clinical exactitude. A launch bustled out from the shore carrying a large black canister in the stern-sheets. Stopping at the point indicated by the patrols, the canister was dropped into the water. For fifteen seconds there was silence. Then, suddenly, there was a dull roar deep beneath the surface and the blast of the explosion threw a great white gusher of water into the air.

Inside *E.7* everything was calm. The depth charge had caused no major damage and the First Officer, having checked the hull for leaks, reported everything still tight. Chancing that the explosion had done more damage to the nets than it had to the submarine Cochrane called for full power again. *E.7* threshed wildly against the heavy steel net but she did not move. By now the port motor was overheating too and the captain had to call off the attempt.

Two hours later another depth-charge swirled towards the bottom, considerably closer than the first, and flakes of cork-packing sprinkled down like snow as the submarine took the full blast of the explosion. But the hull held firm and Cochrane gave the motor another quick burst of power to try and break free.

For the next three hours, at regular intervals, *E.7* strained and threshed against the net but her exertions only seemed to entangle her more tightly. By now the batteries were running down and her captain decided to lie low for a while. The crew rested quietly but they noted with ominous pessimism that Cochrane was carefully destroying the boat's confidential records and secret papers.

On shore the news that a submarine was trapped in the net spread like wildfire. Korvetten Kapitan Heino von Heimburg, commander of the German submarine *UB-15*, was resting in his cabin when he was given the news. Heimburg had once been trapped in a British net and he had evolved his own method of destroying an ensnared submarine. *UB-15* was lying at anchor at Chanak, only a short distance from the net defence, and the German officer immediately decided to take a hand in the proceedings. So taking his cook, Herzig, with him they threw some equipment into a dinghy and rowed over to the Turkish patrol boats. The crew of a gunboat pointed out where they thought the submarine was lying and Herzig, a professional fisherman by trade, swung a plumbline over the side while Heimburg rowed gently along the line of buoys.

After half-an-hour the cook let out a yell as he located the trapped submarine and the two men carefully prepared a mine. They lit the fuse and then lowered it down into the depths. Black diesel oil leaked up to the surface after the explosion and the U-boat captain now knew he had fatally wounded his prey.

The fierce detonation of the mine had shattered every electric light bulb in *E.7* and the crew clattered through the debris in pitch darkness as Cochrane called for diving stations.

'Close main vents. Blow all tanks.'

There was a hiss of compressed air which drowned the sullen gurgling of sea-water leaking into the hull and the submarine began to rise to the surface. The hatch was thrown open and the crew climbed out on deck with their arms raised while Cochrane and the other two officers quickly set the scuttling charges which they had placed ready for use a few hours earlier. Then, reluctantly, they clambered up through the hatch to join the crew lined up on deck. Cochrane, in fact, only just made it in time according to Heimburg's eye-witness account: 'The water was closing over the conning-tower when another figure leaped out of the conning-tower and into the water and swam over to the boat. It was the captain, the last man to abandon ship.'

Cochrane was taken to a civilian prison in Constantinople where his cell-mate turned out to be none other than Lt-Cdr Stoker, the captain of *AE.2* which had been lost earlier in the campaign. Both officers made one abortive attempt to escape but, later, Cochrane succeeded in eluding his Turkish captors and finally returned to England in 1918.

Stocks, of course, knew nothing of *E.7*'s fate and he waited at the rendezvous point for several hours until it became obvious that his new running-mate had failed to get through the Straits. Swinging *E.2* around he headed back into the Marmora to resume his lone patrol.

The daring raid by D'Oyly Hughes had inflamed his imagination and Stocks decided to try a similar landing. After destroying a few small sailing vessels en route he arrived, on the evening of the 7th off a small village three miles west of San Stefano. Lt Lyon was eager to emulate Hughes' daring and, soon after midnight, he was landed on the shore with instructions to blow up a railway bridge.

Stocks cruised up and down off the coast for two days but Lyon did not show up. Finally a battery of Turkish field-guns arrived and forced the submarine to move away from the area. *E.2*'s unfortunate First Officer was never seen or heard of again.

On 14 September Stocks received the recall signal and he set off for his long journey down the Dardanelles. Despite the new Turkish defences the return passage was completed without incident and, in the course of her trip, *E.2* torpedoed and sank an enemy steamer off Bergaz Iskalessi. It had been a relatively quiet period in the Marmora but Stocks was able to report a bag of six steamers and thirty-six sailing vessels when he went to see Keyes on his arrival back at Mudros.

Next into the ring came *E.12*. This was her second patrol and Kenneth Bruce was still in command. She had been fitted with a four-inch gun at Malta and, with the continuing lack of Turkish sea-traffic, it was clear that bombardment tactics against land targets were becoming the order of the day. Bruce used his new toy against the powder-mills at Mudania and then gave the Turks a rude shock by engaging, and defeating, a number of shore batteries. Not that *E.12* was unsuccessful against shipping. On her way up the Straits she had torpedoed and sunk a large steamer and had then fought a torpedo-boat in a surface action and driven the enemy off, badly damaged. A spell of bad weather upset operations but Bruce managed to bag a 3,000-ton supply ship before proceeding to rendezvous with *H.1* on 4 October.

H.1, the first-fruit of Admiral Fisher's emergency building programme on his return to Whitehall in 1914, had been built by Canadian Vickers in Montreal and had then been sailed across the Atlantic to join the Fleet. She displaced 364 tons on the surface, was 150 feet 3 inches long and, built to an American design, was armed with four eighteen-inch bow torpedo-tubes.

Lt Pirie, her Commanding Officer, was ordered to patrol

the eastern basin of the Marmora while Bruce proceeded to Rodosto. Both were in luck. *E.12* destroyed a small steamer and seventeen dhows in the approaches to the town and *H.1* accounted for a steamship at Mudania. They then linked up and cruised to San Stefano where they bombarded the powder-mills and, later, *E.12* claimed another victim when she torpedoed a cargo ship in Lampsaki Bay.

On 20 October Pirie's Canadian-built boat scored two more successes, a steamship of 3,000 tons and another of 1,500 tons near Injeh Burnu, and, two days later, the French submarine *Turquoise* broke through the Dardanelles defences to join her British comrades. On the 23rd Lt-Cdr Warren brought *E.20* into the Marmora and, for a short time, there were four Allied submarines operating in the inland sea.

E.12 had been on patrol for forty days when the recall signal was received, an operational record for the Marmora flotilla. And on his way back down the Straits Bruce broke another record when the Turkish net-defences entangled in the sub-marine's forward hydroplanes, forcing her to sink to the unprecedented depth of 245 feet.

The incident had started when *E.12* tried to ram a net at full-speed, the now-approved tactic for bursting through this form of defence. Somehow a portion of the heavy net ripped away and twisted itself around the submarine's bows sending the boat out of control into the depths. At one hundred feet Bruce ordered the forward ballast tanks to be blown. But it had no effect. At 150 feet she was running into regions deeper than any submarine had ever ventured before and the hull began to creak and groan under the increased pressure of water. At 200 feet the captain, expecting the boat to cave in like a crushed egg-shell at any moment, sent three men forward to work the reluctant hydroplane by hand. They strained at the wheel and *E.12* steadied. But she was still dropping. The thick glass scuttles in the conning-tower cracked under the increasing pressure and water began leaking in. At 245 feet it seemed as if a wilful giant was slowly crushing the submarine in his clenched hand.

Suddenly the men at the hydroplane control succeeded in freeing the wheel and *E.12* leapt for the surface. There was no holding her and, as her conning-tower broke into the daylight, the Turkish patrol boats opened fire. Bruce forced her down again but she was bucking like an uncontrollable child on a toy rocking-horse. Finally, off Kilid Bahr, the submarine grazed a mine-mooring which ripped the net away.

No longer weighed down by the bows she shot to the surface once more and this time the keen-eyed Turkish gunners hit her three times before Bruce regained control and dived for safety. Fortunately none of the shells had struck the pressure hull and, after dodging two torpedoes launched from shore-tubes, *E.12* steered sedately for the exit of the Straits and surfaced off Cape Helles safe and sound.

It had been the wildest passage yet, but the submarine officers had once again shown that their skill and knowledge of the depths was unsurpassed. And Bruce had the pleasure of reporting a personal score of four steamers and thirty sailing vessels when he finally reached Mudros.

On the 27th Pirie sighted a large supply-ship escorted by a gunboat. His torpedo missed the warship and, in the resulting confusion, the steamer high-tailed into Panderma where she hid behind the harbour mole. Determined not to be robbed of his quarry Pirie returned to the town two days later. Boldly steaming down the western shore he swung *H.1* round as he reached the harbour entrance and fired an immaculate shot which struck the Turkish ship on her starboard bow. It was Pirie's swan-song. After 2,000 miles of constant patrols the submarine's engines were beginning to give trouble and, on the 31st, *H.1* returned down the Straits without incident.

On 7 November, 1915, the Germans announced the destruction of the French *Turquoise* and the British *E.20*. The two losses, although separated by several hours, had an unfortunate and sinister link. For despite the German report *Turquoise* had not been destroyed. She had been captured intact.

Running aground near a Turkish fortress on 30 October she had been unable to submerge and her captain, under the threat of the fortress guns, had surrendered with his crew to save unnecessary loss of life. Unfortunately he did not take the precaution of destroying his confidential papers and, when the German naval authorities examined their find, they learned that *E.20* was due to rendezvous with the French submarine that evening. A neatly pencilled cross marked the position of their meeting place on the Frenchman's chart.

When *E.20* arrived at the spot her companion was nowhere in sight but, lurking at periscope-depth 3,000 yards away, was the German submarine *UB-15*.

The British boat was a sitting duck and the torpedo struck her amidships with a roar of flame. Heimburg, *UB-15*'s captain gave a vivid eye-witness account of the sinking after the war:

'We got a perfect shot. A tremendous explosion, a cloud of smoke on the water. When the smoke disappeared no submarine was to be seen, only men swimming around in the water. We picked up nine Britishers including the captain, a young Lieutenant Warren.'

Warren, it seems, had been brushing his teeth when the torpedo struck and he was only half-conscious as he was dragged aboard the U-boat. He was revived by the German sailors who asked him if there was anything he wanted.

'Yes . . .' he replied, 'a toothbrush.' And on being handed one he continued brushing his teeth! Heimburg admitted that he could not vouch for the veracity of the anecdote but 'it's a tip-top yarn whether it's true or not,' he added!

Nasmith arrived in the Marmora for his third cruise on 6 November. *E.11* was now the only Allied submarine left in the area. But, undeterred, he patrolled with his usual vigour.

On 15 November he located two large steamers in Bergaz

Bay. He destroyed one but his second torpedo missed and sank two small dhows instead. At Artaki Bay he found two more and this time, using his deck-gun, he sank one and damaged the other. By the beginning of December he was train-spotting again and shot up a locomotive and a number of goods wagons on his favourite stretch of line where the railway skirted the Gulf of Ismid. The Turks sent the destroyer *Yar Hissar* to find him but Nasmith got in first and the enemy warship went to the bottom after being struck by one of *E.11*'s torpedoes. On the 4th he sank a 5,000 ton steamer off Panderma right under the nose of its escort and then, moving on to Gallipoli, he had a duel with a despatch boat which he left beached and on fire.

Stocks joined him with *E.2* on the 10th and, with the aid of his new four-inch gun, helped *E.11* out by bombarding the railway yards at Mudania. Constantinople still held a golden lure for Nasmith and, as on his two previous cruises, he penetrated the Bosphorus to see what he could find. When he returned a large Turkish steamer had gone to the bottom.

UB-15 tried to ambush the 'Terror of the Marmora' as she was called on Christmas Eve but failed and, after a cruise lasting for forty-seven days, a week longer than Bruce's previous record, Nasmith returned to Mudros having increased his score by five large and six small steamers, a destroyer, and thirty-five sailing vessels. For his efforts he was especially promoted to captain after serving only a year in his previous rank.

The Gallipoli campaign was nearly over. Suvla Bay and Anzac Cove had already been evacuated and the final preparations were being made to withdraw the last troops. The attempt to eliminate Turkey from the war by capturing Constantinople had been finally abandoned and the bloody operation was about to become another chapter in the history books and a line on a war memorial.

Nineteen hundred and sixteen was only two days old when Stocks, commander of the last British submarine operating inside the land-locked sea, received his recall signal and *E.2* passed safely through the Straits for the last time. The Marmora reverted to its age-old calm and Turkish shipping plied the ancient trade routes again without fear of attack by British torpedoes or British guns. Within a week, Cape Helles, last foothold on the arid peninsular, was evacuated in a smoothly-organized operation during which only one man was wounded. After nearly eight months of bloody fighting Gallipoli, and all the horrors conjured up by that name, was over.

Although Nasmith, Boyle, Holbrook and the other leading commanders were called back for service in the North Sea, the battle-tested *E.2*, *E.11*, *E.12* and *E.14*, together with the five veteran 'B' class boats and the six newly-comissioned 'H' class submarines, remained behind.

Three problems faced the Admiralty. The *Goeben* and *Breslau*—to give them their former names—were still based at Constantinople and might try to break out and attack our landing operations in Salonika; the Austro-Hungarian Fleet had to be contained in the Adriatic; and the growing menace of U-boat sinkings in the Mediterranean had to be met.

Of the three problems that of the U-boats was the most urgent for, in the first six months of 1916, they had destroyed 256 ships totalling 662,131 tons. And so, while *E.2* remained on patrol off the entrance to the Dardanelles in case the *Goeben* or the *Breslau* appeared, six were sent to join the Otranto Barrage which was bottling up the Adriatic, and the remaining eight were scattered across the central Mediterranean on anti-U-boat patrols.

The war dragged on in the colourless boredom of routine patrols and periodic sweeps, unenlivened by even the barest glimpse of an enemy target. Only brief episodes of activity attracted attention and even these were few and far between. Death not glory became the reward of the British submarine crews in the Mediterranean.

On 15 July, 1916, *H.3*, one of the boats assigned for duty

with the Otranto Barrage, was lost in the Adriatic and, on 9 August, the veteran *B.10* was sunk during an air-raid on Venice.

For two years *E.2* remained on guard outside the entrance to the Dardanelles to cover an attempted sortie by the *Goeben*, until, worn out by her ceaseless vigil, a propeller shaft broke and she had to withdraw to Malta for repairs. Such are the fortunes of war that, at that precise moment, the Germans, unaware of their good luck, decided to send the battle-cruiser and its consort, *Breslau*, down the Dardanelles for a raid on the Aegean. The two warships left Constantinople at 4 am on 19 January, 1918, all set for a quick success.

Goeben struck a mine before she had even cleared the exit from the Dardanelles but, as the damage was only slight, Admiral von Rebeur-Paschwitz decided to continue. The two ships destroyed several British vessels as they sped through the Greek islands but, chased by a group of destroyers, they ran into another minefield and *Breslau* was sunk. *Goeben* suffered further damage but managed to limp into the Dardanelles where she was reported to have grounded a short distance above Chanak.

In a last desperate effort to destroy the battle-cruiser Boyle's old submarine *E.14*, now commanded by Lt-Cdr White, was brought down from Corfu and, on the 27th, she set out on the hazardous passage up the Straits. The Turkish defences had been greatly strengthened since the halcyon days of Nasmith, Boyle and Holbrook, and *E.14* had to struggle hard to get through the net at Chanak. But when White searched further north he found the battle-cruiser gone. Turning the submarine on to a reverse course he headed back towards the net defences. On the way down the Straits he sighted a Turkish auxiliary and all the glorious exploits of the Marmora submarines flashed into his mind. Unable to resist the temptation White fired a torpedo and, as its bubbling wake streaked across the smooth waters, the Turks knew that a British submarine was, once again, inside the Dardanelles. Patrol boats rushed to the spot and a savage barrage of depth-charges forced the unfortunate *E.14* to the surface. White raised the hatch and leapt into the conning-tower, presumably leading his men to the deck-gun, as a hail of shells swept the surfaced submarine. The captain was killed instantly and, as his body rolled into the water, the crippled *E.14* stuck her stern into the air and plunged down into the depths for the last time. After nearly three years of waiting the Turks had gained at least a partial revenge against Courtney Boyle and the other gallant submarine commanders.

On 23 May the submarines operating in the Otranto area finally achieved success when *H.4* caught the German *UB-52* on the surface. Two torpedoes fired at a range of 250 yards sank the enemy boat in fifteen seconds and only two German sailors survived the attack.

But triumph and tragedy stalked hand in hand. During a similar patrol another 'H' class boat sighted a submarine on the surface and closed to 1,000 yards. Her torpedo blew the target out of the water in a violent explosion. Only when the survivors were picked up was it realized that the Italian submarine *H.5* had been sunk in error.

The spark of war which had burst into flame in 1914 when Holbrook had taken *B.11* into the Dardanelles to sink the *Messudieh* and had been fanned to white-heat by the exploits of Boyle and Nasmith in the Marmora, flickered and died as the weary months of 1918 dragged on. By the end of October the Austro-Hungarian Fleet had surrendered and the ancient Ottoman Empire was in the throes of civil war and revolution. Finally, beaten by the merciless blockade and by the triumphant Allied armies on the Western Front, Imperial Germany signed an Armistice and the struggle was over. The blue Mediterranean resumed its idyllic calm and the worn-out, battle-weary submarines huddled together in Malta's Grand Harbour waiting to be towed to the scrap-yards.

But the memory of their acheivements and the gallant deeds of their heroic crews will live forever in the pages of British Naval History. The Submarine Service had demonstrated the strategic power of the 'damned un-English weapon' and, fortunately for England, the lesson was learned and applied when, twenty-two years later, British submarines again swept the enemy from the Mediterranean in the Second World War.

Afternote:
Lt-Cdr White was awarded a posthumous VC for his attempt to torpedo *Goeben*.

CHAPTER TWELVE

'Unsavoury Tin Cans'

WHEN ROGER KEYES left the 8th Flotilla to take up his new appointment in the Dardanelles the zest went from submarine operations in the North Sea. By 1915 the emphasis was changing from attack to defence, to mining operations and anti-U-boat patrols. It was a change reflected in all aspects of naval policy and was brought about by a multitude of causes, not the least of which was the reluctance of the German High Sea Fleet to seek open battle.

On 4 February, 1915, the German Government issued a formal warning that unrestricted submarine warfare was to begin and, within weeks, a spate of sinkings showed that the warning was no diplomatic bluff. This 'sink on sight' policy was directly contrary to International Law and, when the Germans realized that it was likely to force the United States into the war on the side of the Allies, the Kaiser and his military advisers backed down and called off the campaign.

But merchant ships were not the only targets. A cordon of U-boats ringed the main British Naval Bases and several Grand Fleet ships were lost or damaged in torpedo attacks. In 1915, Jellicoe's numerical superiority over the German Fleet was dangerously slender and these piece-meal losses caused considerable anxiety at the Admiralty and in Scapa Flow. Finally, as part of their terror campaign, the U-boats carried out a series of senseless and murderous sorties against the English fishing fleets and individual trawlers in the North Sea.

It was this aspect of the campaign which gave Admiral Beatty's Secretary, Acting Paymaster Spickernell, the idea of decoying the U-boats to their destruction by ambushing them with the old, obsolete 'C' class submarines which had, by then, been relegated to coastal-defence duties. Jellicoe approved the idea and Captain Haggard, commander of the 7th Flotilla at Rosyth, was instructed to organize and train a number of decoy units. By May, 1915, the scheme was ready to be put into operation.

The plan itself was simple. An armed trawler, cruising in an area where U-boats were known to be hunting, towed a submerged submarine astern with a telephone-line connecting the two captains so that orders could be exchanged when the enemy was sighted. If a U-boat surfaced to attack, the submerged submarine slipped her tow-line and crept into a position where she could torpedo the unsuspecting enemy boat.

Success was slow in coming, although, on one occasion, a U-boat was enticed to the surface by the trawler *Taranaki*. However, by sheer bad luck, *C.27*'s torpedo missed and the enemy submarine managed to escape before a second shot could be fired. But there were better things in store and this time *Taranaki* was again to play the lead.

It was the forenoon watch of 23 June and three bells had just rung on the trawler when a U-boat was sighted on the surface some distance astern. The telephone in *C.24*'s control room buzzed and Lt Taylor heard the voice of the trawler's skipper, Lt-Cdr Edwards, crackling down the line. 'Submarine 1,000 yards astern.

C.24 was lying submerged at a depth of forty feet connected to the *Taranaki* by a three-and-a-half-inch wire rope and a hundred fathoms of eight-inch hawser when the enemy contact report was received and Taylor's crew went into their pre-attack routine. And then the release gear of the tow line jammed! The 'panic-crew' of the trawler were already taking to the boats when the telephone rang on *Taranaki*'s bridge and Edwards learned of the jammed tow line. 'Drop it from your end,' urged *C.24*'s captain.

Edwards knew it was dangerous but there seemed no alternative. If *Taranaki* was shelled and sunk by the U-boat and she was still attached to the submarine, she would drag the unfortunate *C.24* down with her. He gave an order and two men ran aft to release the heavy cables. The submarine's bows sank immediately under the weight of the towing hawsers but Taylor knew that he dare not blow the forward ballast-tanks to restore trim in case the U-boat sighted the high-pressure air bubbling to the surface. Relying solely on the motors and the hydroplanes, he coaxed his boat level and then carefully circled round to the attack position.

U-40 was now lying on the surface while her deck-gun pumped shells into the unfortunate trawler—but *Taranaki* played out her decoy role to the end. With periscope up *C.24* stealthily edged closer until she was within 1,000 yards of the quarry; then Taylor pressed the firing button. There was a slight jolt as the torpedo streaked away and, a few seconds later, the U-boat erupted. It was 9.55 am, just twenty-five minutes since Edwards had telephoned the 'enemy sighted' warning to the captain of *C.24*. After picking up *U-40*'s two survivors, her captain and a petty-officer, *Taranaki* and *C.24* sailed back to Blythe feeling very pleased with themselves.

Not so pleased with his morning's work was Commander Geoffrey Layton, one of the veteran captains of the Harwich Flotilla, who was testing the Navy's first steam-driven submarine, *Swordfish*. This monstrosity, an unfortunte product of the experimental tinkering with steam in the days before the war, was proving as unwieldy and difficult as the experts had predicted.

Condensation in the engine-room was short-circuiting the main switchboard and one member of the crew had already been severely burned. In the cramped confines of the boiler room a flash-back had badly seared the face of a stoker but, what was far more worrying to Layton, the boat had an evil tendency to roll over when she was trimmed down for diving.

But, and this was the crux of the entire experiment, she was fast on the surface.

Both Jellicoe and Beatty had been pressing the Admiralty for some time for fast submarines which could accompany the fleet into battle and, when it was realized that even the new 'J' class boats with their vast thirty-six cylinder diesel-engines would prove too slow, steam seemed to be the only possible answer.

In fact there was no answer to the question, for the question itself was wrong. As events proved time and again submarines were lone hunters. They were not, and should not be, integral parts of a large surface fleet organization. But in 1915 no one was prepared to be so dogmatic even though all the evidence of the recent Battle of Heligoland Bight pointed to the dangers and difficulties of surface ships and submarines operating together.

Even Fisher failed to see the inherent weakness in the argument and he, too, was strongly in favour of fleet submarines. 'Without any doubt,' he had written, 'a fast Battle Fleet which can be accompanied always by submarines under all circumstances would possess an overwhelming fighting advantage.'

But, at the same time, he at least had the sense to realize that steam was not the answer. 'The most fatal error imaginable would be to put steam-engines in a submarine,' he had told Jellicoe in 1913. And by 1915 no one had given him a good reason for changing his mind. Certainly Commander Godfrey Herbert who had sailed in the French steam submarine *Archimede* would have fervently echoed the First Sea Lord's words had he been consulted.

Jellicoe was not concerned with technical problems; he only wanted the most efficient fighting fleet it was possible to produce. And that, in his view, meant the inclusion of fleet submarines. So speed *had* to be found and, with an almost Victorian faith in the supremacy of Man's ingenuity over Nature, the experts confidently prophesied that the drawbacks to steam propulsion could be overcome.

Churchill, always favourably disposed to new technical ideas, was quickly won over to the steam camp and, as early as 28 October, 1914, had written: 'steam-engines may be used to supplement oil engines.' And another factor had entered the ring. Everyone, from Jellicoe downwards, was convinced that the Germans possessed U-boats capable of at least nineteen knots on the surface.

Fisher still wavered while Jellicoe and Beatty kept up their pressure for fleet submarines. Commodore Hall and Sir Eustace D'Eyncourt, Director of Naval Construction, both assured the First Sea Lord that technical problems could be overcome and, finally, Fisher took the plunge and, on 4 May, sanctioned the building of four monster submarines of 1,883 tons each with planned speeds of twenty-five knots. They were to be known as the 'K' class and we shall soon learn more of their tragic history.

The trawler decoys of the 7th Flotilla achieved a second success on 20 July when *Princess Louise* and *C.27* came upon *U-23* off the entrance to the Fair Island Channel. Lt-Cdr Dobson, captain of *C.27*, had already missed a German submarine in a similar ambush on 8 June and this time he was determined to succeed. First intimation of impending action came when the control room telephone rang and Lt Cantile, speaking from the bridge of the *Princess Louise*, reported a 'hostile submarine three points on the port bow, distance 2,500 yards.'

Wishing to get closer to the enemy the trawler skipper added:

'I'm going to steam towards her, sir. Don't slip the tow until I give you the word.' And, at that precise moment, the telephone went dead.

Not daring to raise his periscope in case he was spotted, Dobson weighed up the situation and tried to calculate the best time to slip the tow. Suddenly he heard the sound of shots striking the water as the U-boat began shelling the trawler and he decided to act fast.

The tow was slipped and *C.27* steered to starboard to get clear of the *Princess Louise* before Dobson brought her up to eighteen feet for a quick sweep with his periscope. He could see the enemy boat and he began to close the range as he ordered the torpedomen to flood the tubes in readiness for the attack. The 'C' class boats only had two torpedo tubes so there was little margin for error. If both torpedoes missed the enemy would escape before the tubes could be reloaded.

At 8.11 am Dobson steadied *C.27* and grasped the periscope handles firmly as he moved in.

'Range 500 yards.'

One minute later in the same level tone of voice betraying none of the excitement racing through his blood he snapped:

'Port tube—fire!'

C.27 lurched as the torpedo shot from its tube and Dobson watched intently. The U-boat had spotted their periscope, her engines rumbled to life, and she began to move forward slowly. The torpedo shaved past her stern by inches.

Dobson called a new deflection angle, paused for a moment, and then:

'Starboard tube—fire!'

Again the tense silence while the torpedo was running and then, to the cheers of the crew, it struck *U-23* just aft of the conning-tower. *C.27* surfaced quickly and moved in to pick up the survivors. There were only seven, the captain, two officers and four men. The rest had gone to the bottom in their 669-ton steel coffin.

Dobson won the DSO for his success and later, in 1919, won the VC during operations against the Bolsheviks in the White Sea. *C.27* also ended up in Russian waters.

It did not take the Germans long to learn about the trawler decoy ambushes and, before many more months had passed, they took their revenge.

Four days after *C.27*'s success Cdr C. P. Talbot, the man who had made the first combat patrol by a British submarine on 5 August, 1914, left Yarmouth in *E.16* for the Ems. He arrived on the 25th but was forced to remain submerged all day due to heavy air patrols by German sea-planes, which swooped down to attack each time his periscope broke surface. Crawling along the sea-bed near the Borkum Riff lightship *E.16* became entangled in an anti-submarine net and her bows were dragged down at a dangerous angle. Talbot decided to surface and cut the submarine free by hand. *E.16* rose gently to the surface and her captain threw back the hatch ready to inspect the obstruction. An unusual sound made him raise his head and he found himself staring up at the great silver belly of a Zeppelin floating only a few hundred feet above. The hatch lid thudded down as Talbot hurried below and the water foamed and gurgled as *E.16* sought safety in the depths. And not a moment too soon. As she dived the first bombs whistled down from the Zeppelin and exploded harmlessly on the water.

But the bows were still trapped and, for the next hour, Talbot forced the submarine backwards and forwards in an effort to get free, each frenzied lurch being accompanied by a heavy crump on the surface as the airship dropped more bombs. Finally *E.16* ripped herself free and crawled away to lick her wounds in a quieter place.

The submarine's primitive wireless set could only transmit over a distance of forty miles and was, therefore, quite out of touch with the 8th Flotilla's base at Yarmouth. But Talbot knew that it was imperative to warn Cdr Vavasour-Willet, the Flotilla's CO, of the obstruction so that other boats could avoid the area. And so in an age of submarines, aeroplanes, poison gas, and torpedoes, he sent the warning back to Yarmouth—by carrier pigeon.

26 July dawned clear and sunny and *E.16* set off for the area of Terschelling Island in search of fresh targets. Once again a Zeppelin kept them submerged for several hours and, at about 3 pm, three German destroyers appeared over the horizon having been called in, apparently, by the airship. Talbot should

have dived and escaped his hunters but, brought up in the exciting days of the 8th Flotilla, he decided to attack, which, he reminded himself, is always the best means of defence.

The destroyers were busy quartering the area and, after an hour's careful stalking, *E.16* was within 600 yards of the unsuspecting *V.188*. Talbot's first shot took off her bows and, as her companions rushed in to aid their crippled companion, he stood off and awaited another opportunity. Realizing that they were too busy rescuing survivors to hunt him, Talbot brought *E.16* to the surface for a few moments impudently displaying his presence to the enemy.

Without hesitation the two destroyers broke away from *V.188* and roared in at full-speed to dispose of her attacker. Using *E.16* like a matador fluttering his cape at an enraged bull, Talbot drew them into a suitable position and fired a second torpedo. This time it missed and the two destroyers returned to the crippled *V.188*. Talbot repeated his bull-fighting tactics again and, once more, the German warships charged at him. But the third torpedo also missed, which was not surprising as the enemy ships were moving at over thirty knots, and, reluctantly, he moved away leaving the destroyers to continue chasing their own tails for several profitless hours. The sinking of *V.188* won Talbot the DSO and, as we shall see, he continued to harry the Germans for many months to come.

Things, however, were not going too well for the little 'C' boats and their decoy trawlers. On 4 August, the first anniversary of the war, *C.33* was returning to base with the trawler *Malta*, after an abortive patrol off the Norfolk coast, when they ran into a British minefield near Smith's Knoll. *C.33* struck one of the deadly canisters and she sank like a stone taking Lt Carter and all hands to the bottom. The tragedy was repeated on the 29th when *C29* sank off the Humber after running into a defensive minefield and, as with her sister ship, all hands, including Lt Schofield, her captain, were lost when she went down. From now on the Admiralty ordered all decoy units to keep at least fifteen miles clear of mined areas.

But the little 'C' boats had other troubles and the broken telephone-line which had caused Dobson and *C.27* so much difficulty robbed Lt-Cdr Edwards of a killing. *C.23* was sailing in company with the trawler *Ratapiko* when a U-boat was sighted, but a snarled telephone link delayed *Ratapiko*'s 'enemy contact' report and led to confusion over dropping the tow. The little trawler did her best. The 'panic-crew' abandoned ship while the men at her concealed gun in the stern held their fire until they were at almost point-blank range.

But some sixth sense warned the U-boat captain that all was not as innocent as appearances suggested and he escaped before *C.23* could get into position to fire a torpedo. Soon after this incident the Admiralty learned that the Germans knew all about the 'C' boat decoy units and the scheme was abandoned.

By 1916 a number of submarines, including Talbot and *E.16*, were attached to the Grand Fleet under the direct orders of the Commander-in-Chief and, with the depot ship *Titania*, they were constituted as the 11th (Overseas) Flotilla. Their main task was to patrol across the North Sea to Norway in search of enemy minelayers and, on 12 September, *E.16* left Aberdeen bound for the fjords of the Norwegian coast. To the crew it looked like being another barren, routine patrol but Talbot was full of optimism. Before leaving *Titania* he had been informed that a German submarine, the *U-6*, was cruising in the same area and had sunk three British sailing vessels the preceding week. Talbot wanted *U-6*'s scalp to add to his other trophies.

By all the rules the two submarines should never have met. The sea is a big place and, in the days before radar, contact sightings were limited by weather and visibility. But Talbot had that most essential requisite of the successful submarine commander, a nose for the enemy.

Pouring over the charts in the control room he tried to put himself in the mind of *U-6*'s captain. He plotted the three known sinkings and carefully traced the main trade-routes. Where, he asked himself, would Herr Korvetten-Kapitan pounce next? *E.16* changed course for Stavanger. Talbot's eyes swept the empty sea for sign of the enemy submarine and, just as he was about to hand over the task to his First Lieutenant, he stiffened slightly and peered more intently into the eye-piece. The men in the control room exchanged glances. They knew the signs.

'Down periscope. Thirty feet. Steer starboard 30.'

The needles of the depth-gauges dropped a fraction as *E.16* sank a little lower in the water. The helmsman turned his wheel and repeated the new course back to the captain.

'Group up. Full ahead both.'

The soft hum of the motors changed to a higher pitch as the E.R.A.s obeyed the command and Talbot moved back to the periscope.

'Up periscope—bring her up to twenty feet, Number One—steady—flood bow-tubes.'

In the forward compartment the caps covering the tubes opened and seawater flooded into the narrow cylinders. The First Lieutenant reported: 'Bow tubes ready, sir.'

U-6 was on the surface 1,000 yards ahead, steaming a straight course at a steady ten knots. Talbot could see five men in the conning-tower enjoying a smoke in the crisp air.

'Fire both!'

The propellers of the torpedoes bit into the water as they lurched from their tubes and, building up speed to forty knots, they raced towards the unsuspecting U-boat. They both struck together and the noise of the double explosion was audible even in the submerged *E.16*.

Talbot clicked the handles of the periscope back into place.

'Stand by to surface. Shut main vents—blow all tanks.'

The submarine rose into the clear Norwegian air and the clutches to the diesels were engaged as she sped towards the grave of her victim. Debris and oil-scum sullied the water and

E.16's crew made their way down the slippery steel deck to haul the U-boat's survivors aboard. Only five were saved, the same five Talbot had seen standing in the conning-tower, the rest, including the captain, had gone to the bottom. As the Official Historian, Sir Julian Corbett, noted: 'no more was heard of U-boats in this quarter for a long time to come . . .'

But excitements such as this were rare and most submarines returned from their arduous patrols having seen neither sight nor sound of the enemy. Throughout the rest of 1915 the 11th Flotilla stuck doggedly to its task of snapping up enemy mine-layers while the 8th, operating from Yarmouth, kept up the never-ceasing watch on the Heligoland Bight, its captains always hoping for a glimpse of the elusive High Sea Fleet.

There was little time for boredom, and sea-sickness was one of the greatest problems facing the submarine crews on these wearying routine patrols. One officer, Lt Carr, has left a vivid account of conditions aboard a North Sea submarine of the period: 'Only those who have actually experienced the horrors of sea-sickness can have any conception of the agony men who served in submarines suffered when they were sick as a result of a combination of bad weather, foul air, improper food, and breathing an atmosphere saturated with the fumes of crude-oil and gassing batteries. Imagine trying to work out problems in navigation when your stomach was in such revolt that you worked with a pail beside you and cold, clammy sweat, trickling down from your forehead and drip-ping off the end of your chin, smeared the pages of the work book in which you tried to figure. The greatest agony was that one couldn't always be sick. We had to use every ounce of will-power to get on our feet and do our work.' These were the conditions under which men lived, worked, and fought. Not for hours but for days and weeks at a time.

Talbot in *E.16* scored again on 22 December when he caught a German naval auxiliary between the Ems and the Weser but, four days later, the enemy took their revenge.

E.6, the boat Talbot had commanded in the early days of the war, struck a mine off the Sunk Light Vessel and was lost with all hands.

Such was the saga of the Submarine Service in 1915. As one officer wrote after the war: 'The story of the North Sea operations [was] as much a story of men sealed in unsavoury tin cans, wallowing around the shallow ocean and continually at war with Nature, as it [was] a story of dramatic encounters between craft of opposing navies. In this respect the experiences of German submarine officers and men must have been identical with our own.'

CHAPTER THIRTEEN

'God! Ain't they generous?'

NINETEEN SIXTEEN BEGAN badly for the Submarine Service. On 6 January, *E.17* and, twelve days later, the new *H.6*, under the command of Lt Stopforth, were wrecked off the Dutch coast. But, although lost to the Royal Navy, *H.6* subsequently enjoyed a long, if chequered, career. After salvaging the submarine in February the Dutch interned her at Niewediep and later bought her from the British Government, recommissioning her in the Royal Netherlands Navy as *O.8*. During the Second World War she was scuttled at Den Helder, salved by the Germans, and sailed under the swastika as *UD-1* until she was eventually paid off at Kiel in March, 1943, where she was scuttled two years later.

Nineteen sixteen also saw a new development. The Germans had been operating submarine minelayers for some months and, realizing the advantages of laying minefields in enemy waters from submerged submarines, the Royal Navy took urgent steps to catch up. It was impossible in the time available to design and build minelayers from scratch so the Admiralty decided to convert some 'E' class boats for the purpose.

It was a primitive and dangerous conversion. Mines were loaded into the submarine through two holes cut into the ballast-tanks and they were ejected through a hatch in the stern. Each boat carried eight mines and they were retained in position by means of a primitive bolt system. When the bolt was withdrawn from inside the boat the mine floated out through the flooded stern chamber and was moored into position by its sinker.

E.41 was the first boat to be converted for minelaying and

Lt-Cdr Norman Holbrook, VC was appointed as her captain. She made her maiden trip in March, 1916, and by trial and error the techniques of underwater minelaying were gradually mastered.

The minelayers were grouped together in the 9th Flotilla based at Harwich, first under Captain Waistell, who had originally taken over the 8th from Keyes, and then under Captain Percy Addison. The boats were berthed at Parkstone Quay with *Vernon* acting as mining-depot ship.

Service in the 9th Flotilla was extremely unpopular, which was not surprising in view of the thirty-three per cent casualty-rate, and on one occasion, when it was rumoured that the Admiralty intended to decorate every man who completed eight minelaying patrols in the Bight, a veteran submarine seaman was heard to say:

'God! Ain't they generous? The odds are 100 to 1 they'll never have to decorate anybody.'

E.24 was the next boat to join the flotilla and more followed at regular intervals, usually as replacements for submarines lost. And, as the enemy anti-submarine defences grew stronger, losses became ever more frequent until Harwich acquired the nick-name of 'The Graveyard'.

On 7 March the German cruiser *Strassburg* caught *E.5* in the Heligoland Bight when she was surfaced, re-charging her batteries. The submarine dived at top speed but the enemy was even quicker. The cruiser's sharp steel bow cut deep into *E.5*'s thin-skinned hull and she plunged to the bottom in a gurgling rush of water. On the 24th *E.24* ended her short career by being blown up by a mine; whether it was a German mine or one of her own has never been established. Like so many who were to follow she was just listed: 'Overdue—presumed lost.'

H.8 nearly suffered the same fate two days previously but, thanks to the skill of her captain, she lived to tell the tale. She was patrolling submerged off Ameland Gat when a tremendous explosion threw her out of control. The bows went down as the sea rushed into the gaping hole and she struck the bottom at an angle of thirty degrees in eighty-five feet of water. Within seconds all the watertight doors had been securely closed and the immediate danger of flooding was averted. Her captain, Lt-Cdr Johnson, was an RNR officer, the first to be appointed to command of a submarine, but, despite his lack of experience, his superb seamanship saved the boat.

Johnson was a Canadian who had been serving in the Merchant Navy at the outbreak of war. After training he had been sent out to Halifax to bring *H.8* back across the Atlantic. His trip was so successful that the Admiralty allowed him to remain in command when the submarine entered active service and it was during one of his early patrols that *H.8* struck the mine. Now she lay, a shattered wreck, on the bottom of the Heligoland Bight.

The mine had exploded against the starboard forward hydroplane, ripped off the bow torpedo-tube caps, wrecked the tubes themselves, shattered the forward section of the hull, and torn a gaping hole in the Number One ballast-tank. It seemed impossible that any submarine could survive such damage. But Johnson had no intention of surrendering his proud little command to the sea. Although leaking, the forward bulkhead was holding, and he ordered the motors to be run full-astern, at the same time blowing Numbers Two and Three ballast-tanks. *H.8* backed off the sea-bed and, wallowing like a clumsy porpoise, rose slowly to the surface. There was no time for major repairs; they were only a few miles off the German coast and enemy patrols might appear at any moment; but, using what resources they had, the crew quickly plugged leaks, repaired broken pipes, and replaced blown fuses. Then, despite her near-fatal damage, the crippled submarine limped back to Harwich.

The Flotilla Commander's report on the incident contained the following passage: 'The captain reports that although it appeared obvious to all that the boat was lost, the officers and entire crew proceeded to their stations without any sign of excitement, and all orders were carried out promptly and correctly. I would submit that such conduct in the face of certain death is an example of which the whole service may be proud.'

On 25 April Admiral Scheer launched another of his bombardment raids against the East Coast as part of his strategy to trap an isolated section of the Grand Fleet. Hipper's battle-cruisers threw their eleven-inch shells at Yarmouth and Lowestoft, had a brief skirmish with British light forces, and then scuttled back to the protection of the High Sea Fleet which was supporting the raid some distance in the rear.

Yarmouth was, of course, the main base for the 8th Flotilla and as the Germans swept down on Lowestoft three of its submarines were moving out to intercept the battle-cruisers. But only *H.5*, under the command of Lt Varley, stationed off the Cross Sands Light Vessel, was close enough to the town to see the enemy ships looming out of the early morning mist. Varley dived immediately and, running his motors at full power, he tried to bring *H.5* into range. The great guns of the battle-cruisers began their murderous bombardment and a salvo of eleven-inch shells whistled down on the town. Enormous explosions tore the earth open and rocked the houses. Another salvo whistled in from the sea and the scene seemed set for the massacre of Yarmouth.

Then, suddenly, a signal searchlight winked from the bridge of Hipper's flagship. The guns fell silent and, with the precision of Guardsmen on parade, the battle-cruisers wheeled away from the coast and turned back into the North Sea at high speed. A keen-eyed look-out on one of the German ships had spotted *H.5*'s periscope as Varley brought her in for his attack. And the presence of this single British submarine had saved Yarmouth from a prolonged and devastating bombardment.

The range was too great for Varley's torpedoes, and his

elation at forcing the Germans to break off their bombardment was tinged with disappointment at their escape. Two more submarines, *H.10* (Lt Gay) and *V.1* (Lt Lockhart), were patrolling on a line east-north-east of Smith's Knoll, graveyard of the *C.33*, when Hipper's squadron appeared pounding eastwards at maximum speed. But again the range was too great and no torpedoes were fired.

To make matters more frustrating a group of British aircraft which had taken off in pursuit of the fleeing German battlecruisers sighted the two submarines on the surface and, mistaking them for U-boats, swung around to attack. There was no time for recognition signals and both *H.10* and *V.1* dived sharply beneath the waves as the first bombs fell. Fortunately no damage was done but, for a few weeks, the men of the RFC and the RNAS were decidedly unpopular with the officers of the Yarmouth and Harwich flotillas.

Hipper had been extremely lucky for, not only had he eluded the three submarines, he had also avoided *H.7* (Lt Ebblewhite) which was patrolling in the Haisborough Gat, and *E.37* and *E.53* which were still on passage from Harwich to Yarmouth. A golden opportunity to ambush the battle-cruisers had been missed.

There was still one chance left. Lt-Cdr Hewett in the cruiser *Melampus* was leading five submarines from the 9th Flotilla on an interception course and was placing them on a line through which Hipper's ships were expected to pass. At 6 am the German force appeared over the western horizon steaming well north of the trap and only one submarine, *E.55*, under the command of Lt-Cdr Kellett, who had captured the trawler *Ost* and forced her to tow the crippled *S.1* back to Harwich in 1915, sighted the enemy. But, much to Kellett's dismay, the battle-cruisers were four miles away and there was no hope of making a torpedo attack. Once again Hipper had escaped an ambush by the skin of his teeth.

On balance the Germans had scored a victory. U-boats from

the Flanders Flotilla were patrolling the area to cover Hipper's return across the North Sea when one of them, *UB-18*, located *E.22* and, at 11.45 am precisely, a well-aimed torpedo sent the British submarine to the bottom.

The next major operation involving submarines was planned for early May and was, in part, a repeat of Churchill's Christmas Day raid in 1914, brought up-to-date and with a few new trimmings. Two minefields were to be laid in German home waters, one in the Borkum area by the *Princess Margaret*, the other off the Vyl Light Vessel by the *Abdiel*. A few hours later, at dawn, the sea-plane carriers *Vindex* and *Engadine* were to launch their aircraft for an air raid on the Zeppelin sheds at Tondern. To support the surface ships and sea-planes a group of three submarines was to patrol off the Terschelling Bank with a further six working in the area of Horn Reef with the intention of ambushing any enemy warships sent to intercept the raiding force.

The first part of the operation passed off without a hitch although there had been one early alarm when a group of Zeppelins returning from an air raid on Yorkshire had spotted the British ships steaming hard for the Bight, but, fortunately, no concrete defensive action was taken by the German High Command. By 1.30 am, on 4 May, the minefields were laid and soon after 3 am the sea-planes were being hoisted into the water by their mother-ships. And then things began to go wrong.

Of the nine sea-planes deputed for the raid only two succeeded in taking off and one of these, catching her floats in the wireless aerial of the destroyer *Goshawk*, crashed into the sea drowning its pilot. The sole survivor managed to drop some bombs on Tondern and, nearly two hours later, she returned safely and was hoisted back on board one of the sea-plane carriers. Having completed their mission the entire force reversed course and headed back to England.

Two hours later a silver cigar appeared over the horizon and the Zeppelin *L.7* came into view, apparently scouting for the British ships. *Galatea* and *Phaeton* wheeled away to starboard and tried to drive the German airship off with their guns. By a fortunate chance one of their shells struck home in a vital spot and *L.7* lurched away losing height rapidly as the two cruisers returned to take up station with the main force.

E.31, one of the nine submarines taking part in the operation, was unaware of the incident until, when she surfaced a short while later, Lt-Cdr Feilman raised the conning-tower hatch and found the Zeppelin immediately overhead at a low altitude. Assuming they were about to be attacked he sounded the klaxon, slammed the hatch shut, and dived into the control room. *E.31* slid under the waves while her officers and crew waited tensely for the bombs to explode. But nothing happened.

After a few minutes someone suggested that perhaps the Zeppelin had not spotted them but Feilman knew this was impossible. The submarine had been fully exposed on the surface and the enemy airship was only a few hundred feet overhead. Were they waiting to entice *E.31* to the surface so that she could be bombed more effectively? The officers in the control room were still debating the puzzling behaviour of the Zeppelin when Feilman decided to look around at periscope-depth to satisfy his curiosity. The submarine rose gently, the slim brass stalk of the 'scope poked up above the surface, and *E.31*'s captain carefully surveyed the scene.

The Zeppelin was still there but, so far as he could judge, she had lost height. Feilman switched to his high-power attack lens and searched the great silver gasbag for damage. Suddenly he snapped the periscope handles up and stepped back.

'Stand by to surface.'

'Close all vents. Blow main tanks . . .' The orders echoed down the cramped hull as the men worked the valves and levers.

'Gun crew close up.'

'I think somebody's punctured the Zepp's gasbag, Number One. She's clearly losing height. Make a change to shoot down an airship, eh?'

'Pity we can't use a torpedo on her, sir.'

E.31 broke surface, the hatch swung open, and Feilman followed by the gun-crew clambered up into the conning-tower. The low height of the *L.7* made the attack possible for the submarine's gun had only a limited elevation and, with her enormous bulk, it was an impossible target to miss.

'Load H.E. Maximum elevation. Range 300.'

'Gun ready to fire, sir,' shouted the gunlayer.

'Fire!'

It was an incredible sight. The tiny submarine, rolling gently on the sea, spurting flame as her solitary gun opened fire and, hanging above her like a giant silver sausage, the damaged Zeppelin, seeming to blot out half the sky with its immense, bloated bulk.

Flames began to flicker inside the great fabric-covered hull as the shells exploded and, fanned by the wind, the fire took hold, increasing in intensity until it reached furnace heat. *L.7* staggered and dropped towards the sea—the unnerving roar of burning gas pounding in the ears of the men on the submarine. The Zeppelin's crew were jumping from the gondolas in an effort to escape the searing heat—plunging into the sea a hundred feet beneath like tiny black ants, their arms wind-milling in terror as the waves rushed up to meet them.

Suddenly she crumpled like a punctured concertina, her bow and stern folded inwards as her back broke, and the airship struck the sea with a hissing roar. Steam plumed upwards from the red hot metal frame and *E.31*'s crew stared aghast at the terrible end of their airborne enemy.

German surface ships were rushing to the scene and, leaving the Zeppelin's survivors clinging to the wreckage, *E.31* sank down into the sea and made good her escape. After the terrifying fate of the airship the brightly-lit interior of the submarine seemed snug, warm and, somehow, safe.

On 31 May the two great fleets finally came to grips off the Jutland Bank. The battle left the British in possession of the field but it was no easy victory and controversy has raged ever since over the true winner of the battle. Beatty's battle-cruisers in the first part of the battle were out-gunned and out-fought by Hipper's High Sea Scouting Force but, despite terrible losses, lured Scheer's main force into the arms of the Grand Fleet. Jellicoe's dreadnoughts won a decisive victory when they clashed with the German battle fleet and twice Scheer was forced to reverse course to escape damage.

But at dusk Jellicoe's control of the battle seemed to slip through his fingers. The two fleets steamed on converging courses in the darkness and Scheer, by good luck rather than good management, succeeded in cutting behind the Grand Fleet. He smashed the destroyer flotillas drawn up in the rear and, refusing to delay his flight for a single minute, managed to reach the protection of the German minefields before dawn.

When daylight came Jellicoe found himself master of an empty sea. The enemy had fled, claiming victory even as they retreated towards the Fatherland. On a numerical basis their claim was partially justified and, undoubtedly, Scheer's brilliant leadership had saved their weaker force from complete annihilation by the Grand Fleet. But the Germans ran away and never fought another fleet action. On those grounds victory must be conceded to Jellicoe and the Royal Navy.

Both sides had planned to use submarines as part of their battle tactics but, in the event, underwater warfare played no role in the action. Scheer's U-boats, strung out in a patrol line with the intention of ambushing the Grand Fleet as it steamed from Scapa Flow and Rosyth, were blinded by mist and, in fact, were unaware that the British fleet had sailed.

Jellicoe, as part of his plan, had sent three submarines from the Harwich Flotilla to cover the Horn Reefs, and two boats from the 11th Flotilla to cruise east of the Dogger Bank. Four others, with the destroyer *Talisman*, sailed from Blyth at noon on the 31st.

D.1, *E.55* and *E.26* from the Harwich Flotilla were unlucky. They were assigned to the Amrum channel, on a line from the Vyl Light Vessel in accordance with Jellicoe's original plan drawn up on 28 May. This plan, prepared as part of an operation to draw the High Sea Fleet out into battle, was scrapped when the Commander-in-Chief found the enemy was already at sea but, due to the primitive wireless-sets carried by the submarines, their captains were out of range and could not be advised of the change.

According to their instructions they were to remain submerged on the bottom until 2 June. Unaware of the great battle raging in the North Sea they obeyed and, in the early hours of 1 June, Scheer's battered warships passed directly over the three submarines and reached their bases unscathed. But for the unavoidable breakdown in communications *D.1*, *E.26* and *E.55* would have barred Scheer's escape route to Germany and, in all probability, would have sunk several of his crippled dreadnoughts.

Once again communications had proved the weak link in fleet operations with submarines but, for some reason, the weakness was not apparent to the senior admirals and pressure was still applied to the Admiralty to provide fast fleet submarines.

The 11th Flotilla at Blyth was now brought within the organizations of the Grand Fleet and the newly-built 'J' class boats were assigned to it as each was completed. Britain's best submarine-commanders found themselves tied to the apron-strings of the Commander-in-Chief, no longer lone wolves of the sea but disciplined and organized units of a great and intricate fleet.

Martin Nasmith, VC commanded *J.1* backed up by his fellow VC from the Dardanelles, Courtney Boyle, with *J.5*.

Max Horton, now back from the Baltic, was captain of *J.6*. Other leading commanders joined or replaced them as time went by including Warburton, who had served in the old 'B' class boats in the Dardanelles; Noel Laurence, fresh from his triumphs in the Baltic; Goodhart, a pioneer veteran of the old Oversea's Flotilla; and Ramsey. And most of them found themselves commanding the giant steam-driven 'K' class submarines when the 'J' class boats were replaced.

After Jutland both sides retired to their bases to lick their wounds and there was distinct lack of activity in the North Sea for several weeks although, on 19 June, *G.4* sank the Lubeck-bound steamer *Ems* by gunfire after taking off her crew.

In July the Admiralty finally got rid of the *W1*, *W2*, *W3*, and *W4*, of the Armstrong-Laubeuf type, by selling them to the Italian Government on the grounds that they 'were better suited to conditions in the Mediterranean'.[1] The wheel had turned a full circle and Fisher's outburst in 1914 had now been justified. By the end of 1916 nearly every one of the experimental boats had been either sold or converted for use as surface warships and all British serving submarines were direct descendants of the original 1900 Holland design. Goschen's shrewdness in acquiring Holland's patents at the turn of the century was, at last, vindicated.

On 6 July the Harwich Flotilla's *E.26* failed to return from patrol and was reported 'Overdue, presumed lost'. But Lt Varley was quick to avenge the loss. Varley, captain of the Canadian-built *H.5*, had already endured more than his fair share of frustration and disappointment. Two months previously he had seen the German battle-cruisers steam past, out of range of his torpedoes after the Yarmouth raid, and had been mauled by British aircraft into the bargain.

His assigned patrol position in the Heligoland Bight off Terschelling was, in his opinion, 'not worth a damn' and, fully aware of what he intended to do, he left his official patrol-line

[1] The *S.1*, *S.2* and *S.3* had been sold to Italy in September, 1915.

and set off for Borkum. The result of such indiscipline could be serious but Varley reasoned that if he succeeded in making a killing the powers-that-be would forgive him.

Borkum proved to be as empty of ships as Terschelling but, now committed, there could be no turning back and *H.5* continued her piratical course. In the evening of the 13th Varley sighted a flotilla of enemy destroyers. He dived to attack but the German warships were running at speed and his torpedoes missed.

H.5's luck seemed to have run out. She had wasted several valuable torpedoes and, in addition, her periscope was stiff and could not be fully retracted. She had been forced to crash-dive while repairs were being carried out and had lost her complete tool-kit. The prospect looked extremely gloomy. It took the combined strength of three seamen to turn the periscope when Varley carried out a routine sweep but he refused to turn back. And, on the morning of the 14th, his perseverance was rewarded.

U-51 was sighted as she left her base for an Atlantic patrol and *H.5* stalked her carefully. Finally Varley closed the range to 600 yards and his torpedo blew the enemy submarine out of the water in a spectacular explosion. Anxious to obtain some evidence of his success the young lieutenant came to the surface to pick up prisoners but German patrols which had rushed to the spot at high speed opened fire and forced him to dive.

The shallow waters of the Bight nearly became *H.5*'s grave and, before long, the submarine was rocking under the continual detonation of depth-charges. The Germans also used a wire-sweep which the crew heard scrape along the entire length of the hull but somehow they survived and Varley finally headed for home—more than a little apprehensive of his reception.

Despite his success against the *U-51* Varley got a rocket from his flotilla captain who, at one time, was seriously considering the possibility of having the young lieutenant court-martialled. Varley, himself, was unrepentant and made only a half-hearted apology in his patrol report: 'I very much regret to report my slight transgression from orders . . .'

Fortunately the flotilla captain knew the strains and frustrations which his commanders had to endure and in his report to the Admiralty he showed that he, too, was on Varley's side. 'Lieutenant Varley is a very able and gallant submarine officer,' he wrote, 'and although there is no possible excuse for his disregarding his orders . . . it is submitted that his skilful and successful attack on the enemy submarine may be taken into consideration . . . [and] be considered in mitigation of the offence.'

Varley remained in the Admiralty dog-house for a year until he had, in Their Lordship's view, done sufficient penance. Then in belated recognition of his gallantry he was awarded the DSO.

Holbrook, meanwhile, was still carrying out his hazardous mine-laying patrols with *E.41* and, on one occasion, when it was discovered that the mines were defective and exploding prematurely, he brought half his deadly cargo back to base for inspection even though they were likely to blow his boat to eternity at any moment.

In July, during exercises with *E.4* outside Harwich harbour, *E.41* was accidently rammed by the other submarine whose stem tore a nine-foot hole in her hull. She remained afloat long enough for most of the crew to escape but, when she finally plunged to the bottom in sixty-five feet of water seven members of her complement were still trapped inside.

The only officer left on board, Lt Voysey, called the survivors into the control room and told them to stand underneath the conning-tower hatch. Then, as the water crept slowly up their legs, he quietly explained that the rising water was compressing the air inside the submarine and that, in due course, the hatch would be forced open by the pressure, and they would be swept to the surface in a bubble of air. The water had almost reached their necks before Voysey's theory was proved correct. The hatch suddenly sprang open and three of the trapped men, plus the lieutenant, shot to the surface in the gigantic air bubble where they were picked up by the destroyer *Firedrake*.

Three men now remained inside the doomed *E.41*, Stoker Petty Officer Brown, a stoker rating, and an engine-room artificer. They could see the glimmer of daylight through the open hatch and, diving into the water, they swam towards it. The stoker and the E.R.A. succeeded in clambering through the narrow opening but, as the pressure inside and outside the submarine was now equal the hatch closed again before Brown could follow them.

Built of solid steel and forced down by the weight of the sea, the hatch was too heavy for one man to open, and Brown swam back to the engine-room to try the forward torpedo-hatch. Chlorine gas was now seeping through the boat from the shattered batteries and the submarine was in complete darkness but the Stoker Petty Officer did not intend to give in without a fight.

His only hope of escape, however, depended on building up the air-pressure in the engine-room compartment so that, like the conning-tower party, he would shoot to the surface in a bubble of air when the pressure had built up sufficiently. Aided by his intimate knowledge of the submarine's interior Brown began to slowly free the clips and gearing of the hatch so that it could open when the compressed air was ready to do its job.

It was a nightmare task. Everything was pitch-black. The air was strongly tainted with chlorine gas, the oily seawater was up to his waist, and great blue sparks kept flying from the fuses and connections as the water short-circuited the current. Finally the hatch was freed and Brown faced the most critical moment of all.

In order to build up the air-pressure it would be necessary to admit more water into the flooded submarine; the slightest error would drown him. Brown moved to the stern and tried to open the rear door and the cap of the stern tube, but both refused to budge. Crawling back past the main switchboard he received several severe shocks from the exposed terminals but he persevered and attempted to unfasten the weed-trap of the circulating inlet. The butterfly nuts would not loosen and he moved on to the muffler valve. Here, at last, he had success and, as the water surged into the submarine, he crawled back to the torpedo-hatch, climbed on top of the engines, and waited underneath while the air pressure built up.

But the compression was insufficient and, although he managed to lift the hatch three times, it would not raise sufficiently for him to get out. He had earlier dropped the hatch clips on to the floor and they now lay under several feet of water but he knew they must be recovered so that the hatch could be secured or his precious compressed air would seep through the gap and escape. Diving down into the cold, oily water he searched for the clips, located them, and climbed back on top of the engines again to fasten the hatch down tight. When this had been done he set off into the submarine and opened the scuttle of the engine-room bulkhead to admit more water into the compartment. Once more he settled down and waited for the pressure to build up.

At what he judged to be the right moment he struck the clips free and raised the heavy steel door. It lifted a few inches and then slammed down trapping his hand. Using all his strength he forced it open a few inches to release his injured hand and, once more, waited. Finally, after an hour and a half inside the sunken submarine, Stoker Petty Officer Brown succeeded in raising the hatch and he, too, was swept to the surface in a pocket of air. But, before being taken away for medical treatment, he insisted on giving a detailed account of the damage inside the submarine to the salvage officers including details of which valves were open and which bulkhead doors were closed. Then, and only then, did he agree to go below for treatment. As a result of Brown's heroic efforts *E.41* was raised a week later and, after refitting, resumed operational duties with the Harwich Flotilla where she earned fresh laurels the following year.

In August, Scheer made a half-hearted sortie to prove that the High Sea Fleet was still capable of battle after its battering at Jutland, and the submarines were ordered to sea in an attempt to ambush the enemy on their return to base.

Lt-Cdr Turner with *E.23*, Varley, now dutifully obeying orders, in *H.5* and Lt Williams-Freeman in *H.9*, were already on routine patrol in the western approaches to the *Ems* and they were quickly reinforced by Jessop's *E.38* and Talbot's *E.16* who were told to take station along the swept channel between the Amrum Bank and the west of Heligoland.

Six more submarines drawn from the Yarmouth, Lowestoft and Harwich flotillas under Captain Waistell of the 9th joined the destroyer *Firedrake* to take up a position in the southern part of the North Sea, while a further three boats sailed for the Corton Light Vessel with the destroyer *Hind*. It was a tremendous feat of organization and, within two hours of the enemy leaving his bases, all the submarines were heading for their assigned war stations.

There proved to be no contact between the opposing surface fleets despite Jellicoe's high hopes of a major action but the submarines did succeed in inflicting some damage on the enemy. An hour before dawn on the 19th Turner in *E.23* sighted the High Sea Fleet about sixty miles north of Terschelling. He had a grandstand view of the great armada and, having allowed the light-cruisers to pass, he fired a torpedo at Hipper's battle-cruisers as they steamed past. Although the range was only 800 yards the torpedo missed and *E.23* had to dive to avoid a counter-attack from enemy destroyers.

At 3.30 am a further group of darkened ships passed across his periscope and, at 4.37 am, he fired at a second group. This time the range had increased to 5,000 yards and success again eluded him. But Turner felt his luck must turn soon and he remained in position at periscope-depth waiting for the rest of the High Sea Fleet. Half an hour later he was rewarded. A well-aimed torpedo struck the battleship *Westfalen* on her starboard side and her speed dropped away as she struggled to stay in the line. Unwilling to be saddled with a lame-duck Scheer ordered five destroyers to escort the damaged battleship back to Wilhelmshaven and the Fleet steamed on.

Turner turned and followed *Westfalen* and her escorts in the hope of administering the *coup de grâce* but, although he fired two more torpedoes, both missed and the 18,900-ton dreadnought reached harbour safely for repairs. Satisfied that no further attacks were possible *E.23* came to the surface and wirelessed details of Scheer's strength and course back to Harwich for transmission to Jellicoe in the *Iron Duke*. Then, his mission completed, Turner resumed routine patrol.

On the 22nd *E.16* struck a mine and sank to an uncharted grave at the bottom of the North Sea but, by the end of the month, Cdr Raikes and the *E.54* had come upon no less than three U-boats and had sent one, *UC-10*, to the bottom.

Later the same month Scheer's ships set out on another raid —this time with Sunderland as the target. When Jellicoe realized the probable area to be attacked he ordered the 2nd, 3rd and 11th Flotillas, stationed on the Tyne and at Blyth, to sail immediately and patrol seawards between Sunderland and Newcastle while surface forces from Scapa and Rosyth speared southwards searching for the enemy.

But Scheer, in fact, never closed the English coast and the great fleet was soon making its way back to Germany after a brief and indecisive sortie. Passing through the Bight the German warships were sighted by Lt-Cdr John de Burgh Jessop who was patrolling the area in *E.38* of the Harwich

Flotilla. Just after 6.30 am on 19 October he spotted the battle-cruisers steering westwards. They were too far away for attack but Jessop, rapidly calculating an interception course, brought *E.38* to the surface and headed at full-speed for a better position.

Twenty minutes later a group of light-cruisers and destroyers appeared from the east. Diving under the destroyer screen Jessop fired two torpedoes but, thrown off his aim as the submarine momentarily lost trim, they missed. The next time he surfaced he found the entire German Battle Fleet steaming past but, despite his efforts to get into an attacking position, they faded into the distance before the range had been sufficiently reduced.

Then, just as he thought the enormous procession of ships had come to an end, a three-funnelled light-cruiser and four destroyers hove into view. Once again he dived beneath the destroyer screen and as he emerged the other side he found the *München* square in his sights.

Two torpedoes hissed from *E.38*'s bow-tubes and, a few minutes later, two explosions were heard inside the submerged submarine. Thanks to her stout construction the cruiser did not sink and, as Jessop crept quietly away, the destroyers were towing her back for repairs. *E.38* made two further attacks, one on another cruiser, and one on a U-boat, but in both cases the torpedoes missed and Jessop had to return to Harwich only half-satisfied with his results. The Admiralty, however, were more than satisfied and *E.38*'s commander was awarded the DSO for his exploits.

In November two U-boats had grounded near the Bovbjerg Light and, for some reason best known to himself, Scheer took a large segment of the High Sea Fleet out to support the salvage operations.

Noel Laurence, whose original successes in the Baltic with *E.1* were related in an earlier chapter, was now serving with the 11th Flotilla and on 5 November he was on patrol off

Horn Reef in the new 'J' class submarine *J.1*. Just after noon Laurence sighted four German battleships through his periscope at an estimated range of 4,000 yards. There was a heavy swell on the surface and depth-keeping was tricky but *J.1* went to the attack. At one point the heavy swell caused her bows to break surface but, by great good fortune, the German look-outs failed to see her and Laurence drove her down by running his motors at maximum power. It was at this precise moment, as the submarine was diving at full speed, that the enemy dreadnoughts came into his sights.

It was a situation that demanded instant decision and, Laurence fired all four bow-tubes with a five-degree spread as *J.1* thundered towards the bottom. As the torpedoes fanned out he kept his fingers crossed. Everything had been done off balance and in the heat of the moment. Could he, with luck, score a hit with one of them?

Fortune favours the bold and, by incredible chance, two of the four torpedoes struck home. One on the *Grosser-Kurfürst*, the other on the *Kronprinz*. It was impossible to sink an armoured dreadnought with a single puny eighteen-inch torpedo but damage beneath the waterline would take a long time to repair and that, in itself, was an important achievement.

Kaiser Wilhelm was furious with Admiral Scheer for risking his major units to salvage two relatively unimportant U-boats and the German Commander-in-Chief received a sharp rebuke. 'To risk a squadron, and by so doing nearly to lose two armoured ships in order to save two U-boats, is disproportionate, and must not be attempted again.' Laurence also reflected ruefully on his success and later told a fellow officer: 'How I wish I had fired both torpedoes at one ship and made sure of her ... but I thought I could bag them both.'

And so, in a brief flash of success, the British submarine campaign in the North Sea for 1916 came to a close. But not, sadly, before two more boats, *E.30* on 22 November and *E.37* on 1 December, had joined their many comrades on the bottom.

CHAPTER FOURTEEN

'What's your end doing, Sir?'

IT WAS APPROPRIATE that Commander Ernest Leir, the man who was known as the 'humourist of the 8th Flotilla' in the pioneer days of 1914, should have been appointed as captain of *K.3*, the first of the new 'K' class to go into service. For the gargantuan steam-driven 'K' boats were a joke, and a very bad joke at that. Leir, himself, once said: 'The only good thing about 'K' boats was that they never engaged the enemy.'

K.3 was commissioned on 4 August, 1916, and her trials were an augury of things to come. The temperature in the engine-rooms reached alarming heights even with the hatches open on the surface and she also seemed to be a bad sea boat. As a final touch of irony, she was shelled by a friendly patrol-boat off the Isle of Man.

The giant submarine was just as unhappy, apparently, under water. On one occasion the future King George VI, then a very junior officer in the Royal Navy, was taken on a trip when she was being put through her paces. Leir prepared to dive but, instead of gently nosing under the surface, *K.3* dug her bows down hard and headed for the bottom at a steep angle. She hit the seabed with a resounding thump and stayed put with her bows deeply buried in the mud. The water was only 150 feet deep in the bay and, with her enormous length, the submarine's stern poked up out of the sea, her bronze propellers still whirling. Fortunately she was released without damage and, twenty minutes later, was floating obediently on the surface like a regal, if ugly, swan.

Leir took her up to Scapa to join the Grand Fleet and earned the disapproval of Admiral Beatty by saluting the flagship, not with his ensign in the correct manner, but by dipping his funnels. Not even the contrariness of a 'K' boat could quench Leir's sense of humour.

January, 1917, found her on patrol in the North Sea steaming at ten knots in a beam sea with a fresh wind whipping the waves into white crests as the submarine buried her bows into the water. Suddenly an unexpected wave smacked against the port side, sloshed down the funnels, and quickly extinguished the boiler fires. Without power the submarine broached to and tons of water cascaded down the funnels before the crew could close off the hatches. Fortunately Leir still had a small diesel-engine intended for use as an auxiliary and, employing this as a surface propulsion unit, he brought *K.3* safely back to Scapa.

In the middle of 1916 the Admiralty had divided the North Sea into four submarine patrol areas. The Maas patrol (one boat) and the Terschelling patrol (five boats) were supplied by the Harwich Flotilla, and the Horn Reef and Skagerrak patrols, each consisting of four boats, were maintained from the flotillas at Tyne and Tees.

Beatty, the new Commander-in-Chief, disliked the organization and complained that of the eighty-six submarines available, seventy-six were being held back as coast-defence vessels against a possible, but highly unlikely, German invasion. He wanted forty of the newer boats attached to the Grand Fleet leaving only the old 'C' class submarines for coastal defence duties.

The Admiralty did not refuse Beatty's request, but neither did they accept it. After two years of relentless sea war they were still undecided as to what constituted the correct role for the Navy's growing number of submarines and the new Commander-in-Chief was told, rather lamely: 'Submarines now constitute our principal defence against raids of all kinds.'

It seems incredible that the lessons of offensive submarine warfare had not been assimilated by the Admiralty despite the evidence provided by the operations of the Baltic and Marmora Flotillas. And, as we have seen so far, the Home submarines had had little, if any, success against German raiding operations. Yet, in Their Lordships' eyes, the submarine was 'our principal *defence*'.

All energies were now directed against the U-boat menace, a prime example of offensive submarine operations, and, choosing to interpret Beatty's request as one asking for submarines for anti-U-boat patrols, they proceeded to demolish it by statistics. British submarines on patrol, they said, had made contact with enemy U-boats on fifty-six occasions. They had attacked them six times and had only had three successes. But even the Admiralty's statistics were wrong. British submarines had already sunk *U-6*, *U-23*, *U-40*, *U-51* and *UC-10* by January, 1917.

As usual the matter was shelved and it was not until March that Beatty's request was partially satisfied by a general reorganization of the flotillas.

On 19 January *E.36* was lost after a collision in the North Sea following a mining patrol and on the 25th *E.45* was sent to the northern exit from the Bight where she laid a new field. The mines claimed half a dozen innocent fishing-trawlers but failed in their main purpose—that of sinking U-boats travelling to and from their bases.

The anti-U-boat role was stepped-up in other directions. A new flotilla of eight 'C' boats was formed at Harwich 'to intercept enemy minelayers from Zeebrugge' and Beatty's Grand Fleet submarines were strung out on continuous patrol between the Long Forties and the Skagerrak to catch U-boats using the northern route into the Atlantic. Having proved by statistics that anti-U-boat patrols by submarines were a relative waste of time, the Admiralty had proceeded to throw nearly all our submarine strength into precisely that type of operation.

Meanwhile the elephantine 'K' boats were still suffering from their never-ending teething troubles. *K.2*, commanded by Baltic veteran Noel Laurence, caught fire during her first trials in Portsmouth dockyard. She had submerged in a dock basin for diving-tests when a sudden explosion sent a sheet of flame searing through the engine-room. With typical lack of foresight there were no fire extinguishers aboard and Laurence brought her back to the surface so that the crew could douse the flames by tipping buckets of water down the hatch.

At Devonport *K.6* was carrying out her first diving-trial in one of the basins and, having gone down, refused to come up again. After two hours trapped inside the submarine a dock-yard inspector traced the fault to the compressed air system and *K.6* returned to the surface like a lamb. Having witnessed the near-tragedy many of the dockyard workers refused to go down a second time and it was several days before the next test could be carried out.

K.4 went aground during her initial trials and *K.11* was quickly back in the repair yards for a new generator after an influx of salt water had ruined the original.

But on 29 January the 'K' boats suddenly ceased to be a joke. From that day onwards 'K' stood for *Killer*. At eight o'clock that morning Lt-Cdr Godfrey Herbert joined *K.13* at Fairfield Shipbuilding Company's yard for her final acceptance trials. Aided by tugs the great submarine was carefully edged out into the Clyde and, after an embarrassing brush with the steamer *Sonnava*, set off for Gareloch where she was to carry out her diving-tests.

K.13 was well-loaded. In addition to her regular crew of fifty-three, she also carried fourteen directors and employees of Fairfields, thirteen other civilians, and the captain and engineer officers of the *K.14*. On her arrival at Gareloch she picked up another of Fairfield's directors and Professor Percy Hillhouse, the company's naval architect. Everything went smoothly on the first run down the loch and, by lunch-time, signing of the acceptance forms looked like being a mere formality. Leaving two of the Fairfield's men behind *K.13* set out for her final dive with eighty people aboard.

Herbert took her down at 3 pm after a leisurely but very careful check that everything was functioning correctly. One indicator was seen to be flickering but Engineer Lt Lane said this was due to faulty wiring causing a bad contact. It was an important indicator. It showed whether the engine-room ventilators were fully shut before diving. *K.13* dipped under the water with the unhurried ease of a slothful whale and Herbert ordered her to be trimmed for twenty feet. Suddenly the quiet routine was broken.

'The boiler room is flooding freely, sir.'

The E.R.A. slammed and secured the water-tight door to the boiler room behind him as he delivered his spine-chilling message and, almost at the same moment, Lane shouted up the voice-pipe:

'Surface at once. The boiler room is flooding.'

Herbert was the last man on earth to be ruffled by an unexpected emergency, his past experiences were proof of that, and he immediately gave the order to blow tanks and surface.

The crew worked manfully. Wheels were spun, valves were turned, and levers were moved. The forward ten-ton keel was dropped and compressed air hissed from the ballast-tanks. The submarine should have risen but the depth-gauges told a different story—they were still sinking. At that moment Coxswain Oscar Moth confirmed Herbert's worst fears.

'She's out of control, sir.'

K.13 came to rest with her stern on the bottom, fifty feet down, inclined upwards at four degrees. As Herbert gave the order to stop motors spouts of water shot out of the voice-pipes and they had to be quickly plugged before the control room was flooded as well. Then a fire broke out on the main switchboard and the men had to beat it out with their bare hands. By now it was clear that the entire after-end of the boat was flooded and *K.13*'s captain decided to take a roll-call. Only forty-nine of the eighty men on board the stricken submarine answered as their names were called out.

Professor Hillhouse, the naval architect, produced his slide-rule and began calculating how much air was left and how long it would take for forty-nine men to consume it. His answer was not encouraging—only eight hours at the most.

By four o'clock the men on the surface were getting worried at the submarine's failure to reappear and Michell, the captain of *E.50* which had also been undergoing trials that day, sent an urgent message back to the Clyde reporting a probable accident to *K.13* and requesting salvage apparatus. Six hours later the gunboat *Gossamer* set out for Gareloch and the salvage vessels *Tay* and *Thrush* were also ordered to leave.

The confusion was incredible. *Gossamer* arrived at midnight with a diving-suit but no diver and, when one was finally found, the suit proved to have perished with age and nearly drowned its occupant. *Thrush*, too, arrived with neither a suit nor a diver.

After an eternity of waiting, when every minute was precious to the men trapped below, one of Fairfield's divers made the descent and began inching his way along *K.13*'s hull. A morse message tapped out from inside the submarine was picked up and relayed back to the surface: 'ALL WELL BEFORE ENGINE ROOM BULKHEAD.'

Inside the submarine conditions were worsening. The air was slowly poisoning the trapped men and many of them were just lying down awaiting the inevitable end. According to the Professor's calculations they had run out of time.

Herbert, however, was still confident that salvage was possible and he discussed various schemes with Goodhart, the captain of *K.14*, who was travelling as a passenger for experience. Together they planned to get into the conning-tower, build up the air pressure, and then open the hatch so that Goodhart would be blown to the surface. Herbert decided he should remain behind with his men.

A detailed report was written indicating conditions inside the *K.13* and a list of survivors was appended. The paper was placed in a small metal cylinder for safety, and preparations, which included cutting a hole in the side of the conning-tower and fitting an improvised sea-cock, were begun for Goodhart's escape attempt.

At midday the two climbed into the conning-tower and closed the lower hatch. All now depended on their nerve and skill. Goodhart opened the valve to let in the water and, gradually, the air pressure built up under the compression. When the water-level had reached their waists Herbert turned on the compressed air and, while he held on to the steel supports, Goodhart pulled the clips and opened the hatch.

He swept out of the compartment as the air caught him and Herbert caught a quick glimpse of his body streaking up through the water. Then, surprised by the power of the compressed air, *K.13*'s captain found himself being forced upwards through the hatch as well. There was nothing he could do to resist the pressure and, covering his face with his hands for protection, Herbert allowed his body to be swept out of the submarine.

On board *Thrush* the first knowledge of the escape attempt was a tremendous upheaval in the water as the air rushed to the surface from the open hatch. Suddenly a head bobbed into view, someone made a grab, and Commander Herbert was dragged to safety. But there was no sign of Goodhart.

Once he had been revived Herbert told the salvage officers the precise condition of the crippled submarine now lying on the bottom of Gareloch fifty feet below. Compressed air was their only hope of survival—compressed air to help support the leaking bulkhead from the engine-room, to replenish the poisoned atmosphere inside the *K.13*, and, most important of all, to enable the survivors to blow the forward ballast-tanks so the bows could be brought up to the surface.

High pressure air-hoses were taken down but the divers

could not find any way to connect them. Capt. Frederick Young, the Naval Salvage Adviser, who had just arrived from Liverpool suggested making an escape tube. And, while the men on the surface pitted their wits to find a solution, the men trapped inside *K.13* were slowly dying.

Hopes rose at six that evening when the divers finally managed to connect the air-hoses to the submarine but they were quickly dashed when it was found that, for some reason, the air was not getting through the valve. And as they worked and sweated the divers could hear the pathetic morse-code taps from inside the hull: GIVE US AIR. GIVE US AIR.

Soon after midnight the trouble was located in the air-hose itself which was blocked with ice. In a matter of minutes it was cleared and air began hissing into the crippled submarine.

The effect on the crew was little short of miraculous. Men who had for hours been lying half-dead on the steel floor roused themselves and helped fill the compressed-air bottles while others checked valves and gauges ready to blow the tanks. Finally, just after 3 am, the bows lifted off the mud.

A trawler passed a stout six-and-a-half-inch wire under the forward part of the submarine to prevent her sinking back to the depths again but, despite their efforts, the bows themselves were still five feet below the surface. A further tube was fitted in place by the divers so that air and food could be passed down to the trapped men while the salvage operations continued. By 6.30 am they had established voice communication with the survivors.

Some of the salvage officers considered that time was now on their side. The men inside the submarine had food and air in unlimited quantities and preparations to lift the *K.13* could proceed slowly so that every precaution could be taken. But both Michell and Herbert disagreed. The vital bulkhead was still leaking and, under the tremendous pressure of water inside the engine-room it must soon collapse. Time, in their view, was just the thing they did *not* have.

Once again the heavy steel wire latched under the submarine's hull was tautened and slowly, inch by inch, the forward end of *K.13* was lifted until the bows were ten feet clear of the surface. Herbert decided to bring the men out through the torpedo-tubes but, before any instructions could be passed, the submarine lurched, slid back slightly, and came to rest with the bottom of the tubes two inches under water.

K.13 was at an angle of sixteen degrees with her stern rammed deep into the muddy bottom of the loch. The main fuse had blown on the switchboard and the interior, lit only by a solitary light and three torches, was otherwise in complete darkness.

After a great deal of argument amongst the experts on the surface they accepted Herbert's suggestion that a hole should be cut in the bows with an oxy-acetylene torch. Once again there were delays and set-backs and it was three o'clock in the afternoon before the first hole, two feet square, had been cut through the outer skin of the forward deck. There was another delay when it was found that the space between the outer and inner hulls was flooded and it was some time before the men inside the submarine could work the valves for the water to drain away.

But, finally, the torch bit through the steel of the inner skin and the escape hole was ready. Then, one by one, the exhausted men were helped out of the submarine until all forty-seven were safely aboard the fleet of motor-boats which had gathered in readiness. Just fifty-seven hours had elapsed since Herbert had taken *K.13* down on that fateful dive.

The salvage men found Goodhart's body wedged inside the wheelhouse. He had apparently been blown through the hatch with such force that his head had struck the roof of the bridge and, knocked unconscious by the blow, he had drowned. His death was a sad blow to the Royal Navy. An experienced submarine captain, he had taken *E.8* out on the first combat patrol of the war and, later, while serving in the Baltic with Horton, had sunk the armoured cruiser *Prinz Adalbert*. Now he was gone, a victim of the evil hoodoo of the 'K' boats.

His place as captain of *K.14* was taken by Cdr Ferdy Feilman, the man who had shot down Zeppelin *L-7* when he was in command of *E.31*. Herbert, however, left the Submarine Service completely and took over a flotilla of armed trawlers. Having survived disasters in *A.4*, *D.5* and *K.13* it seems that the Admiralty did not want to strain his luck too far. But he never forgot his pioneer days with the Submarine Branch and, in the Second World War, he returned to Fort Blockhouse where he carried out a number of important experiments in connection with the development of Chariots, the two-man human torpedoes.

K.13 the villain of the piece, was towed back to Fairfield's yard, refitted, and commissioned back into the Royal Navy as *K.22*. Her new captain was Charles de Burgh, a former commander of *G.8*, and Oscar Moth, who had spent fifty-seven hours trapped at the bottom of Gareloch, rejoined her as coxswain. But, although re-numbered, *K.22* was to figure in another 'K' boat disaster before many more months had passed.

Early in March two submarines of the 10th Flotilla were sent to patrol the U-boats' exit route from the North Sea. *G.13*, despite her number, had a lucky trip. A U-boat was sighted on the surface off Muckle Flugga and Lt Bradshaw, after a copybook attack, sank her with a single torpedo. His victim was the *UC-43* outward bound for her hunting grounds along the busy shipping-routes of the North Atlantic.

Although never officially confirmed, Bradshaw also attacked and damaged the giant submarine *Bremen* which, with *Deutschland*, acted as underwater freighters shuttling between New York and Germany. *G.13* sighted the U-boat at long range and her first two torpedoes, fired from bow-tubes, missed. Bradshaw swung round the submarine and fired his starboard beam-tube and, when this also failed to score, came around in a complete circle to aim a pot-shot from his port beam-tube.

But this too, missed the target, and with *Bremen* rapidly vanishing into the distance, Bradshaw played his last card. Bringing *G.13* end-on to the U-boat he released his last torpedo from the stern-tube. The range was 7,000 yards and any chance of success seemed impossibly remote, even assuming that the torpedo would travel that far under its own power. But the law of averages swung his way and in the distance he heard the sound of an underwater explosion.

The Admiralty, however, were not convinced and refused to credit *G.13*'s captain with a positive sinking. It was only after the war that Bradshaw's claim was vindicated. The *Bremen* had been struck by a torpedo but she did not actually sink. Despite serious damage her crew succeeded in getting her back to Germany for repairs and she was still afloat in 1918, converted to a surface vessel.

But triumph, as always, was balanced by tragedy. When Bradshaw returned to the 10th Flotilla's depot-ship anchored in the Tees he learned that *E.49* had struck a mine in the Balta Sound on the 12th and that his friend Lt Beal and all hands were missing.

Later the same month the long-awaited reorganization of the submarine flotillas was announced. Beatty's repeated request for more submarines at Scapa Flow was ignored and, instead, the Admiralty concentrated the main flotilla strength on trade protection duties. Although Jellicoe was now First Sea Lord, it was clear that Whitehall still regarded the submarine as a defensive weapon.

Beatty was furious with the Admiralty for refusing to supply the Grand Fleet with what he considered to be adequate numbers of submarines and, as if to demonstrate his power as Commander-in-Chief, he took over the entire 10th Flotilla, transferring it lock, stock, and barrel, from the Tees to Scapa Flow. But if Bradshaw, Warburton, and the other eager young captains of the 10th thought that service with the Grand Fleet meant offensive operations they were doomed to disappointment. Beatty, like the Admiralty, only wanted submarines for anti-U-boat duties.

Even the new 12th Flotilla comprising *K.1*, *K.2*, *K.4*, *K.6*, *K.7* and *K.8* found themselves relegated to anti-U-boat patrols, a situation so farcical that it can be compared with an elephant hunting a flea. Although capable of twenty-five knots on the surface the unwieldly 'K' boats took four minutes to dive and, once submerged, were in many cases slower than their German targets. To pit one of these steam monsters against an agile well-handled U-boat was the height of absurdity yet, so skilled were their captains, that even the ridiculous sometimes worked.

Operation B.B. designed 'to force enemy submarines to dive through certain areas occupied by destroyers, so that they would be on the surface while passing through adjacent areas occupied by our submarines' was one of Beatty's brain-waves. Forty-nine destroyers and seventeen submarines took part and the 'K' boats were assigned a prominent role.

On 16 June *K.7* was running submerged in the Fair Isle Channel when the destroyers *Observer* and *Rocket* located her. She was mistakenly identified as a U-boat and, within minutes, depth-charges were exploding all around her. Her captain, Gilbert Kellett, managed to get clear before coming to the surface and plaintively signalling that he was 'on their side'. Later that same day *K7* found a U-boat on the surface running south. Kellett's first torpedo missed but, determined to chalk up the 'K' boats' first victory, he let go with four more torpedoes seventeen minutes later. One of the group struck the U-boat amidships but, with typical 'K' luck, it failed to explode. Deciding that *K.7* might do better on the surface Kellett brought her up and, using his superior speed, began closing the enemy boat.

A torpedo hissed from the starboard tube but *U-95* dodged

it with casual ease and then crash-dived out of further trouble. Now it was *K.7*'s turn to be exposed on the surface. But Kellett decided not to play any more. Black smoke belched from the submarine's funnel and she steamed away from the area as fast as she could.

K.1 also got into trouble during Operation B.B. Her captain, Cdr Charles Benning, took her into a shallow anchorage near Bow Rock and ran her aground. She was not seriously damaged but, in accordance with the Royal Navy's disciplinary regulations, Benning faced court-martial. His plea that rats had eaten the chart of the anchorage was accepted by the board and the charges were dismissed. It was an excuse that only a 'K' boat captain could have got away with.

One favourite story in the 12th Flotilla concerned the First Lieutenant who, during a diving trial, telephoned the captain from his control position in the stern and exclaimed excitedly: 'I say, sir. My end's diving. What's your end doing?'

July, 1917, was a mixed month with success and disaster equally shared. On the 21st *C.34*, engaged on anti-U-boat patrols near the Shetland Islands, was an unfortunate victim of her prey when, while cruising on the surface, she was torpedoed and sunk by *U-52*.

Across the North Sea in the Heligoland Bight Norman Holbrook had just completed laying a new minefield with *E.41* when he sighted a German auxiliary escorted by several patrol-boats. Using all the skill and cunning which he had previously demonstrated while captain of *B.11*, Holbrook brought his new boat into an excellent attacking position, and his first torpedo struck the auxiliary fair and square amidships. Then, as his victim listed to starboard with clouds of steam erupting from her shattered boilers, he brought *E.41* to the surface and, as Talbot had done on several occasions, invited the escorts to charge in for a counter-attack.

The Germans were only too delighted to oblige and, as the patrol-boats steamed towards the submarine, Holbrook swung eastwards and, still running exposed on the surface, drew them in the direction of the newly-laid minefield. On reaching the fringe of the field *E.41* dived sharply hoping to lure the patrol-boats over the mines as they continued the chase. But the enemy swung away as the submarine dived, doubtless fearing a torpedo attack, and Holbrook's very gallant ruse ended in failure.

During 1917 the decoy trawler system had been extended to some of the 'Q' ship operations and, on 15 August, Lt-Cdr Richardson in *D.6* was cruising in company with the top-sail schooner *Prize*, a decoy-ship well armed with concealed guns, 150 miles north-west of Rathlin Island. *U-48*, unaware that the innocent-looking sailing-boat was a Royal Navy warship, closed in on the surface while Richardson, about three-quarters of a mile astern, dived for a counter-attack. Suddenly *Prize* hauled down her decoy Swedish flag, hoisted the White Ensign, and opened fire on the U-boat. Heavy seas prevented *D.6* from getting close enough to launch her torpedoes and, having been struck by two shells, *U-48* quickly submerged to seek safety in the depths.

But this was not the end of the story. Now aware of the true identity of the little schooner the U-boat captain followed her to the north-west and, at 1.30 am on the 14th, a well-placed torpedo blew her to pieces. *D.6* was following two miles astern and the men on her bridge saw the explosion but, although they hurried to the scene, not a single member of the 'Q' ship's crew survived.

After their initial successes the 'Q' ships were a complete failure and, although they continued operating until the end of the war, no U-boats were destroyed either by decoy-ships working independently or in conjunction with submarines after August, 1917.

But, despite their lack of success, the steady drain of losses to the submarine flotillas continued unabated. *E.47* failed to return home from a North Sea patrol on 20 August and, less than a month later, G.*9* was sunk by one of our own destroyers in an unfortunate sequence of mistaken identities.

The submarine had been the first offender. Seeing the destroyer a few hundred yards away she had failed to identify her correctly and fired a torpedo which, for some reason, did not explode. The abortive attack, however, warned the destroyer that a submarine, presumably German, was in the vicinity and, cramming on full-speed, she swung round to ram. Her sharp steel bows cut into G.*9*'s hull and the submarine was ripped completely in half. Only one man, a stoker, out of her thirty-one man crew was saved.

Defensive patrols remained the primary function of the submarine flotillas throughout the autumn and by the end of September a total of thirteen submarines, with the depot-ships *Vulcan* and *Platypus*, were stationed at Buncrana on Loch Swilley to escort the inward-bound Atlantic convoys through the U-boat-infested waters north and west of Ireland. The inclusion of a sea-plane carrier in the escort organization did, however, indicate that the Admiralty was, at last, beginning to understand the correct principles for countering the U-boat menace.

Although well clear of the convoy areas British submarines continued to score a few successes against the enemy and, in October, *E.45* discovered and destroyed *UC-62*. The action was fought at dawn and began when Lt-Cdr Watkins sighted shell flashes on the horizon. Arriving at the scene on the surface he found *UC-62* shelling a neutral Dutch merchantman and, before he was sighted by the enemy, he took *E.45* down to periscope-depth to attack.

The submarine crept to within 400 yards of the U-boat before firing and the torpedo exploded directly beneath the conning-tower. There was a tremendous flash and *UC-62* plunged to the bottom like a stone, joined a few minutes later by the unfortunate Dutch ship which had been holed beneath the waterline by the German's shells.

Such successes, although obtained solely by chance, encouraged the Admiralty in their mistaken belief that submarines were the most effective weapons for use against the U-boats and, for ten days in October, four submarines from the 10th and 11th Flotillas *G.3*, *G.4*, *G.7* and *G.11* were assigned to watch a gap in the minefields through which U-boats were thought to be passing.

It was an elaborate operation involving more than one hundred surface ships ranging from flotilla leaders to drifters but bad weather marred many aspects of the plan and, in fact, the four submarines did not make a single enemy contact during the entire period. The special mined nets appear to have been more successful and, when the operation was concluded, the Admiralty claimed to have sunk *U-50*, *U-66* and *U-106*, a claim later confirmed by the Germans.

Although the submarines had failed to play any part in the sinkings they continued to obtain isolated successes, usually in lone-wolf operations when the dice of chance rolled in their favour. It was during one such incident that Lt P. Phillips and *E.52* caught and sank the *UC-63*.

The U-boat was cruising on the surface at night and, according to the sole survivor, the men on the bridge were chatting to each other instead of keeping look-out. *E.52*'s torpedo was not sighted until it was only yards away and *UC-63* had no time to take evasive action. Even more remarkable was the fact that the British submarine was running on the surface throughout the entire attack. As one of *E.52*'s officers said afterwards: 'Victory goes to the alert and the conning-tower of a submarine is no place in which to gossip or doze. The attention of the Officer of the Watch on the *UC-63* had probably not been distracted for more than a few seconds, but it was long enough to cause death to all but one of her crew.'

Further south, in the area covered by the 5th Flotilla and the Dover Patrol, the old coast-defence submarine *C.15* enjoyed similar luck when she sank *UC-65* while she was trying to force the barrage across the Straits. *UC-65* was luckier than her two sisters *UC-62* and *UC-63* in that two officers and three seamen survived the sinking.

Lt Blacklock in the Harwich Flotilla's *E.29* also had a brush with a U-boat but, on this occasion, the enemy got away. It was a thrilling chase and one which exemplified the courage of the British submarine captains in their dangerous task. The U-boat was sighted on the surface at 1,000 yards but, as Ronnie Blacklock took *E.29* down to attack, the U-boat commander sighted the British submarine and began diving at precisely the same time. Now that both boats were submerged it became a game of blindman's buff and Blacklock used the hydrophones to pick up the sound and direction of the U-boat's engines. 'If we pick him up,' he told the crew, 'we'll try to ram him underwater.' Fortunately for *E.29* the enemy boat was not located and, after a long search, the hunt was called off. Had she rammed the enemy as Blacklock intended it is highly likely that she would have plunged to the bottom alongside her victim.

On 16 November the 12th Flotilla was ordered to sea with the Grand Fleet for an offensive sweep towards Denmark. Led by the light-cruiser *Blonde* the boats behaved quite well although there were inevitable difficulties in station-keeping when the submarines were running in line ahead. But it was too good to last.

At approximately 10 pm on the 17th *Blonde* altered course in accordance with operational orders. *K.1* slowed down rapidly as the cruiser swung away and, as the line bunched up, *K.4* running immediately behind, rammed the boat ahead. There was a sickening crunch of torn metal and *K.1*'s stern began sinking as water flooded in. Prompt action by the crew in closing the watertight doors saved the submarine from the immediate danger of sinking but it was clear that she was crippled. *Blonde* came alongside, took off the crew, and tried to take the battered *K.1* in tow but as the weather deteriorated during the night it became clear that the submarine could not be saved and, at 10 pm, the cruiser's guns opened fire to finish her off.

Back at Scapa the morale of the 12th Flotilla fell to a new low when it was learned that all the 'K' boats were to be fitted with new bulbous bows. The inference that they were not seaworthy in their present condition did nothing to allay the fears which the men felt for the lumbering monsters each time they left harbour.

The men of *K2* nearly rose in mutiny over an imagined grievance concerning Ship's Prayers and when the crew of a 'J' class boat were ordered to transfer to the new *K.22*, the refitted and rechristened *K.13*, a number of them reported sick with a mysterious illness which enabled them, fortuitously, to evade the draft.

In December the steam-driven boats were transferred from Scapa to Rosyth and reconstituted into two flotillas, the 12th under Capt. Charles Little, one of the original Harwich veterans, in the cruiser *Fearless*; and the 13th under the irrepressible ex-captain of *E.4*, Ernest Leir with the cruiser *Ithuriel*. But, once again, disaster was awaiting just around the corner.

Errors and accidents were not, however, confined to the 'K' boats. Lt Coltart in *G.6* was returning to Devonport on 18 December when she came to the surface 500 yards from a convoy. The American destroyers escorting the convoy took her to be a U-boat and they turned towards the submarine with their guns blazing. There was no time to exchange recognition signals and Coltart dived *G.6* deep hoping to escape. The destroyers thundered overhead dropping depth-charges and the sea boiled and erupted in fountains of froth as they exploded deep under the surface. *G.6* was thrown about like a cork but, by the skilful control of her captain and crew, she held her depth and escaped serious damage. Finally, convinced that he had made a kill, the destroyer captain swung away and returned to Plymouth.

When Coltart and his officers entered the officer's mess that evening they found the commander of the destroyer explaining to all and sundry how he had sunk the 'U-boat': 'She broke surface right under our bows. We fired a couple of shots that seemed to strike home; then we rammed her and, to make sure, dropped three depth-charges right over the spot where she had disappeared.'

G.6's captain elbowed his way over to the American. 'Sorry to disillusion you, old chap,' he said languidly, 'but it was my boat you tried to scupper. If a whisky-and-soda will make up for the DSO you won't get, you're welcome to one on me.'

CHAPTER FIFTEEN

'Remain on Patrol'

JANUARY, 1918, was the Submarine Service's blackest month since the beginning of the war. On the 6th the Canadian-built *H.5*, the submarine which had sunk *U-51* in 1916, was lost following a collision in the Irish Sea and, eight days later, *G.8* failed to return from a North Sea patrol. *H.10*, another of the Canadian-built boats, was lost on the 19th and, as recorded in Chapter Eleven, Geoffrey White's *E.14* was sunk by the Turks on the 28th. The last day of the month witnessed the destruction of *E.50*.

This latter boat had enjoyed an exciting career and had been on trials in Gareloch on the day *K.13* had sunk. On one occasion, when under the command of Kenneth Michell, she had accidently rammed a U-boat. Both submarines had been running blind underwater and, by chance, *E.50*'s bows had cut into the enemy's bow quarter. The U-boat rolled under the impact and the British submarine somehow rode up so her bows were resting on top of the German's forward deck.

Realizing that the U-boat was trapped, and hearing her pumps working flat-out to try to combat the water flooding into her hull, Michell turned to his First Lieutenant. 'Must be more damaged than we are,' he observed, 'it sounds as if he's leaking badly—and he seems damned anxious to get topside. Flood all our tanks. We'll keep him down.'

As *E.50*'s ballast-tanks filled with water she sank towards the bottom taking the damaged U-boat with her. The crew could hear the German sailors frantically pumping and blowing their tanks in an effort to regain buoyancy but gradually, the sounds died away into ominous silence. Michell waited a few minutes and then, deciding that the U-boat was now flooded, he went astern to allow his enemy to sink to the seabed on her last dive. After the war, however, it was learned that the U-boat had managed to survive the collision. Although badly damaged she had succeeded in limping home and, after a spell in dock, had returned to active operations.

But five losses in a single month were insufficient to satisfy the evil hoodoo that brooded over the steam driven 'K' boats and February saw a spectacular disaster involving no less than nine of the smoke-belching monsters of the 12th and 13th Flotillas.

Their Rosyth base now housed nearly every prominent captain in the Submarine Service. Noel Laurence, the first man into the Baltic with *E.1*, commanded *K.2*; Geoffrey Layton, skipper of the experimental steam-submarine *Swordfish*, had *K.6*; Claude Dobson, who had sunk *U-23* with the little *C.27*, was in *K.10*; and David Stocks, whose veteran *E.2* had seen valiant service in the Dardanelles, was in command of *K.4*. *K.8*'s captain was Ross-Turner who, in 1916, had torpedoed the *Westfalen* with *E.23*, and *K.14* was skippered by Thomas Harbottle, one of the 'E' boat commanders from the Mediterranean. Samuel Gravener from the old 'B' class boats in the Dardanelles had *K.7* and Charles de Burgh, another North Sea veteran, commanded *K.22*. The other captains, Herbert Shove, John Hutchings, Thomas Calvert, John Bower, Brownlow Layard, and Henry Hearn, were all experienced submarine-commanders although they were not so well known to the public as the others.

The saga of disaster began when Beatty's staff devised Operation E.C.1, a cruiser exercise involving almost the entire Grand Fleet *and* the two 'K' boat flotillas. Sir Hugh Evan-Thomas, leader of the famous 5th Battle Squadron at Jutland and now commander of the Rosyth Force, led his ships out of the Forth in the afternoon of 1 February bound for a rendezvous with Beatty's fleet.

The 12th Flotilla under Capt Little comprised *K.4*, *K.6*, *K.7* and *K.3* while the 13th, led by Leir in *Ithuriel*, consisted of *K.11*, *K.12*, *K.14*, *K.17* and *K.22*. *Courageous* was at the head of the long, snaking line followed by Leir's flotilla. Then came four battle-cruisers, the four submarines of the 12th Flotilla, and the battleships.

It was dark by the time they reached the mouth of the estuary and, to add to the difficulties of night navigation, a light mist hung over the water. Leir's boats were travelling at nineteen knots each following the shaded, blue stern-light of the submarine ahead. Then, suddenly, as they approached the vicinity of May Island a group of minesweeping trawlers, ignorant of the fleet operation in progress, steamed across the line.

K.11 cut speed and turned to port. *K.17* followed suit but Harbottle in *K.14*, third submarine in the line, held a straight course although he, too, reduced speed to thirteen knots. Realizing that he was getting too close to the boats ahead he ordered *K.14* to starboard but, at that crucial moment, the 'K' boat hoodoo jammed the helm. She swung out in a wide circle and, by good fortune, *K.12*, the boat immediately astern, passed clear. *K.22*, however, had lost sight of *K.12*'s stern-light and, unaware of what was happening a few hundred yards ahead, de Burgh held his course.

'Hard a'starboard.'

K.22's captain suddenly saw a red navigation-light two hundred yards ahead passing across his bows. It could mean only one thing. A ship was lying broadside on directly in his path.

The submarine reacted only sluggishly to the helm and, still moving at nineteen knots, her sharp prow cut deeply into port side of *K.14* just behind the forward torpedo-compartment. Both crews acted swiftly and, as the two submarines drew apart, all the watertight doors were slammed and secured. There was no immediate danger of sinking although the forward compartments in both boats were flooded and they lay together rolling gently in the swell as their wireless-operators tapped out urgent collision signals.

Harbottle and de Burgh's greatest worry was the approaching battle-cruisers. When they finally arrived on the scene they tore past at twenty-one knots and the submarines rolled violently in their wash. But they all passed safely—all, that is, except *Inflexible*, the last in the line.

She struck *K.22* in the bows bending thirty feet of metal like putty, ripping off the external ballast-tank on the starboard side, and almost rolling the submarine over. Then she ran clear leaving the stricken *K.22* wallowing in the water like a wounded whale. Several members of the crew remembered that their boat was the original *K.13*, the killer of Gareloch.

Almost half-an-hour passed after the second collision before Leir, in *Ithuriel*, learned of the accidents and, even then, he received only a garbled report. Anxious to assist his crippled submarines he turned on all the cruiser's navigation-lights and swung south followed by the remnants of his flotilla—*K.11*, *K.12* and *K.17*. But they were soon in dire trouble.

The battle-cruiser *Australia*, steaming at high speed, loomed suddenly out of the mist narrowly missing the little group and only a miracle saved her from ramming *K.12*. Then, as the great ship was swallowed up again by the mist, they ran into a group of destroyers and weaved in wild confusion before plunging on into the darkness in search of their comrades.

'Tiny' Little, commander of the 12th Flotilla, had also picked up news of the accident and *Fearless* flashed a warning to *K.3*, *K.4*, *K.6* and *K.7*, to watch out for the damaged submarines. Fifteen minutes later they had passed clear of May Island and Little felt relieved that they had avoided the area of the collision without incident. What he did *not* know, however, was that Leir and the survivors of the 13th Flotilla had reversed course and were now heading back towards him.

Suddenly the men on the cruiser's bridge saw lights ahead

and the approaching ships swung safely to starboard so that they would pass port to port in accordance with the rule of the sea. All, that is, except the third ship in the line which held a straight and steady course. *Fearless* was doing all of twenty-one knots and, although her engines were put full astern, a collision was inevitable.

Her victim was *K.17*, the third boat of the returning 13th Flotilla, and the cruiser's bows ripped into the submarine a few feet forward of the conning-tower. *K.17* twisted clear and reeled away into the darkness sinking fast while the men on *Fearless*'s bridge, dazed and shocked by the crash, stared in dumb horror as she vanished into the night.

True to the traditions of the Submarine Service *K.17*'s crew remained at their stations calmly carrying out their emergency drill and closing the watertight doors. But it was obvious that the boat could not remain afloat for more than a few minutes and, as the order came down from the bridge, they filed up on deck to abandon ship.

There was utter confusion in the rear. *K.3* nearly rammed *K.4*; only Shove's prompt order to swing hard a'port saved a collision; and both flotillas merged in a wild mêlée of weaving, jinking ships.

K.6 and *K.12* narrowly avoided a head-on collision but, in the excitement, the men on *K.6*'s bridge lost sight of their flotilla companion *K.3*. Spotting a white light ahead Lt Sandford, officer of the watch, assumed it to be *K.3* and brought his own submarine around to keep station on her stern. When Layton arrived on the bridge a few minutes later, however, he realized the error. It was not *K.3*—it was *K.4*. And she was lying broadside across their path.

'Hard a'port. Full astern.'

But it was too late. *K.6*'s bows cleaved deeply into the side of the unfortunate *K.4* nearly slicing her completely in half and, locked together in a fatal embrace, both submarines began to sink.

Layton ordered all watertight doors to be closed and he turned on full power to break free. Fortunately *K.6* had not been badly damaged by the collision and, as her propellers bit into the water, she began to pull free. There was a screeching whine of torn steel as she backed away from her victim, and by the time she had drawn clear, *K.4* had taken her last plunge into the depths.

K.7, arriving on the scene within seconds, also found *K.4* directly in her path but she sank so rapidly that Gravener's boat passed right over the spot where she vanished without even scraping her keel. *K.7* was brought to a stop, her engines reversed, and she moved slowly astern to pick up the survivors, not of *K.4*, but of *K.17*, who were still swimming around in the darkness calling for help.

The 5th Battle Squadron, although warned by wireless of the collisions, was unaware that both flotillas were milling around directly ahead and Gravener's men were still trying to pick up the survivors from the earliest disaster and the dreadnoughts swept on to the scene at twenty-one knots. What followed was probably the greatest tragedy of all during that terrible night.

The escorting destroyers ploughed straight through the helpless men swimming in the water, cutting them to pieces with their propellers, and by the time they had passed clear only nine men remained alive. No one was to blame for this final horror —except possibly the men at the top who had originally created the 'K' boats and sent them to operate with the fleet. Not a single man escaped from the *K4* and, of the nine men rescued from *K.17*, one died a short while later. Such was the price paid by the Submarine Service for the stupidity of the Admiralty.

The Court of Inquiry convened on board *Orion* five days later placed the blame squarely on the shoulders of the submarine captains and their officers, a travesty of justice typical of the times. And one officer was court-martialled following the

Inquiry's report. But dangers, disasters, and injustice, could not quench the spirit of the submarine crews.

When Layton handed over *K.6* to William Crowther, who had been on board her during that tragic night off May Island, he told her new captain that the disasters had been good experience for him and were 'a bloody good introduction to "K" boats'.

The chapter of accidents continued although, by now, the hoodoo of the steam submarines was apparently having a few week's rest after its exertions on the night of 1 February.

D.7 on patrol in the North Sea under the command of Lt Tweedy sighted the destroyer *Pelican* through her periscope. Themen on the destroyer's bridge had, at the same moment, spotted the submarine's 'scope and, unable to identify it, assumed it to belong to a U-boat. As *D.7* dived away the destroyer heeled over sharply and raced through the water to ram.

Tweedy's prompt evasive action saved the submarine from the danger of *Pelican*'s tough steel bows but he could do nothing to avert the depth-charge attack that followed. The explosions were uncomfortably close and when the third charge shattered the light bulbs *D.7* was forced to surface. Fortunately the submarine's crew were able to flash a recognition signal before any further attack was made and everyone was happy, especially the Admiralty's explosives experts who now had a first-hand account of how it felt to be at the receiving end of British depth-charges.

Later the same month the new submarine *L.2* had a similar escape. In her case the attackers were the American destroyers *Paudling*, *Davis*, and *Trippe* now serving as convoy-escorts following the United States entry into the war on the side of the Allies. *L.2* was misbehaving and, despite all Lt-Cdr Ackworth's attempts to control the boat, she kept losing trim and porpoising to the surface. The look-outs on the American destroyers only caught a momentary glimpse of the submarine's conning-tower but it was sufficient to bring them into action.

Swinging away from the convoy they opened fire while Ackworth took his boat down to ninety feet in an effort to escape.

When the depth-charge attack started L.2's captain sought safety at 200 feet but even this was insufficient. A near-miss jammed the after hydroplanes and she went down at a steep angle by the stern, hitting the bottom at 300 feet with her bows angled up at fifty degrees. More depth-charges floated down and Ackworth fought to save his nearly-crippled boat.

Finding that the forward hydroplanes were unable to restore trim he blew tanks. The submarine lurched off the bottom and, thrown out of control by the jammed hydroplanes at the stern, she shot to the surface at a steep angle. As soon as she appeared the destroyers opened fire with everything they had at a range of 1,000 yards and quickly scored a direct hit on the pressure hull just behind the conning-tower. The situation was fast becoming desperate for, with her hull holed, L.2 could no longer escape by diving.

Ackworth threw back the hatch and leapt into the conning-tower, Verey-pistol in hand, to fire his recognition signals. By good fortune the American look-outs recognized him and, as the lights hissed into the air, they stopped firing.

As if the hazards of Allied surface ships were not enough, on 15 March the unfortunate D.3 was attacked and sunk by a French airship, when on a routine patrol off the Flanders coast. But, given the chance to carry out their proper tasks as lone hunters, the submarines were still chalking up their own successes against the enemy.

In April, Admiral Scheer decided to launch a full-scale sortie against the British Scandinavian convoys. The High Sea Fleet, preceded by Hipper's battle-cruisers, left their bases early on the morning of the 23rd in heavy mist. As they passed through the Bight they were sighted by J.6 but Warburton, her captain, could not identify the great, grey warships steaming through the mist and, assuming them to be units of the

Grand Fleet, he made no attack. In the circumstances it was probably the wisest thing to do but Warburton's subsequent action is open to doubt. Guarding against the fact that they were British ships, he decided not to surface and wireless a sighting report to the Admiralty in case it would reveal their presence to the Germans. Thus Scheer was able to continue northwards towards the convoy-route leaving the British unaware that he was even at sea.

V.4 and *J.4*, two more submarines operating in the area, did not see the enemy at all and it was only an unfortunate mechanical breakdown by *Moltke* which forced Scheer to break wireless-silence and thus alert the Admiralty to his presence. The Grand Fleet went to sea immediately and the Harwich Force swept eastwards in the hope of cutting off Scheer's retreat. At the same time. *E.42* was ordered to take up position in the northern sector of the Bight.

Unwilling to venture further with his crippled battle-cruiser Scheer reversed course. Heading back, with the *Oldenberg* towing the *Molkte*, he ran slap into Lt Allen waiting at periscope-depth in *E.42*. The submarine fired four torpedoes as the long line of ships passed across its bows and the last scored a direct hit on the *Molkte* which, having slipped its tow, was crawling eastwards at slow speed on its damaged engines. The German destroyers launched an immediate counter-attack on the submarine but, after an hour, they gave up and Allen was able to creep away and return to Harwich.

Molkte reached the Jade River safely despite the torpedo-hit but it was Scheer's last throw. The High Sea Fleet never again left its protected harbours until, in November 1918, it sailed across the North Sea to surrender at Scapa Flow.

Roger Keyes, now promoted to Rear-Admiral, renewed his acquaintance with the Submarine Service when he took over the Dover Patrol from Reginald Bacon, who had been the first Inspecting Captain of Submarines in 1902. Keyes was concerned with the failure to prevent the U-boats escaping through the Channel and, in typical style, he evolved a scheme to bottle them up before they even reached the sea.

At that time the Germans had developed a large submarine base at the inland port of Bruges complete with repair shops, armament stores, and concrete bunkers. The U-boats reached the Flanders coast by means of the Belgian canal system and their two main exits were at Zeebrugge and Ostend.

If we seal off the exits, Keyes reasoned, the U-boats will be trapped inland and the submarine offensive in the Channel and Western Approaches will die away like a limb withering from loss of blood.

The events of the St George's Day raid on Zeebrugge are outside the scope of this book and the grand panorama of the operation must be restricted to the exploits of Unit 'K', the two submarines selected to sail with the armada.

Both submarines were old, almost the oldest to take part in active operations at this late stage of the war, and each was packed with explosives. *C.1*, under Lt Newbold and *C.3* under Lt Sandford were selected from the 6th Flotilla at Portsmouth; Sandford's elder brother, Francis, a Lieutenant-Commander, acted as the unit-commander in a French-built picket-boat.

The odds against their return were not encouraging and Keyes insisted that the crews of both submarines should be reduced to two officers and four men each. Their target was the viaduct linking the Zeebrugge Mole to the mainland and, although one boat carried enough explosives to demolish the structure, the second submarine was brought along as a back-up unit.

Just after midnight Unit 'K' arrived at their pre-arranged positions having previously slipped their tows. But as Dick Sandford spotted the viaduct ahead he realized that *C.1* and the picket-boat were nowhere in view, having separated during the run-in to the target. Timing was crucial and he decided to press on alone.

C.3's primitive petrol-engine roared defiantly as he swung towards the viaduct and, in the bows, Leading Seaman Cleaver, turned on the smoke canisters in an effort to conceal their approach. An off-shore wind, however, swept the smoke away leaving the tiny submarine unprotected as it closed on the girdered bridge.

Suddenly a flare rose into the sky and, as it died away, three seachlights picked out the low bulk of the submarine easing through the water. Yet, incredibly, the enemy guns held their fire and, within minutes, *C.3* rammed full tilt into the gaunt steel skeleton of the viaduct.

All six men were on the tiny bridge, to ensure that they would not be trapped below if anything went wrong; under their feet was five tons of Amatol. Only when Sandford heard the German guards laughing did he realize why his boat had been spared the merciless shelling he had expected. The enemy thought that the submarine had been trying to sail under the viaduct and had unintentionally become trapped.

Taking advantage of this unexpected hiatus Sandford lit the fuses while the others scrambled to release the motor-skiff they were carrying ready for their escape. Once the twelve-minute fuse was burning Dick Sandford jumped into the skiff, and, as the six men pulled away, the Germans finally opened fire at point-blank range.

Stoker Bindall was hit first and, as Sandford reached forward to help him, a machine-gun bullet shattered his hand. Now there was a further set-back. The skiff's propeller had been damaged during launching and their only hope of escape lay in their skill at the oars. Harner and Roxburgh grabbed an oar apiece and tried to propel the flimsy little boat away from the explosive-packed submarine, but the tide was running against them and progress was pitifully slow.

Another burst of machine-gun raked the skiff and Petty Officer Harner slumped forward against the oar. Cleaver pushed him aside, seized the handle, and took over rowing. Sandford, too, had been hit again, this time in the thigh, and

Lt Howell-Price replaced him at the tiller. The bottom of the boat was awash with blood and, as the pump laboured to drain it clear, the sea around the skiff was dyed bright red.

Pom-pom guns joined in the barrage from the shore but Cleaver and Roxburgh stuck to the oars. Sandford, white-faced with agony, urged them on while Howell-Price con-contrated on the steering. Bindall was unconscious and Harner, badly wounded but anxious to help his companions, dragged himself into a corner where he would not impede the movements of the oarsmen.

Their own courage saved them from further agony. A deafening sheet of flame erupted alongside the viaduct and a tremendous clap of thunder indicated that *C.3* and her cargo had gone up on schedule. With the viaduct went the German machine-gunners, pom-poms, and searchlights. Ten minutes later Francis Sandford and the picket boat located the men from *C.3* a few hundred yards off the harbour mole and the wounded were lifted to safety.

Newbold and *C.1* never reached the viaduct. The submarine lost its tow and the hawser threatened to snag the propellers. Newbold stopped the boat while Beyford, his First Lieutenant, went forward to free the rope. It was pitch dark and the submarine was rolling in a heavy swell. Losing his footing on the slippery steel deck Beyford was swept overboard but, clutching the heavy towing hawser he had been sent to retrieve, he managed to climb back on board *C.1* having successfully accomplished his task.

Next Newbold found himself being fired at by a destroyer and, only after an exchange of recognition signals, was he allowed to proceed towards his target. The various delays had, however, put him twenty minutes behind schedule and aware of the vital need for split-second timing, he decided to lie off the area and keep observation rather than smash his way forward at the risk of collision with other boats in the raid.

He saw the flash of *C.3*'s self-destruction but, not hearing the attendant sound of the explosion, he could not be sure that Sandford had succeeded. Then, as he was about to close in and make a run for the viaduct, he saw *Vindictive* steaming back to Dover and, assuming that the raid was either over or a failure, he decided to turn around and follow her. *C.1*'s part in the great Zeebrugge raid was over.

Dick Sandford was awarded the Victoria Cross for his part in the operation, the fourth and last member of the Submarine Service to win it in World War One.

After Zeebrugge, submarine activity once more reverted to routine patrols, occasionally punctuated by success. On 12 May *D.4* trapped *UB-72* in Lyme Bay and sent her to the bottom with a well-placed torpedo. *G.2* bagged *U-78* during a similar patrol and the newly-built *L.12* disposed of *UB.90* with a neatly-executed attack in the early hours of the morning while the enemy boat was on the surface charging its batteries.

In addition to these three sinkings, D'Oyly Hughes, Nasmith's First Lieutenant in the Dardanelles and now captain of *E.35*, torpedoed *U-154*.

The attack lasted two and a half hours and D'Oyly enjoyed a narrow escape at the end. *U-154* was quartering the surface apparently waiting to rendezvous with another U-boat when *E.35* spotted her and, due to the enemy's frequent changes of course, it took a long time to get the German submarine square in the sights. D'Oyly fired two torpedoes just to make sure and both struck home causing such a violent explosion that several of *E.35*'s own electric light bulbs were shattered by the blast. The British submarine surfaced to pick up survivors but, sighting a periscope, she dived immediately and, while she was still sliding beneath the surface, the hydrophone operator reported the sound of a torpedo passing close by.

Apparently *U-154*'s companion had been near at hand when the torpedoes struck and, remaining beneath the surface, she had tried to ambush the British boat as she came to the surface searching for survivors. It was a lucky escape and showed, once again, the dangers and hazards of submarine operating against submarine.

L.10, too, scored against one of the German's rarely-seen surface-ships when she put a torpedo into the destroyer *S.33*. But the High Sea Fleet was now so securely locked inside its harbours that the submarines patrolling the Bight had little hope of repeating such successes. When enemy surface ships were sighted the submarines often became the hunted rather than the hunters and, in fact, *L.10* was sunk by German destroyers on 3 October when she attempted to repeat her earlier achievement.

Enemy minefields also continued to take their toll and on 20 July *E.34* met her end in the gloomy depths of the North Sea after running into an uncharted minefield while on a routine patrol in the Bight.

Meanwhile the 'K' boats were still fighting a private war against their own crews. *K.16* ended up on the bottom of Gareloch during diving trials but, more fortunate than the ill-fated *K.13*, her captain, Charles de Burgh, managed to blow the ballast-tanks and bring her to the surface without incident. It was, however, a frightening few minutes for the men trapped inside her hull.

In May the newly-completed *K.15* lived up to the steam-submarine's reputation when running on a patrol line. A beam-sea entered the funnel intakes, swamped the fans, and extinguished the boilers. With great presence of mind Vaughan Jones, her commander, ordered the submarine to be shut off for diving. Even so sufficient water had entered the boiler-room to destroy the ship's buoyancy at the stern and she sank slowly to the bottom stern first, her great bulbous bows sticking out above the surface.

The valves jammed and it took eight hours to free the pumps before her stern slowly lifted off the seabed and she regained trim. The fault was found to be in some ports in the funnel superstructure which opened both ways. All the other 'K' boats had been modified but, by some strange quirk, *K.15*'s ports were not altered even though she had only left the builder's yards a few weeks earlier. It was such technical inefficiency that led to so many 'K' boat disasters. They were so complicated that nothing could be left to chance—yet it too often was.

Herbert Shove also had an unpleasant moment when *K.3*, a survivor of the May Island disaster, lost her trim and plunged to the bottom on 2 May. This took place in the Pentland Firth where there was an unusually deep hole in the sea-bed and, being a 'K' boat, it was inevitable that she should choose this precise spot for her involuntary dive. The submarine hit the bottom at 266 feet and it says much for her solid construction that, apart from crumpling her many stays, stanchions, and angles, she survived the tremendous pressure and was brought back to the surface safely.

On 10 June, despite all the weight of contrary evidence, the Admiralty ordered six more 'K' boats from the builders, their numbers being *K.23* to *K.28*. Fortunately the war was over before they were completed and only one, *K.26*, was commissioned into service.

Meanwhile more monsters were being created. *K.18*, *K.19*, *K.20* and *K.21* were suspended and their plans were revised to make them 'submarine monitors', or, as the Navy preferred to call them, 'Dip-Chicks'. They stemmed basically from Fisher's fertile mind and he had claimed, when first proposing them, that they would 'end the war'.

Known as the 'M' class, these new submarines carried a single twelve-inch gun which was capable of being fired underwater. The only snag was that they had to come to the surface each time the gun was reloaded. In fact the only saving grace about the monitor submarines was that their main propulsive units were diesel and not steam-engines—although exactly why the Admiralty decided this in view of their subsequent orders for more steam submarines is not clear.

Max Horton, the scourge of the Baltic in 1914 and 1915, was

appointed captain of *M.1*, but he has left no record of his personal feelings about his unusual command. For, like the 'K' boats, the 'M' class submarines had a similar record of disaster and Horton was fortunately no longer in command when *M.1* finally sank to the bottom for the last time in 1925 following a collision off Start Point.

What is even more astonishing is that, having created the idea of monitor submarines, the Admiralty would not use them operationally in the North Sea for fear that the Germans would copy the design.

And so the war at sea came to an end, not in the fury and excitement of the battle but in dull, monotonous routine. When, in 1914, Fisher had remarked, 'I have not yet mastered on what basis our submarines harm the enemy more than themselves,' he was, in fact, prophesying the fate of the Submarine Service in those last months up to the Armistice when there were many more losses than gains and when there seemed to be more accidents than actions.

C.25 was a typical victim. A group of German sea-planes returning from a raid on Lowestoft spotted her cruising on the surface while on patrol off the south-east coast. Climbing high into the sun to blind the eyes of the submarine's look-outs the five aircraft swooped down on their unsuspecting victim with machine-guns blazing.

C.25's crew scrambled to action stations. Their sole defence against this new menace from the sky was a single puny Lewis-gun but, before they could reach it, the conning-tower rattled under a hail of Spandau bullets and they were cut to pieces. Bell, the young lieutenant in command of the submarine, and two other men were killed instantly, while a fourth, Leading Seaman Barge, fell mortally wounded.

Delay meant disaster and, true to the traditions of the service, Barge offered himself as sacrifice to save the ship. 'Dive, sir,' he told the First Lieutenant. 'Don't worry about me. I'm done for anyway.'

DUW-R*

But, although every second spent on the surface added to their danger, the crew struggled to drag their wounded comrade below despite the bullets from the circling aircraft. Sadly it was labour in vain for the gallant Barge was dead by the time they got him into the control room.

An even more macabre incident was to follow. As the C.25 was being prepared for diving she rolled in the swell and the body of one of the dead sailors on the conning-tower slid down the sloping deck and came to rest with his leg protruding through the hatch opening. It was impossible to shut the hatch until the lifeless limb had been removed and the crew sweated and strained to push the corpse clear. Two more men were killed in the struggle to free the hatch and, in desperation, the First Lieutenant ordered the leg to be amputated.

By the time this gruesome task had been completed the seaplane's bullets had ripped open the pressure hull and smashed the submarine's electric motors. It was now impossible to escape by diving and it was only the timely and unexpected arrival of an 'E' class boat which saved them by driving off the German aircraft with her four-inch gun. She then took the shattered C.25 in tow and brought her back safely to base.

An identification error so simple that it seems incredible brought about the loss of Horton's old submarine J.6 when she was sunk by a 'Q' ship on 15 October. At the subsequent Court of Inquiry the 'Q' ship's captain was exonerated of all responsibility for the sinking when the unfortunate mistake was explained in evidence. Apparently something hanging down from the side of the submarine's conning-tower made the 'J' of her identity number look like a 'U' and, satisfied that it was the U-6, the 'Q' ship opened fire. A large white tablecloth was waved from the after-hatch and a morse-lamp on the conning-tower flashed: 'H-E-L-P ... H-E-L-P ...' But the hidden guns of the 'Q' ship did not waver in their murderous fire and the unfortunate submarine floated off into the fog sinking rapidly from a dozen shell holes punched through her pressure hull. Only when the survivors were picked up, the 'Q' ship rescued fifteen of *J.6*'s thirty-four man crew, did they realize they had been shelling a British submarine.

That such mistakes were accepted by the men of the Submarine Service without rancour or bitterness was exemplified at the Court of Inquiry. As the 'Q' ship's captain and officers left the room the survivors of *J.6* came to attention and saluted them.

On 1 November the last British submarine to be lost by enemy action, *G.7*, failed to return to her base after a routine patrol in the North Sea. She, too, had paid the price of victory and added her name to the long roll of the Royal Navy's submarines whose only entry in the records were the three words: 'Overdue—presumed lost.'

For the men of the Submarine Service who were fortunate enough to be ashore on Armistice Night the celebrations were riotous. At Harwich a ship's band was loaded on board a railway truck and pushed down the jetty by a mob of jubilant seamen and officers. All was well while the truck remained on the private railway lines inside the naval base but, somehow, it got pushed through the gates and out on the main line. A railway signalman spotted the singing matelots cruising down the line with their band playing and, sticking his head out of his box, yelled:

'Don't you bastards know the London express is coming along here in a few minutes?'

The whole spirit of the Submarine Service was crystallized in the reply he received from the celebrating sailors:

'Hurrah for the London express! Let's ram it!'

For those still at sea an extra tot of rum had to suffice. The Navy on duty could not afford to relax its eternal vigilance. When the captain of *R.12* wirelessed for permission to return from patrol so that he and his crew could join in the celebrations he received a curt reply from his flotilla commander: 'Remain on patrol until ordered to return.'

For that was the Royal Navy. As ready for action in peace as it had been in four long years of war. As Commodore Hall said in a General Signal to the Submarine Service on 12 November, 1918: 'We leave the war with a record as proud as any that war has ever produced. Submarines were the first at sea on the outbreak of war; they have been continually in action while it lasted; they will be the last to return to harbour.'

It was an appropriate valediction for the 'damned un-English weapon'.

APPENDIX ONE

SUBMARINE FLOTILLA DISPOSITIONS
(Number of boats in brackets)

Flotilla	Aug 1914	Dec 1914	Jan 1915	Aug 1916	Mar 1917
1st	Devonport (2)	Devonport (2)	Devonport (2)	Rosyth (4)	Hawkcraig (1)
2nd	Portsmouth (4)	Portsmouth (4)	Portsmouth (8)	Tyne (8)	Tyne (4)
3rd	Dover (6)	Yarmouth (5)	(Cancelled) (-)	Humber (10)	Humber (2)
4th	Dover (8)	Dover (10)	Dover (10)	Nore (6)	Nore (3)
5th	Nore (6)	Nore (6)	Nore (6)	Dover (12)	Dover (5)
6th	Humber (6)	Humber (7)	Humber (8)	Portsmouth (3)	Portsmouth (2)
7th	*Tyne (3)	Leith (4)	Leith (8)	Clyde (3)	–
8th	Harwich (19)	Harwich (22)	Harwich (21)	Yarmouth (12)	Yarmouth (10)
9th		Clyde (4)	Clyde (3)	Harwich (25)	Harwich (28)
10th		Tyne (5)	Tyne (4)	Tees (12)	Tees (12)
11th				Blyth (12)	Blyth (12)
12th				Scapa (7)	Scapa (9)
13th				Scapa (7)	Scapa (2)
Platypus					Queenstown (8)
Vulcan					L. Swilley (6)

* Plus a further six boats at Leith.

APPENDIX ONE *(cont.)*

In addition flotillas abroad consisted of:

August 1914	Gibraltar	(3)
	Malta	(3)
	Hong Kong	(3)
	Australia	(2)
March 1917	Mediterranean	(15)
(Approx)	Hong Kong	(3)

Note Number of submarines assigned to flotilla is shown by figure in brackets under the beside of the base.

APPENDIX TWO

BRITISH SUBMARINES FROM 1914 to 1918

Class	Holland	'A'	'B'	'C'	'CC'	'D'
Number completed						
Before 1919	5	13	11	38	2	8
After 1919	–	–	–	–	–	–
Lost in action	–	–	1	8	–	3
Lost accidentally	1	4	1	2	–	1
Prototype date	1902	1903	1905	1906	1914	1910
Surface Tonnage	104	165	280	290	313	550
Submerged ,,	122	180	313	320	373	620
Length (in feet)	63½	100	135	145	144	162
Engines	Petrol	Petrol	Petrol	Petrol	Petrol	Diesel
Horsepower	160	450	600	600	600	1750
Screws	1	1	1	1	1	2
Surface speed	8	11½	13	14	13	16
Submerged ,,	5	7	9	10	10½	10
Torpedo tubes	14″	18″	18″	18″	18″	18″
Number torpedo ,,	1	2	2	2	5	3
Guns	–	–	–	–	–	2 12 pdr
Complement	7	11/14	16	16	?	25
					CC-2 3-TT	D.1 smaller

APPENDIX TWO (cont.)

Class	'E'	'S'	'W'	'V'	Naut-ilus	Sword-fish
Number completed						
Before 1919	58	3	4	4	1	1
After 1919	–	–	–	–	–	–
Lost in action	25	–	–	–	–	–
Lost accidentally	3	–	–	–	–	–
Prototype date	1913	1914	1915	1915	1917	1916
Surface tonnage	660	265	340	364	1270	932
Submerged ,,	800	386	508	486	1694	1475
Length (in feet)	181	148	171	147	242	231
Engines	Diesel	Diesel	Diesel	Diesel	Diesel	Steam
Horsepower	1600	650	710	900	3700	3750
Screws	2	2	2	2	2	2
Surface speed	16	$13\frac{1}{4}$	13	14	17	18
Submerged ,,	10	$8\frac{1}{2}$	$8\frac{1}{2}$	9	10	10
Torpedo tubes	18″	18″	18″	18″	18″ 21″	18″ 21″
Number ,, ,,	5	2	2	2	4 2	4 2
Guns	1 12 pdr	–	1 small	1 small	1 12 pdr	2 12 pdr
Complement	30	18	19	18	42	42
	Six fitted as mine-layers					

APPENDIX TWO (*cont.*)

Class	'F'	'H.1'	'H.21'	'J'	'K'	'M'
Number completed						
Before 1919	3	20	10	7	17	2
After 1919	–	–	14	–	1	1
Lost in action	–	2	2*	–	–	–
Lost accidentally	–	2	3	1	5	2
Prototype date	1915	1915	1918	1916	1916	1918
Surface tonnage	353	364	440	1210	1883	1600
Submerged ,,	525	434	500	1820	2565	1950
Length (in feet)	151½	150¼	171	275½	338	296
Engines	Diesel	Diesel	Diesel	Diesel	Steam	Diesel
Horsepower	900	480	480	3600	10500	2400
Screws	2	2	2	3	2	2
Surface speed	14½	13	13	19½	23	15½
Submerged ,,	9	10	10	9½	9	9½
Torpedo tubes	18"	18"	21"	18"	18"	18"
Number	3	4	4	6	8	4
Guns	1 small	1 small	1 small	2 3"	2 4" 1 3" AA	1 12" 1 3" AA
Complement	18–20	22	22	44	50–60	60–70
			*Both sunk WW2		K.17 2 5.5"	

APPENDIX TWO (cont.)

Class	'G'	'L.1'	'L.9'	'L.50'	'R'
Number completed					
Before 1919	14	8	8	1	10
After 1919	–	–	11	6	–
Lost in action	2	–	1	1	–
Lost accidentally	2	–	2	1	–
Prototype date	1915	1917	1918	1918	1918
Surface tonnage	700	890	890	960	420
Submerged ,,	975	1070	1080	1150	500
Length (in feet)	187	231	$238\frac{1}{2}$	235	163
Engines	Diesel	Diesel	Diesel	Diesel	Diesel
Horsepower	1600	2400	2400	2400	240
Screws	2	2	2	2	1
Surface speed	$14\frac{1}{2}$	$17\frac{1}{2}$	$17\frac{1}{2}$	$17\frac{1}{2}$	$9\frac{1}{2}$
Submerged ,,	10	$10\frac{1}{2}$	$10\frac{1}{2}$	$10\frac{1}{2}$	15
Torpedo tubes	21" 18"	18"	21" 18"	21"	18"
Number ,, ,,	1 4	6	4 2	6	6
Guns	1 3" AA	1 4"	1 4"	2 4"	1 4"
Complement	31	36	36	40	22
			Five fitted as mine-layers		

APPENDIX THREE

ACKNOWLEDGEMENTS & SOURCES

THE AUTHOR would like to acknowledge his debt to the following published works which have provided much of the source material in this book. Titles marked with a * have been used extensively while the others have provided background material or individual details of personalities or incidents. For the reader who wishes to learn more about the naval history of the First World War and the role played by British submarines this list will prove a useful bibliography.

---

*Naval Memoirs by Admiral of the Fleet Sir Roger Keyes (Thornton & Butterworth, 1934–35)

* The World Crisis by Winston Churchill (Thornton & Butterworth, 1923–1931; Odhams Press 1939)

*Smoke on the Horizon by Vice-Admiral C. V. Usborne (Hodder & Stoughton, 1933)

HM Submarines by Lt-Commander P. K. Kemp (Herbert Jenkins, 1952)

Raiders of the Deep by Lowell Thomas (Heinemann, 1929)

Fighting under the Sea by Captain Donald Macintyre (Evans Brothers, 1965)

* The 'K' Boats by Don Everitt (George G. Harrap, 1963)

*Dardanelles Patrol by Peter Shankland and Anthony Hunter (Collins, 1964)

Subs & Submariners by Arch Whitehouse (Muller, 1961)

* The Most Formidable Thing by Rear-Admiral William Jameson (Rupert Hart-Davis, 1965)

*Official History of the War. Naval Operations. (Volumes 1 to 5) by Sir Julian S. Corbett and Sir Henry Newbolt (Longmans, 1923)

Memories by Admiral of the Fleet Lord Fisher (Hodder & Stoughton, 1919)

Lord Fisher by Admiral Sir R. H. Bacon (Hodder & Stoughton, 1929)

My Naval Life by Admiral of the Fleet the Earl of Cork and Orrery (Hutchinsons, 1943)

*My Naval Life by Commander Stephen King-Hall (Faber and Faber, 1952)

The Life and Letters of David Beatty, Admiral of the Fleet by Rear-Admiral W. S. Chalmers (Hodder & Stoughton, 1951)

Sea Fights of the Great War by W. L. Wyllie and M. F. Wren (Cassells, 1918)

Roger Keyes by Cecil Aspinall-Oglander (The Hogarth Press, 1951)

*Max Horton & The Western Approaches by Rear-Admiral W. S. Chalmers (Hodder & Stoughton, 1954)

APPENDIX THREE (cont.)

Sailor in the Air by Vice-Admiral Richard Bell Davies (Peter Davies, 1967)
Sea Flyers by C. G. Grey (Faber & Faber, 1942)
The Times History of the War Vols 1-22 (*The Times*)
*Warships of World War I by H. M. Le Fleming (Ian Allan)
The Russians at Sea by David Woodward (William Kimber, 1965)
The Grand Fleet, 1914-1916 by Admiral of the Fleet Earl Jellicoe (Cassells, 1919)
Command the Far Seas by Keith Middlemas (Hutchinson, 1961)
Zeebrugge by Barrie Pitt (Cassells, 1958)
Naval Battles of the First World War by Geoffrey Bennet (Batsford, 1968)
Fear God and Dread Nought. The correspondence of Admiral of the Fleet Lord Fisher edited by Arthur J. Marder (Jonathan Cape; 1952-1959)
From Dreadnought to Scapa Flow. (Volumes 1-4) by Arthur J. Marder (Oxford University Press, 1961)
*By Guess and by God by William Guy Carr (Hutchinson, 1930)
The Riddle of Jutland by Langhorne Gibson and Vice-Admiral J. E. T. Harper (Cassells, 1954)
The World's Warships by Fred T. Jane (Sampson Low & Marston, 1915)
The Great World War (Volumes 1-9) edited by Frank A. Mumby (The Gresham Publishing Co, 1916-1920)

And to countless other books, magazines, and newspaper articles, which have all contributed some small part to my understanding of submarine warfare and naval history.

Index

(NB. Ranks shown are contemporary.)

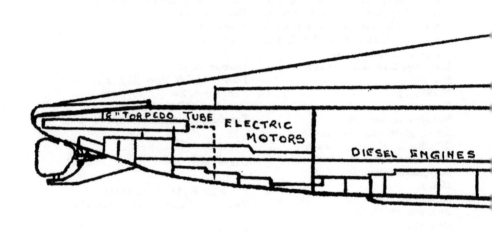

18" TORPEDO TUBE   ELECTRIC
MOTORS   DIESEL ENGINES

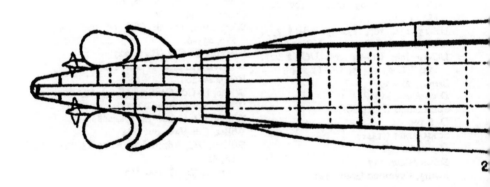

2

"E" CLA

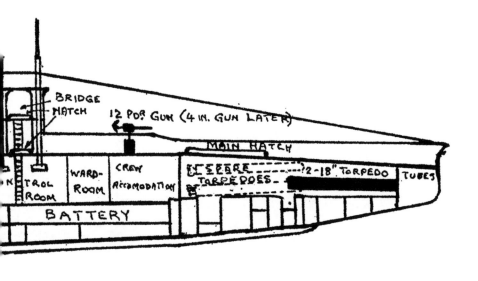

BRIDGE
HATCH

12 PDR. GUN (4 IN. GUN LATER)

MAIN HATCH

CONTROL ROOM

WARD-ROOM

CREW ACCOMODATION

SPARE TORPEDOES

2-18" TORPEDO

TUBES

BATTERY

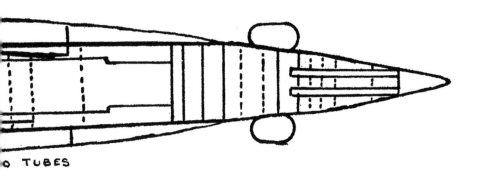

O TUBES

SUBMARINE

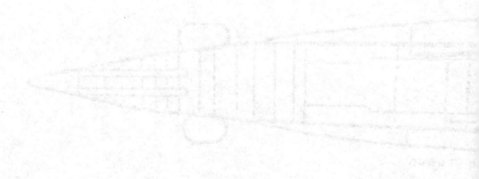